T0247755

A PHILOSOPHY OF NE.

Appeals to need abound in everyday discussion. People make claims about their own needs all the time, and they do so in a way that suggests these should have a certain moral force. Needs also play an important role in contemporary popular discourse about social justice, climate change, obligations to future generations, dealing fairly with refugees, treating animals humanely, and critiques of consumerist lifestyles – to name just a few of the many examples. The idea of need is present in an increasing number of debates and domains. There is interest in need from several disciplines, not just philosophy, which also include psychology, economics, political science, social work and sociology. This volume, then, offers a fine introduction to an increasingly important concept in day-to-day life. In a new Foreword, Gillian Brock discusses the continuing significance of several innovative chapters in the book, indicating how they presaged new directions in philosophical conversation.

SORAN READER (1963–2012) was Reader in Philosophy at Durham University. She was the author of *Needs and Moral Necessity* (2007).

GILLIAN BROCK is Professor of Philosophy at the University of Auckland and a recent Fellow at the Edmond J. Safra Center for Ethics at Harvard University. She has published widely on ethics, political and social philosophy, and several applied ethics fields, along with a number of more inter-disciplinary areas. Her latest book is *Justice for People on the Move* (2022).

TALKING PHILOSOPHY

General Editor: Edward Harcourt

The Royal Institute of Philosophy has been, from the very start, a fundamentally outward-facing organization. In 1924, Sydney Hooper – main mover behind the establishment of the Institute – realized that outreach to a wide interested public was a vital part of the value (whether social, cultural or intellectual) that philosophy at its best can impart. The Institute's first executive committee actively promoted that broad pedagogical message through accessible civic talks, and included in its ranks many of the most eminent luminaries of the day: not just professional philosophers but also sociologists, physicians, politicians, evolutionary biologists and psychologists. The Institute, from its foundation, has thus been rooted in an egalitarian community of people devoted to the principles of learning, debating and teaching philosophical knowledge in the broader service of what Hooper called 'the most permanent interests of the human spirit'. Talking Philosophy maintains this noble tradition. A book series published under the joint auspices of the Institute and Cambridge University Press, it addresses some of the most pertinent topics of the day so as to show how philosophy can shed new light on their interpretation, as well as public understanding of them.

Books in the series:

Moral Philosophy
The Philosophy of Mind
Ethics
A Philosophy of Need
Karl Popper
Spiritual Life

A PHILOSOPHY OF NEED

EDITED BY

SORAN READER
University of Durham

WITH A FOREWORD BY

GILLIAN BROCK
University of Auckland

CAMBRIDGE
UNIVERSITY PRESS

CAMBRIDGE
UNIVERSITY PRESS

Shaftesbury Road, Cambridge CB2 8EA, United Kingdom

One Liberty Plaza, 20th Floor, New York, NY 10006, USA

477 Williamstown Road, Port Melbourne, VIC 3207, Australia

314–321, 3rd Floor, Plot 3, Splendor Forum, Jasola District Centre, New Delhi – 110025, India

103 Penang Road, #05–06/07, Visioncrest Commercial, Singapore 238467

Cambridge University Press is part of Cambridge University Press & Assessment, a department of the University of Cambridge.

We share the University's mission to contribute to society through the pursuit of education, learning and research at the highest international levels of excellence.

www.cambridge.org
Information on this title: www.cambridge.org/9781009230162

DOI: 10.1017/9781009230179

First published as Royal Institute of Philosophy Supplement: 57, The Philosophy of Need, 2005, Paperback ISBN 9780521678445.

This edition first published 2024.

A catalogue record for this publication is available from the British Library.

A Cataloging-in-Publication data record for this book is available from the Library of Congress

ISBN 978-1-009-23016-2 Paperback

CONTENTS

LIST OF CONTRIBUTORS

Sabina Alkire

David Braybrooke

Gillian Brock

Jonathan Lowe

Sarah Miller

John O'Neill

Soran Reader

Christopher Rowe

Garrett Thomson

David Wiggins

Bill Wringe

FOREWORD

GILLIAN BROCK

Appeals to need abound in ordinary discourse. People make claims about their needs all the time, and they do so in a way that suggests their needs should have a certain moral force. Needs also play an important role in contemporary popular discourse about social justice, climate change, obligations to future generations, dealing fairly with refugees, treating animals humanely, and critiques of consumerist lifestyles, to name just a few of the many examples. The idea of need seems to be appealed to in an increasing number of domains and debates. There is interest in need from several disciplines, including psychology, economics, philosophy, political science, social work, and sociology. And so it is no surprise that many might turn to a work such as *The Philosophy of Need* in search of philosophical wisdom concerning this ubiquitous concept.

When Soran Reader edited *The Philosophy of Need*, originally published in 2005, she did an excellent job assessing the state of philosophizing about need and collecting some of the best work being done at that time in the field. She marked her assessment of the state of play by looking back at some of the questions I originally posed in my earlier collection on the philosophy of need, *Necessary Goods: Our Responsibilities to*

Meet Others' Needs,[1] published in 1998. As she summarized the questions posed there, there are four categories:

1. Which needs are morally and politically important?
2. What importance do they have?
3. How can opponents be persuaded to accept the importance of these needs?
4. How can sceptical doubts be resolved?[2]

Reader reports that at the philosophy of need conference, held in Durham in 2003, which gave rise to the essays collected here, 'there was a newly confident consensus that some needs are morally significant, ... that such needs entail substantial political and moral responsibilities'.[3] This is not surprising, given that we were a bunch of needs-enthusiasts all already predisposed to think needs, in some form, were important and could ground significant responsibilities! But it is also not surprising that our confidence in needs was not uniformly shared with colleagues across our various fields. In fact, all of those four categories of questions posed in 1998 still dominate literature today.

At any rate, on Reader's assessment in 2005, the field had moved on significantly and she summarized these

---

[1] G. Brock (ed.), *Necessary Goods: Our Responsibilities to Meet Others' Needs* (Oxford: Rowman and Littlefield, 1998).

[2] S. Reader, 'Introduction', *The Philosophy of Need* (Cambridge: Cambridge University Press, 2005), 3. For the original, longer formulations of concerns, see Brock (ed.) *Necessary Goods*.

[3] Reader, 'Introduction', 4.

developments by framing new questions that she correctly imagined would shape continuing debate. These were:

1. What mistakes do opponents make in neglecting need? What is it that they dislike about need?
2. Where beyond political and moral philosophy might needs matter? What is the fundamental nature of needs? How do they fit into human nature?
3. How should we best frame, and how should we best meet, our moral responsibilities in relation to needs?[4]

These questions orient the original introduction to this volume, and Soran Reader situates the chapters in offering answers to these questions. It might be worth mentioning in particular that, in their important essays, Christopher Rowe, Sarah Miller, and Soran Reader draw attention to the important role the concept of needs has played in understanding the history of philosophy. And Jonathan Lowe makes a powerful argument that the concept of need plays a uniquely important role in the explanation of actions. Indeed, there is much scope for more work in highlighting the prominent role that needs can and have played across domains and in philosophizing through the ages. Reader's first two groups of questions remain as pressing today as they were in 2005. The same can be said for her third question, which has preoccupied needs theorists for millennia.

---

[4] Reader, 'Introduction', 4.

As I have noted, Reader was perhaps overly optimistic about the progress that had been made in accepting needs as an important concept ready to take its place with other core notions in normative domains. She believed that needs theorists had become less defensive in their positions, no longer having to expend as much energy on clearing away scepticism about needs, and misconceptions about these ideas. However, there has been a reversal in any gains that might have been made at the 2003 conference. Needs theorists continue to have to do much ground clearing before they can advance their views. And they are drawn back into some of the core issues that have long plagued theorizing about needs. The innovative work collected in this volume offers important and innovative approaches that can be used to shore up answers to some of the dominant recurring questions for needs theorists. Many of these contributions are highlighted in Reader's introduction.

Here, I turn my attention to some of the ways in which debates have evolved since the volume was originally published. As I see it, debates concerning needs have developed in several consequential ways, and here I identify a few important areas as key examples.

There has been substantial work in political philosophy on a variety of topics relevant to the study of needs. Notably, significant work has been done in analysing notions of how to distribute according to needs.[5] As Marx famously

---

[5] For some examples, see David Miller, 'Needs-Based Justice: Theory and Evidence', in A. Bauer and M. Meyerhuber (eds.), *Empirical Research and Normative Theory* (Berlin: De Gruyter, 2019); Nicole Hassoun,

advocated, a just society is one in which there would be distribution according to need. But what would this actually entail? There are numerous difficulties that should be considered even when we limit our attention to distribution according to needs. For instance, should strict priority go to the most needy? Should we, rather, give priority to those whose needs can be efficiently or effectively met with limited resources? When there are conditions of scarcity, should we simply observe a principle of equal provision for needs even though all will remain needy? Is there ever scope for meeting needs via lotteries? How should (say) housing needs be ranked, relative to (say) needs for education or health care, if choices must be made with limited budgets?

Another area of political philosophy where needs have gained considerable attention is in the debate between egalitarians and sufficientarians. Advocates for equality have been engaging extensively with proponents of a position known as 'sufficiency'. Whereas egalitarians promote a conception of justice that favours equality, sufficientarians typically claim that what justice requires is that everyone get sufficient for a good life, and needs have a prominent role in defining what is sufficient. The contemporary debate, sparked off by Harry Frankfurt, arises because he claimed that having *enough* rather than an *equal amount* should be

'Meeting Needs', *Utilitas* 21 (2009), 250–75; and Gillian Brock and David Miller, 'Needs in Moral and Political Philosophy', *Stanford Encyclopedia of Philosophy* (Summer 2019 Edition), Edward N. Zalta (ed.), URL = <https://plato.stanford.edu/archives/sum2019/entries/needs/>.

the focus of justice. Indeed, the focus on equality is harmful and misguided, according to Frankfurt. There is much to learn from this lively debate, but also, in my view, many ways to resolve the alleged tensions between the two opposing sides.[6] Needs have a distinctive role to play in understanding justice. And understanding what is important about the idea of equality has a central role to play as well. There is interesting work being done, and to be done, in tracing the important and subtle ways in which concern with needs and equality should be connected.[7]

Normative philosophers have also been much more engaged with global concerns over the last decade or so. For political philosophers, responsibilities to meet needs in the global sphere have been a prominent concern, with many different kinds of views being proposed. The debates about distributive justice, begun in the 1970s with Rawls's seminal work *A Theory of Justice*, originated in a context where the state largely defined the scope of justice. However, if we adopt a global perspective, how should this alter our account of distributive justice? There are many interesting accounts of how the global extension does or does not matter, and

[6] For excellent treatment of the debate between sufficientarians and egalitarians, see, for instance, Paula Casal, 'Why Sufficiency Is Not Enough', *Ethics* 117 (2) (2007), 296–326, and Liam Shields, *Just Enough: Sufficiency as a Demand of Justice* (Edinburgh: Edinburgh University Press, 2016).

[7] For some possibilities, see Gillian Brock, 'Sufficientarian and Needs-Based Approaches to Distributive Justice', in Serena Olsaretti (ed.), *The Oxford Handbook of Distributive Justice* (Oxford: Oxford University Press, 2018), 86–108.

innovative work has been done on showing the role of how needs combined with other salient considerations might affect responsibilities in the global domain.[8]

Following other trends in philosophy, there has been considerable interest in doing empirical work on needs. By studying ordinary folks' beliefs about needs, we can often gain some useful insights and much-needed correctives to more abstract philosophical approaches and positions.[9] Experiments have been designed to test people's convictions about how needs matter in a range of contexts. Research suggests that claims of need carry considerable weight when ordinary folks are asked about their views concerning such matters as social justice, fair distributions, and the like. Many experiments show that concern for needs is robust. However, as one might expect, justice is a multi-faceted concept and several considerations are relevant to our thinking about what justice requires, notwithstanding our views that needs carry significant weight in many contexts. So, researchers have been refining our knowledge of when and

---

[8] For some particularly interesting or different accounts focusing on the relationships between those who are needy and those in a position to assist, see Richard Miller, *Globalizing Justice: The Ethics of Poverty and Power* (Oxford: Oxford University Press, 2010); David Miller, *National Responsibility and Global Justice* (Oxford: Oxford University Press, 2007); John Rawls, *The Law of Peoples* (Cambridge, MA: Belknap, 1999); and Gillian Brock, *Global Justice: A Cosmopolitan Account* (Oxford: Oxford University Press, 2009).

[9] For an excellent summary of key points, see, for instance, Miller, 'Needs-Based Justice: Theory and Evidence'.

how needs matter, especially relative to other concerns that are relevant to justice.

Another noteworthy influence on the field since 2005 is the contribution Soran Reader herself made to theorizing about needs before her unfortunate death in 2012. In her book, *Needs and Moral Necessity*, Reader makes a number of bold claims about the role needs should play in moral philosophy. For instance, Reader claims that we should understand ethics as 'the practice of meeting needs'.[10] In order to understand the practice, we should understand four features of the moral terrain. These are: the agent; the act; the end that action is aimed at achieving; and the patient. While consequentialists focus on ends, deontologists on acts, and virtue theorists on agents, in the moral domain, the patient – the being who has needs – is sorely neglected.[11] Reader argues that examining the patient and her needs gives us important insights into successfully understanding the moral domain. Drawing on Aristotle, she develops an account according to which needs are those things that are central to a being. Human beings are not just biological beings, but rather have different identities – as, perhaps, a parent, a farmer, or a householder. All these needs central to identity can be morally demanding needs, but they are demanding only within the context of moral relationships. However, Reader's account of moral relationship is somewhat idiosyncratic, since it turns out that

[10] Soran Reader, *Needs and Moral Necessity* (New York: Routledge, 2007), 27.
[11] Reader, *Needs and Moral Necessity*, 42–4.

encounters, even brief ones, count as a form of moral relationship on her view. But some might wonder whether this not only stretches the idea of relationship, but rather dissipates the concern she was aiming to address in trying to limit the demandingness of needs. At any rate, Reader's provocative claims on how needs should transform our understanding of moral matters have provided much food for thought.

At least one other place where Soran's views did much to stimulate debate can be found in the influential paper that might help to revive interest in a needs-based approach in global public policy. Her paper, 'Does a Basic Needs Approach Need Capabilities?',[12] takes aim at some of the criticisms of needs concerning their so-called conceptual inadequacies. She argued that there is more conceptual richness in the concept than critics suppose. In particular, she has done much to advance understanding on the relative strengths and weaknesses of a needs-based approach, compared with its main rival based on 'capabilities'. This matters to global public policy. A basic needs approach played an important role in global public policy in the 1970s and early 1980s. However, the capabilities approach came to replace it in the late 1980s.[13] Indeed, the capabilities approach is a dominant framework used by the most influential organizations within which international development issues are

[12] Soran Reader, 'Does a Basic Needs Approach Need Capabilities?', *Journal of Political Philosophy* 14 (3) (2006), 337–50.

[13] For more on this approach, see the essay by Sabina Alkire in this volume.

implemented in policy and practice.[14] But, as Reader shows, many of the original criticisms of a needs-based approach were misguided – or, where they did have force, were criticisms that could have been avoided through better implementation policy. As she carefully documents, many of these criticisms simply do not hit their targets and are based on misunderstandings about needs-based views and their necessary commitments. Given Reader's important work in this area, it is possible we might see renewed interest in a needs-based approach to matters of global public policy.

As we look ahead at some new directions that needs theorizing might usefully take in the future, it is worth noting that there is important work on needs taking place in several disciplines. Needs theorists might profitably consider some of this literature, as there is much we can learn from such ventures. Of course, there have always been important cross-disciplinary approaches to the study of needs, and these have made influential contributions to the field. The work of Len Doyal and Ian Gough is particularly noteworthy in this regard. Their ground-breaking book *A Theory of Human Need*[15] has been prominent in the literature for almost three decades. Philosophers interested in needs should show more willingness to engage with and

---

[14] The most prominent of these is the United Nations, which makes use of capabilities in such important instruments as the UN Development Index and the UNDP Poverty Index. All of these are playing key roles in steering international development policy.

[15] Len Doyal and Ian Gough, *A Theory of Human Need* (Houndmills: Macmillan, 1991).

learn from colleagues working in other fields. In this regard, there are important contributions to understanding needs being made in psychology,[16] human development and development ethics,[17] social and public policy,[18] and social work,[19] to name just a few of these significant areas. There should be more appreciation from philosophers that we might learn something important about needs by looking across disciplines. Indeed, many disciplines have useful insights to offer which can improve our philosophizing about needs.

[16] See, for instance, Richard Ryan and Edward Deci, *Self-Determination Theory: Basic Psychological Needs in Motivation, Development and Wellness* (New York: Guilford Press, 2017).

[17] Des Gasper, *The Ethics of Development: From Economism to Human Development* (Edinburgh: Edinburgh University Press, 2004).

[18] Ian Gough, *Heat, Greed and Human Need: Climate Change, Capitalism and Sustainable Well-being* (Cheltenham: Edward Elgar, 2017).

[19] Michael Dover, 'Human Needs', in E. Mullen (ed.), *Oxford Bibliography Online: Social Work* (New York: Oxford University Press, 2010); and Michael Dover, 'Human Needs: Overview', in C. Franklin (ed.), *The Encyclopedia of Social Work* (New York: Oxford University Press, 2016).

Introduction

SORAN READER

The concept of need plays a significant but still relatively unexplored role in philosophy. In September 2003 The Royal Institute of Philosophy funded a conference held at Hatfield College, Durham, England, where philosophers from around the world devoted an enjoyable weekend to further exploration.[1] In everyday political life, scepticism about the importance of needs seems to be abating, perhaps reflecting an increased confidence among needs-theorists, grounded in years of painstaking analysis and argument on the margins of mainstream philosophy. This increased confidence freed participants at the conference to work less defensively and more constructively, and to extend their depth and range of their work. One happy result is that

[1] Thanks to the Royal Institute of Philosophy for funding the conference, and to Anthony O'Hear, James Garvey and everyone else at the Institute who helped for their generous and timely help with the final preparation of this manuscript for publication. I would also like to thank everyone who came to the conference, and those bodies which contributed extra funding: the Aristotelian Society, the Mind Association, and the Analysis Trust (who provided funds to enable graduates to attend). Staff at Hatfield College also helped to make it a memorable event.

new aspects of the philosophy of need are identified and explored in this volume.

In this introduction I highlight three topics that struck me as central concerns at the conference. I don't claim that my topics exhaust important concerns in the philosophy of need, or that the developments I identify are by any means the only or most important ones to have occurred in recent years. My aim is simply to highlight topics discussed at the conference which may be of wider interest.

Several speakers would tackle aspects of a topic in their papers, and questions and discussion would return to each of these topics again and again. The first topic is the mistakes that are involved in neglecting need. What are those mistakes, exactly? And what might lead philosophers to make mistakes like that? The second topic is the role of need outside political philosophy. What is the significance of need in the history of philosophy? What role might it play in the philosophy of action, or in the philosophy of psychology? What is the metaphysical nature of needs, and how are human needs related to which aspects of human nature? The third topic concerns efforts to find the best way to characterise our responsibilities in relation to needs, given that people still tend to be wary of claims from need. Must we talk in terms of need, or is some other language preferable, for example the language of rights or capabilities? How can we ensure needy people are not patronised when they are helped? How can we ensure autonomy and freedom are respected?

In 1. I set these new topics in the context of some recent developments in the philosophy of need. In 2.–4. each new topic has a section of its own, in which I sketch the claims and arguments of papers that concentrate on that topic, and set the claims of each paper in the context of claims made by other participants. I also note relevant points from papers that make their main contribution on a different topic. I don't offer a full philosophical discussion of the arguments of every paper, but I do make brief comments, mentioning some possible objections and flagging up what strike me as intriguing questions, or promising lines of further inquiry on the topic. In 5. I conclude with thoughts about where the philosophy of need might go next.

My hope is that this introduction will enable readers to see which chapters they will need to read in full, which they should turn to first, and how each chapter, and the volume as a whole, are related to current debates in the philosophy of need and beyond. Another hope, of course, is that this volume will inspire readers to take the philosophy of need forward in their own work.

1.   Developments in the Philosophy of Need

In everyday life it is once again generally accepted that the concept of need is politically important. Needs are no longer so quickly dismissed as 'things you want, but aren't prepared to pay for'; liberal and capitalist worries that policies based on need will harm beneficiaries by being unduly paternalistic, or harm donors by fostering dependency and excessive demands, are no longer so widely, loudly or persistently voiced in political discussion. This change may be largely a matter of changing political fashion, a conceptual shift that has nothing to do with philosophical argument—but it is surely also in part at least thanks to the work on need of analytic philosophers, and political activists like the founders of the pragmatic Basic Needs Approach to international development.[2]

One way to reveal developments in the philosophy of need, is to compare contemporary questions with those treated a while ago. These developments can usefully be summed up with reference to an earlier collection of papers, *Necessary Goods*, edited by Gillian Brock in 1998, where Brock identifies the following questions as central concerns in the philosophy of need at that time:

1. Which needs are morally and politically important?
2. What importance do they have?
3. How can opponents be persuaded to accept the importance of these needs?
4. How can sceptical doubts be resolved?[3]

The task set by Brock's first question was to identify the central category of morally important needs ('essential', 'vital', 'absolute' or 'basic' needs).[4] The task set by her

---

[2] See for example the work of Dharam Ghai and others at the ILO in the 1970s, and the further work by Paul Streeten, Frances Stewart, S J Hurki, Mahbub ul Haq and Norman Hicks for the world bank, which resulted in *First Things First* (Oxford: Oxford University Press World Bank Research Publications, 1982).

[3] G. Brock, *Necessary Goods* (Lanham: Rowman and Littlefield, 1998).

[4] See D. Wiggins, 'Claims of Need' in *Needs, Values, Truth* (Oxford: Oxford University Press, 1987), 1–57, and G. Thomson, *Needs* (London: Routledge, 1987).

second, was to characterise the kind of moral importance such needs might have in political contexts (grounding rights, entailing obligations, or being a valuable aspect of well-being).[5] The task set by her third question was to find arguments to resist political opponents (for example, by arguing that commitments to freedom, equality, justice or well-being entail a commitment to meet needs).[6] The task set by the fourth question was to deal with sceptical objections about the need concept (such as that it is contestable, and vulnerable to paternalism and manipulation).[7]

At the conference it was evident that concerns had shifted since Brock posed her questions in 1998. There was a newly confident consensus that some needs are morally significant, and that what makes them significant is their necessity for the life and activity of the needing human being. There was consensus that such needs entail substantial political and moral responsibilities, and much less time was spent on convincing opponents or dealing with sceptical doubts than used to be felt necessary. This increased

---

[5] Several philosophers address these issues in their contributions to *Necessary Goods* and elsewhere, including David Wiggins, Onora O'Neill, Robert Goodin, David Braybrooke, Gillian Brock and James Sterba.

[6] See for example David Braybrooke's work, particularly *Meeting Needs* (Princeton: Princeton University Press, 1987), the work of Paul Streeten in *First Things First* and elsewhere, and that of Frances Stewart, Len Doyal, Ian Gough and Des Gasper.

[7] Most analytic writing on need pays considerable attention to sceptical doubts. In 'Claims of Need' David Wiggins addresses a particularly wide range of doubts.

confidence is liberating for needs-theorists. No longer limited to proposing and defending their approach, they are now free to expose and diagnose the mistakes which led their opponents to ignore or dismiss need. They are free to explore the concept more deeply, to show how it contributes to a wider range of areas of philosophy (like action theory, philosophy of psychology, metaphysics, and history of philosophy), and to give detailed attention to the practical political problems of implementing a needs-responsive public or private ethic.

We might sum up these developments by framing a new set of questions:

1. What mistakes do opponents make, in neglecting need? What is it they dislike about need?
2. Where beyond political and moral philosophy might needs matter? What is the fundamental nature of needs? How do they fit into human nature?
3. How should we best frame, and how should we best meet, our moral responsibilities in relation to needs?

Each of these questions furnishes the topic of one of the sections below.

2.   What mistakes are made in neglecting need, and why?

In this topic, we see a change in tone from defensive to critical. Rather than trying to persuade opponents by addressing their doubts, as needs-theorists did in answering Brock's third question 'How can we persuade opponents?', participants use powerful arguments to expose the mistakes involved in failing to give needs their due (Wiggins and Brock). Another change is from defensive to diagnostic. Rather than offering arguments to show why liberals, libertarians, utilitarians and classical economists must take account of needs, participants begin to explore the interesting question of what it is about needs that opponents dislike (O'Neill), and what might be done about it.

David Wiggins recalls a time when 'everyone knew in practice what need meant, knew a need from a mere desire, and knew a vital need from a need which was less than that' (p. 26). When the primacy of need began to give way to the maximisation of economic goods like wealth and time-savings, Wiggins was led to the philosophy of need, in search of ways to restore the concept to its rightful place. Outraged for example by the way, in 1960s proposals for new ring roads for London, the disvalue of the destruction of people's homes and communities was 'swamped ... by the simple numerosity of a vast sum of time savings for persons driving motor-vehicles' (p. 27), Wiggins began a lifelong search for arguments for need that sceptics and critics of the concept would not be able to ignore. Of course, as Wiggins points out, sceptics and critics of need continued as if deaf and blind to such arguments, however rigorous, however reasonable. And as he also points out, they continue still. The increased acceptance of the concept of need amongst philosophers, political theorists and development thinkers that I noted above has so far had little influence on the thinking of governments, economists, or executives of powerful corporations. The mistake such agents make is a moral one: they deny and ignore something of obvious and fundamental moral importance.

But conceptual and empirical mistakes have also contributed to the marginalisation of need, for which philosophers and political theorists must share some responsibility. Wiggins focuses on the conceptual mistakes, seeking to demonstrate the indispensability of the need concept to any adequate theory of rationality. He first tackles prudential rationality, using Richard Hare as his example. For Hare, prudently self-interested agents have to be consistent, which he takes to require valuing others' preferences or interests as they value their own. This generalised prudence Hare argues is equivalent to classical Utilitarianism, which would make utilitarianism a requirement of rationality. But, Wiggins protests, Hare's project must fail since he relies on a false picture of individual prudential reasoning:

> Is "maximise the satisfaction of my preferences" really the thing a rational deliberator actually intends in practising individual prudence? Surely a rational deliberator asks himself constantly not so much *how to maximise* his preference-satisfaction but *what to prefer* ... Indeed, one might think that he will be foolish not to interest himself always in the question *what really matters here? what does a person such as I am (and such as I aspire to be) vitally need*? [This is a] miserably attenuated ... conception of the ordinary rationality of ordinary first-person deliberation. (p. 35)

Wiggins makes similarly fundamental criticisms of John Rawls' account of political rationality. Rawls invites us to imagine a group of free, rational, self-interested deliberators behind a veil of ignorance of their own social positions and conception of the good, charged with the task of rationally deciding principles to govern the basic structure of their society. The first question Rawls has them ask, is by what principle they will be able to accept inequalities resulting from contingencies. Wiggins objects that a question about need, like 'what guarantees of what strength ... [can be made] to ensure that the worst bad luck anyone encounters will be alleviated?', is what rationality actually requires, because 'what harms the dispossessed or destitute is not so much inequality as dire unsatisfied need' (p. 38). A principle aimed at preventing inequality misses what people really care about, which is that no-one should suffer unnecessary harm. Rationally grounded social justice, Wiggins argues, will begin with thoughts about need, and will 'go by a direct route against contingency', and be 'essentially ameliorative'.

Wiggins then considers economic rationality, and proposes that the precautionary principle, often cited as a requirement of economic rationality, ought to be understood in terms of need. The principle requires that where human activities risk environmental damage, they must be restrained even in the absence of full scientific certainty about the negative effects. Wiggins champions Hans Jonas' version of the principle, which requires us to 'act so that the effects of our actions are not destructive of the possibility of economic life in the future' (p. 44).

We must give priority not just to present vital needs, but to the needs of that on which all earthly things depend to meet their needs: the earth itself. Our reluctance to protect the earth may be rooted in a fear that we will be unable both to meet needs, satisfy desires, and leave enough and as good for the future. Wiggins points out this fear may be unfounded: there is hope for sustainability. But even if sacrifices from the present generation are required, he argues, they are indeed *required*—and by practical rationality itself, not by any particular philosophy or creed. Given that our generation is but one moment in history, we cannot afford to be ignorant or reckless about what the world needs from us if it is to be sustained for future generations.

With these brief but powerful sketches, Wiggins reveals 'just some of the possibilities . . . of setting free the serious notion of need and giving it its independence' (p. 41–2). Where Wiggins focuses on the moral and conceptual mistakes involved in ignoring need, Gillian Brock highlights some empirical mistakes, arguing that the most popular current liberal theories of justice underestimate the priority rational political deliberators will give to need. Brock first outlines a veil of ignorance device which she argues will plausibly help rational deliberators to be impartial, by concealing from them what will be in their immediate self-interest.[8] With the usefulness of the veil of ignorance established, Brock draws our attention to the experimental work of Norman Frohlich and Joe Oppenheimer.[9]

---

[8] Brock's veil of ignorance is structurally and procedurally similar to Rawls' well-known one, but Brock makes different assumptions, and so draws different conclusions, to Rawls.

[9] N. Frohlich and J. Oppenheimer, *Choosing Justice: An Empirical Approach to Ethical Theory* (Berkeley: University of California Press, 1992).

Frohlich and Oppenheimer set out to test empirically what principles of justice rational deliberators behind a simulated veil of ignorance would actually choose. They were particularly interested to see whether deliberators would prefer John Rawls' difference principle of maximising income for the worst off, or John Harsanyi's principle of maximising average income; two further principles were included as options: maximising the average with a floor constraint, and maximising the average with a range constraint. The experiments were detailed, and were repeated in different cultural contexts. Their striking results should give supporters of both Rawls and Harsanyi pause.

'Interestingly', Brock says in a most understated piece of criticism, 'the principles chosen in the experiment do not support either Rawls' or Harsanyi's models. Indeed, there was almost no support for the Difference Principle' (p. 59). Only 1% supported the difference principle which was championed by John Rawls as a principle deducible a priori behind the veil of ignorance. Only 12% supported the average-maximisation principle favoured by John Harsanyi again on the basis of a priori arguments. 9% supported the range constraint. 78% supported the floor constraint. The conclusion about needs that Brock draws is hard to avoid. Even behind a veil of ignorance, rational deliberators will seek first and foremost to ensure that essential needs are met. Reduction of inequality or maximisation of income do not matter as much as seeing to it that everyone has enough to avoid harm. Deliberators do not care as much about the relative well-being of Rawls's difference principle, or the average income of Harsanyi's, as they care about the absolute deprivation that the floor constraint is conceived to prevent. These experiments also showed that deliberators don't just prefer a needs-meeting principle when behind a veil of ignorance. When they are required experimentally to 'live by' the need-principle in various scenarios in later stages of the experiment, this increases their confidence in it.

Why do so many philosophers neglect need? Every participant at the conference felt the pressure to answer this question. The costs appear to be high, with moral compromise, conceptual weakness and poor fit with the facts already on the list. Persistent sources of doubt about needs include the thoughts that needs seem passive, that meeting them seems paternalistic, and that demanding they should be met seems apt to be manipulative and to avoid the issue of desert. Sabina Alkire considers the passivity and vulnerability to paternalism of the need concept, and argues the 'capability approach' of Amartya Sen provides an important corrective supplement. David Braybrooke confronts the worry about desert, arguing we should avoid the term 'need' when dealing with people who feel this doubt—other terms will elicit their help more effectively. Wiggins adds the suggestion that the sheer power of the concept might be what repels philosophers: if they let it in, it will take over, derailing their theories.[10]

---

[10] If Wiggins is right, in place of classical Utilitarianism, Hare would have had a needs-based ethic; in place of the difference principle, Rawls would have a principle of needs-meeting, and economists using the precautionary principle would have had to acknowledge their reliance on a concept they claim to dispense with in favour of preference.

John O'Neill concentrates on something else about needs that may put philosophers and politicians off: claims from need appear to humiliate the claimant. O'Neill distinguishes between talk of need as a principle of justice, which says people must have what they need as a matter of justice (as for example in the need principle endorsed in Frohlich and Oppenheimer's experiments), and talk of need as a principle of community or solidarity, which says meeting needs is constitutive of relations of care within a society. The liberal worry about need as a principle of community, distinct from worries about passivity, paternalism and desert, is that making needs-meeting central to social relationships may be incompatible with recognising the autonomy and independence of individuals. Correspondingly, needs based criticisms of the market may fail to recognise the ways markets foster independence and autonomy.

O'Neill considers the arguments of Adam Smith against the appeal to necessities in economic life, which in turn draw on the Stoic values of self-sufficiency and independence. Speaking from need is humiliating. Depending on others and appealing to their benevolence to meet one's needs is humiliating. Worse, such dependency 'tends to corrupt and enervate and debase the mind' (p. 79). Yet vulnerability to need, and mutual dependency between members of any society, are, as Smith also recognises, ineliminable facts of life. Smith's solution is the market: 'through market exchange individuals can meet each others' needs without benevolence' (p. 81). This is because the market avoids the appeal to benevolence. Rather than appealing to the benevolence of the person to whom I sell my labour,

I appeal to their self-interest. This is how I can preserve my independence and dignity. There are objections—the independence thus achieved is an illusion, as I now depend on the system of exchange, and if that fails to meet my needs, it is no longer clear that there is anyone to whom I can appeal.

This independence depends on my having something somebody wants to pay for, and, notoriously, for the most needy in society this condition will never be met. Not everyone can play market. But the objection that O'Neill develops focuses on Smith's concept of self-sufficiency. Smith himself acknowledged that to believe in the self-sufficiency presupposed by the market requires self-deception, but insisted it is necessary for economic development:

> [The 'invisible hand' metaphor refers] to the indirect and unintended link between the self-deception of the rich, 'their natural selfishness and rapacity' in the pursuit of 'vain and insatiable desires' and 'the distribution of the necessaries of life' across the whole population and hence the general improvement of the condition of the poor through the encouragement of commerce and industry. (p. 95)

O'Neill argues that Smith's claims in support of this self-deception cannot be sustained. First, self-deception (like dependency, which Smith wants us to avoid for this reason) corrupts the mind. Second, autonomy and independence are represented as virtues, but they are only contrasted by their defenders with vices of deficiency—heteronomy, as lack of autonomy, and dependency, as lack of independence.

O'Neill points out that a virtue must be contrasted with vices of excess, as well as vices of deficiency, and suggests that the excesses of autonomy and independence, which are fostered and thrive in the market economy, have been given insufficient attention by supporters of autonomy and independence.

The missing vice O'Neill christens 'arrogant self-sufficiency'. Autonomy 'can take the excessively individual-istic form which fails to acknowledge necessary dependence on others: the resulting conceit is as much opposed to autonomy as excessive dependence' (p. 96). Modern market societies don't just fail to theorise and warn against any such vices, but actually present them as virtues. The individual self and its wants are made sovereign. The remedy O'Neill proposes is an egalitarianism founded on the existence and recognition of common vulnerability. Only if human beings recognise common vulnerability to need, can the humili-ation involved in speech from need be eliminated. Only if we allow it could happen to any of us, will neediness cease to be shameful, and the resulting impulse to avoid the needy, and blame them for their plight and our discomfort, be overcome.

3. **Where might needs matter beyond political philosophy? How are they related to human mind and nature?**

In this topic, we see a shift of emphasis. Rather than con-sidering which needs are morally or politically important, as did those addressing Brock's first question, 'Which needs are important?', participants take for granted that existence needs are morally and politically important. Some branch out from there to explore the role need can play outside political philosophy, for example in the history of philosophy (Rowe, Reader and Miller), or the philosophy of action (Lowe). Others consider the nature of needs more deeply, exploring its connection with interests and desires (Thomson), and question the assumption that morally important needs are especially connected with human agency, rather than with human life more broadly conceived.

a.   History of Philosophy

Christopher Rowe, Sarah Miller and I explore the role that the concept of need has played, albeit largely unremarked hitherto, in the history of philosophy. Rowe considers the implications for our understanding of needs of a view he attributes to Aristotle, that there is no necessary connection between being a biological human being, and being rational and potentially virtuous. Rowe points out that this leaves open the possibility that those lacking what we moderns call needs may be sub-human. The accidents of human life, instances of occurrent essential need, that result in a lack of rationality or virtue, such as deprivation in childhood or misfortune in later life, are seen from Aristotle's perspective as accidents that deprive their subject of full humanity, because full humanity is defined in terms of rationality and virtue. This explains Aristotle's distasteful doctrine of natural slavery, and his relegation of 'necessary people' (farmers, labourers, traders and craftsmen) to lesser status, leaving full rational humanity the sole prerogative of those with sufficient leisure time to conceive and pursue their own projects. On Rowe's view, for Aristotle neediness impinges on humanity. Rowe contrasts this with an earlier Socratic or Platonic view, according to which human beings are necessarily both rational and virtuous.

For the Socrates and Plato of the *Lysis*, the text Rowe draws on most heavily, human beings as such inalienably desire only the actual good, and, by implication, necessarily have only one real need, the need for the wisdom required to acquire the good. The view does not deny that human beings may have felt desires for the bad—but it does insist that those are not desires properly speaking, they are to actual desire as illusion is to veridical perception. Rowe argues that this view has the political advantage against Aristotle's, of preserving the idea of a valuable core of all human beings as such which is intrinsically set on the real good, and by implication must always be respected. But the implications for our understanding of needs are less immediately attractive. The Socratic view suggests that the things we normally take to be human needs are only ever circumstantially good, and so only ever circumstantially desirable. Even a physically healthy life, assumed by contemporary needs-theorists to be an essential need if anything is, is only a circumstantial need on the Platonic view. The only unconditional need turns out to be not any basic or vital need of human life, but wisdom: the knowledge of human nature and good which will tell us what, in any actual circumstance, is good for us, thereby telling us what we need, which is to say, what we in fact desire there.

I explore Aristotle's views about needs in more detail. Aristotle's account of human needs is valuable because it describes the connections between logical, meta-physical, physical, human and ethical necessities, but Aristotle does not fully draw out the implications for human needs and virtue. Like modern sceptics about need, Aristotle was ambivalent about necessities. He thought the absolute necessities of God and eternal cyclical motion were a good thing, but he was hostile to many of the necessities we call 'human needs', and I argue that this prevented him from seeing the constitutive role meeting needs must play in human virtue. Aristotle regards many ordinary human necessities, including labouring, farming, trading and craft, as mere necessities, not really proper parts of human life; but he regards other more grand necessities, including war, politics and religion, as necessities that are proper parts of human life, and proposes virtuous people should not meet ordinary needs, but should leave that to those others Rowe charges Aristotle thought fall short of full humanity.

I argue Aristotle was wrong to downgrade ordinary needs: they are as apt to be proper parts of a good life as the grand ones, and the Aristotelian good man must be able to recognise and meet needs. I then argue that Aristotle was led into error, first because his conception of life and action as aimed at leisure is flawed; second because his conception of human self-sufficiency as having fewer or no needs, rather than met needs, is incoherent; third, because his claim that self-sufficiency might consist in having the power to get others to meet your needs, rather than the ability to meet them yourself, is false. The proper Aristotelian conclusion, is that far from being an inferior activity fit only for slaves, meeting needs is actually the first part of Aristotelian virtue.

Sarah Miller turns to more recent history, and describes a problem in the ethics of care which she suggests can best be resolved by drawing on the account of true human needs and what must be done about them that is to be found in Kant's moral philosophy. Philosophers working from the perspective of the ethics of care notice that the needy require care, and argue that caring is constitutive of an agent's goodness. Good care must also be interactive, rather than active on the part of the carer and passive on the part of the cared-for. Whilst the recognition of need, respect for the dignity of the needy, and recognition of the value of what needs-meeters do are all extremely valuable original contributions to contemporary moral philosophy uniquely made by care-ethicists, Miller argues that they do not go quite far enough, to the extent that they do not establish, beyond the virtuousness of caring, a binding duty on all moral agents to care. Kant's moral philosophy, she argues, provides just the resources necessary for such an argument.

Kant establishes a duty of beneficence. But because the Kantian duty of beneficence is a wide, imperfect duty, it requires supplementation, some of which we can find in Kant (specification of precise actions, limitations of scope and sacrifice, reciprocity of care, and promotion of agency for the pursuit of the agent's own ends), but some of which we must return to the ethics of care to find: an account of sympathy for the needy, moral perception of need, and the need to care for the dignity of the needy when care-giving.

Both elements, Miller argues, of a form of moral duty which has sympathetic, perceptive, well-judged and dignifying care as its content, are vital to an adequate and comprehensive moral philosophy.

b.   Philosophy of Action

Jonathan Lowe argues that the concept of need may be uniquely equipped to play a role in the explanation of actions. Externalist accounts of reasons for action usually cite 'facts' or 'states of affairs' as the ontological categories to which such reasons belong. But problems arise for such accounts. Facts or states of affairs, to function as reasons for action, would have to be normative; but this would violate the fact/value distinction. In addition, a normative fact would be a metaphysically 'queer' entity in the sense made famous by J L Mackie. Pursuing an analogy with the explanation of belief in theoretical reasoning, Lowe argues that to avoid these difficulties we should see facts, where they function as reasons, as reasons for belief rather than for action. My beliefs have propositional content, as when my belief that it is raining has the propositional content 'it is raining'. Just so, Lowe proposes, we should take my actions to have 'actual content' which are acts, as when my action of giving you a gift has the actual content 'gift-giving'. Just as different beliefs may have the same propositional content, so different acts may have the same actual content. Just as a true belief is one whose propositional content corresponds to a fact, so, Lowe argues, a good action should be thought of as one which 'corresponds'—or perhaps rather 'answers'—to a need.

As theoretical reasoning aims at truth, so practical reasoning aims at goodness. With this framework in mind, differences between the logic of belief and the logic of action are shown to follow from fundamental ontological differences between facts and needs. Where facts cannot conflict, needs can. Another metaphysical implication is that we will no longer be able to conceive of the world as a totality of facts or states of affairs: we will have to see it as permeated by needs also. Whether such needs can be understood naturalistically is a question Lowe leaves open, but Thomson and others suggested a naturalistic interpretation of needs may be plausible.[11]

Doubts might be raised about Lowe's claim that needs can have an especially fundamental role to play in understanding actions. It might be argued that rather than needs or facts, states of affairs, as possible worlds which may or may not be realised as facts and brought about by actions, are the ontological category into which reasons for action should be taken to fall.[12] But even if Lowe's strong claim

[11] Lowe's account of the relationship between the logic of action and the logic of belief is reminiscent of G E M Anscombe's arguments, where she refers to the shared structure as 'the great Aristotelian parallel'. But Lowe goes further than Anscombe, who does not see any special role for need, and does not attend to the metaphysical problems that might be raised by taking practical reasons to be facts. See G. E. M. Anscombe, 'Practical Inference', in *Virtues and Reasons*, ed. by Hursthouse, Lawrence and Quinn (Oxford: Clarendon Press, 1995), 1–34.

[12] Jonathan Dancy has made this kind of point in *Practical Reality* (Oxford: Oxford University Press, 2000), and more recently in correspondence.

(that all reasons for action as such must be needs) may have to be weakened, perhaps to include good-making affordances less demanding than needs (interests, capacities to benefit, or to realise capabilities, for example), claims for 'states of affairs' may be underspecified. Not any state of affairs can be a reason for action—states of affairs which could not be brought about by an agent, or could not be known about or experienced, could not be reasons for an agent to act. If the metaphysical category must be narrower than 'states of affairs', but may have to be broader than 'needs', perhaps 'states of affairs affording opportunities to do good' is the best way to specify the relevant category. Needs will then form a substantial part, if not the whole, of that category.

c.   Philosophy of Mind and Human Nature

Rather than beginning with an intractable philosophical problem, and proposing a new role for needs in solving the problem, as Lowe does, some participants began with the notion of a morally important need, and sought to give a fuller philosophical account of the nature and significance of such needs. In this spirit, Garrett Thomson explores how our essential needs are related to our interests and desires. Thomson defines essential needs as inescapable necessities. Inescapable necessities are things without which it follows causally inescapably that the subject will suffer serious harm. The subject cannot forgo their fundamental needs, and it is this that gives the concept of fundamental need practical leverage, and shows the connection between such needs, the essential nature of the needing being and what it is for such a being to suffer harm.

Thomson then turns to explicating the notion of harm. He argues that the familiar desire theory of harm, popularised by economic utility theory, which defines harm as the deprivation of that which we desire, want or prefer, is inadequate because it invites a counterintuitive uncritical attitude to desire. In its place, Thomson offers his own 'general motivating interest' theory of harm, according to which we suffer harm when we are deprived of that which it is in our core interests to have. Core interests are then defined, drawing on Freud's theory of underlying motivation, moderated by a critical, hermeneutic approach to desires, as the motivational source of desires. Interests explain why we want the particular things we do, as when hunger explains a trip to the fridge, but they are not themselves desires (because they are independent of beliefs, and because they do not determinately motivate specific, particular actions). Neither, however, are they metaphysically separate entities—interests are 'facets of our wants' (p. 181). Some of these interests are inescapable:

> [Such interests] demonstrate in what sense our well-being consists of living in accordance with our nature, rather than … getting what we desire [they] set limits to how radically and deeply we can change ourselves, and … determine ends that must be taken as given in prudential deliberation. (p. 185)

Thomson emphasises the connection between essential nature and what will count as true needs. Our true needs

23

are the natural necessities of our essential nature, those things we must have in order to be what we are. The notion of nature in use here might benefit from some refinement and clarification. Thomson conceives the nature which fixes our inescapable interests as that about us which is given, which we cannot change. But Thomson also hints that he is aware of another, intriguing aspect of human nature made much of by Aristotle and neo-Aristotelian philosophers, which is that as well as what we might call the 'first nature' that is more or less absolutely inescapable, of raw constitution and brute environment, human beings acquire 'second nature'—characteristic ways of being and acting—through induction into some of the many distinctive forms of life characteristic of first-natural human beings.

Thomson refers to human second nature as 'the more optional sides of our nature'. But I wonder how 'optional' our second-natural identities can be. Consider my second-natural identities as a philosopher, a citizen, a mother, a musician. Depending on how complete my induction into the form of life has been, and how much it pervades and shapes my life, it may be that the fundamental interests, needs and desires arising from my second nature are more inescapable, in a morally important sense, than those arising from my first nature as a human being. If I do not get what I need to be the mother or the philosopher I am, in what sense can I, the unique individual I am, survive?

Other participants also touched on questions about how morally important needs are related to which aspects of human nature. Christopher Rowe raised the challenge of whether we truly ever unqualifiedly need anything but wisdom. Others challenged an assumption long held by philosophers of need, that morally important needs are necessities for agency. Sarah Miller, Gillian Brock, David Braybrooke and Sabina Alkire continued to emphasise the connection between morally important needs and agency. But in discussion several contributors questioned this. John O'Neill pointed out that requirements for existence are not co-extensive with requirements for agency. When I need pain-relief, for example, this need does not have to be explained in terms of a privation and restoration of agency, but might be better explained with reference to some broader notion of human life. This broader notion of human life might include simply being, experiencing in characteristic ways, manifesting, expressing or presenting one's nature or character, and engaging in relationships. All of these aspects of human life richly conceived might be sources of morally important needs, on a par with the capacities for action already taken to ground important needs.

One source of the assumption that essential needs serve agency suggested in discussion, might be that this assumption provides uniquely effective conceptual leverage against sceptics about need. Libertarians, liberals and capitalists all value free agency highly. Establishing that even they had to care about needs, was one of the most central projects of earlier philosophical work on need, and the topic of several papers in Brock's anthology. But if, as many at the conference suspected, this argument has more or less been won, we may now be in a stronger position to broaden out our conception of the bases of morally important need.

It was also suggested in discussion that the focus on agency might reflect a 'western' cultural bias. Sabina Alkire suggested an approach to essential needs which defines them in more specific detail, as necessities of particular human capabilities, understood as 'dimensions of human flourishing' which may be passive or active, might avoid the cultural imperialism of preoccupation with individual freedom and production, whilst retaining a commitment to self-determination and dignity of those seeking to meet their needs.

4. How should we frame our responsibilities to meet needs? How to meet them?

With this topic, once again, we see a shift of emphasis. Where those addressing Brock's second question, 'What importance do needs have?', and her fourth question, 'How can we allay scepticism?' were concerned to establish some genuine obligations arising from needs, and tied up in answering sweeping sceptical doubts, participants at the conference felt confident enough to set sceptical worries aside. Taking for granted that needs ground significant rights and obligations, participants turn their attention to considering how best to frame those obligations, and how best to meet them in practice (Wringe, Braybrooke and Alkire).

Are responsibilities relating to needs a matter of obligation, or rights? As we saw above, Sarah Miller draws on Kant to argue for a universal imperfect duty to meet needs which is necessary to complete our understanding of what it is to care. Developing this idea, Bill Wringe argues we have a collective obligation to meet needs, grounded in a positive subsistence right of the needy to have their needs met. To make the case, Wringe starts by taking issue with the arguments of Onora O'Neill in 'Rights, Obligations and Needs'.[13] Onora O'Neill argued that although it makes sense to speak of a universal imperfect duty to meet needs (of the sort Miller describes) it does not make sense to speak of any positive right of the needy to have their needs met.

Subsistence rights, for Onora O'Neill, are 'empty manifesto rights',[14] because for her a right, to be coherent, must fall into one or other of two categories—universal rights and special rights. Universal rights, such as the right not to be killed, impose a duty on every moral agent which all can consistently respect. Special rights, such as the right to be repaid a debt, impose a duty only on a specified individual moral agent. Subsistence rights, she argues, fall into neither category, which she takes to entail that they cannot be rights at all. In the light of this, she recommends we shift the focus in our discourse about how to frame helping action to meet needs, from talking about rights or entitlements of the needy, to talking about the duties or obligations of agents able to help.

Bill Wringe argues that O'Neill is wrong to insist that well-formed rights must be either universal or special. He argues that subsistence rights generate obligations which fall into a distinctive third category, which he calls 'collective obligations'. A collective obligation is one that can only be discharged by the collaborative, co-ordinated action of a

---

[13] O. O'Neill, 'Rights, Obligations and Needs', *Necessary Goods*, G. Brock (ed.) (Lanham: Rowman and Littlefield, 1998), 95–112.

[14] Ibid., 12.

group comprising more than one agent. The skills, knowledge and well-placedness of the different members of the collective are complementary, and are all irreducibly essential to the collective needs-meeting action required to respect subsistence rights.

It might be objected that the difference between Wringe and Onora O'Neill seems merely rhetorical—where Wringe prefers to speak of rights, O'Neill prefers to speak of obligations. But the differences are philosophically and ethically deeper than this. Philosophically, O'Neill denies the coherence of subsistence rights. Ethically, this denial might be cited to justify the dismissal as incoherent of claims of right made by needy individuals and groups, which would compound their humiliation (see the discussion of John O'Neill's paper, above). Further, Onora O'Neill's Kantian account of the obligation to meet needs, like Sarah Miller's, puts it on a par with other imperfect obligations such as the obligation to develop my own talents, and does not explain why it is intuitively so obviously more important to see to it that subsistence needs are met, than it is to see that my talents are developed.

Where Wringe argues that essential needs constitute rights, Gillian Brock argues needs are more fundamental, so that needs could and perhaps should displace rights: 'in order to draw up a sensible list of our human rights we must have a sense of our basic needs' (p. 65), second, needs-talk is more universally recognised and valued: 'while talk about human rights is popular in some cultures, particularly in the West, it does not always enjoy good resonance in many others' (p. 66). The question of whether talk of need should be integrated into a discourse of rights or obligations, or whether it should rather replace them, forming a complete normative discourse of its own, remains to be addressed.[15]

One way to understand the debate between Miller, O'Neill, Wringe, Brock and others about talk of needs *versus* talk of rights and obligations, might be to see it as a debate about which conceptual framework has the greatest moral force. Brock discusses the relative merits of talk of rights *versus* talk of needs and concludes that needs have wider moral force; Miller argues that talk of duty is an essential supplement to talk in the ethics of care of the virtue of needs-meeting care; Wringe argues against Onora O'Neill that talk of subsistence rights is well-formed and politically important: just as Miller argued the Kantian duty to care is necessary to give need its full moral force, so Wringe argues the language of rights adds a layer of force to needs which would otherwise be lacking.

This question of moral force was David Braybrooke's central concern at the conference.[16] But rather

---

[15] Gillian Brock and I argue in 'Needs-centered Ethics' (*Journal of Value Inquiry*, 2002, 425–434) and in 'Needs, Moral Demands and Moral Theory' (*Utilitas*, 2004, 251–266) that talk of need is indispensable to any adequate normative moral theory. This entails that both rights-based and obligation-based deontological theories must mention needs; but it leaves open a possibility we mention but have not yet explored, that any rights- or obligation-based theory (or indeed a value- or virtue-based one) might actually be replaceable without remainder, by a comprehensive normative theory based on need.

[16] Braybrooke has long argued that the concept of need has an important role to play in political deliberation, where it functions well as a

than defending his well-known Schema, Braybrooke here considers the question of moral force more generally. Braybrooke's notion of moral force is highly context-dependent—something has moral force only if it is accepted by the relevant population in four respects (it is taken to express emotion, express an imperative, have a perlocutionary effect, and be supported by moral arguments) (p. 227). Braybrooke assumes what is now once again more generally accepted, even by opponents of need: needs for most people in most communities have quite strong moral force.

Braybrooke does not claim that to be genuine a normative statement must have uncontestable universal force, whoever makes it, at whatever time and under whatever conditions. He is open to the idea, now generally accepted by philosophers of need, that moral force is contestable and must be politically negotiated. He is thus well-placed to allow the possibility that other 'vehicles' for the expression of normative claims may work better, for certain

surrogate for utility. A surrogate for utility is needed, Braybrooke argues, because *contra* the claims of economists, the concept of utility is obscure and difficult to measure, whereas the concept of need is familiar, well-understood and relatively simple to measure. Over years, Braybrooke has developed a schema describing mechanisms which capture the moral importance of needs. His aim has been both descriptive and normative. As well as making explicit how the concept of essential need may function in actual political deliberation, the schema is also intended to offer a framework for reflection on political policies and priorities which Braybrooke recommends. The best-known presentation of his views is *Meeting Needs* (Princeton: Princeton University Press, 1987).

people, at certain times and under certain conditions. He focuses in particular on persons who do not feel the moral force of needs—who find 'neediness ... a tiresome subject' and suspect that the needy may often have got that way 'through their own current shiftlessness' (p. 211). To get them to feel the moral force of a situation, he suggests we may need to avoid talk of need, and make use of other 'vehicles' which have more 'moral force' for them (just as talk of needs for most of us is a vehicle with more force than talk of utility). Talk of 'episodic' (or occurrent, unmet) need may work, and such talk need not mention 'need', instead referring directly to actual shortfalls, the 'specific instances where help is urgently called for: thirst, starvation, exposure, illiteracy' (p. 220). When we try to get needs met, we might refer to the resource that will meet the need (say, food), the actual shortfall (say, injury, or starvation), the end state (say, being nourished, or free to be nourished), or some other aspect of the situation. So long as the need is met, Braybrooke suggests, it matters less than is commonly thought which vocabulary we use.

Braybrooke's account of the range of forms moral talk can take, suggests the possibility of a kind of pluralism. He discusses the pros and cons of talk of capabilities *versus* talk of needs, and argues that in general talk of need has greater moral force, because it is well-understood and in everyday use, while talk of capability is even rarer and less well-understood than talk of utility. Also, because essential needs refer to absolute deprivation, where capability refers to the full range of human capacities to benefit, Braybrooke suggests the moral force of capability as such will be weak.

One can ask why one should care about whether or not a person has the opportunity to expand their capability; one cannot so naturally wonder why one should care about whether or not a person has what they need to live.

Sabina Alkire writes as someone practically engaged in political efforts to get needs met, so she considers what will be the best conceptual framework, in the light of the practical standard of what will most help the needy understand and meet their own needs, and what will most help those charged with helping them. Alkire focuses on the question of whether it is preferable to frame helping action in terms of meeting needs, or expanding capabilities. The founder of the capabilities approach to economics and development, Amartya Sen rejected the idea that a needs-based approach to development policy could be sufficient with quite cursory arguments in the 1980s, charging that talk of need is commodity-focused, paternalistic, and passive, where the capability approach he prefers makes human freedoms to do and be central, respects autonomy and is active.[17] Alkire recommends a more conciliatory view. She shares in the new confidence that essential needs are morally important. But equally, she insists the work of Amartya Sen and others using the capability approach has an essential contribution to make. The advantages of both forms of discourse, for her, are evident.

In Alkire's view, current international coordinated action on poverty, such as that which advances the

[17] A. Sen, *Resources, Values and Development* (Oxford: Basil Blackwell, 1984), 509–532.

Millennium Development Goals, demonstrates the political salience of talk of need. But to be effective and sustained, institutional responses to needs have to have some account of the role of localized human participation, both in the definition of needs, and in the measures taken to redress them. For her, needs-talk needs supplementation, by an account of how needs are to be identified and met at the local and concrete (as opposed to global and abstract) level. In her view, talk of capability has similarly evident political salience. But like talk of need, it cannot stand alone. To be efficiently put into operation, talk of capability requires the identification and prioritization of basic capabilities or functionings.

Here Alkire sees the possibility of a useful complementarity, to which both components—capability and need—are indispensable. She proposes that the identification and prioritisation of unmet needs, and responses to them, might best be approached as an iterative sequence of activities. To start discussion, she sketches a possible sequence. First, general important achievable goals should be articulated. Second, long-term valued goals should be identified. Third, vital needs required to realise those goals should be identified. Fourth, a strategy should be designed and implemented safeguarding negative freedoms and allowing goals and strategies to be revised by public debate in an ongoing way. Fifth, steps should be found and taken to mitigate capability contraction in the course of meeting vital needs. Alkire explores how an understanding of need would fruitfully inform this sequence, while arguing that the capability approach, which clearly identifies the intrinsic importance of agency, provides a more adequate overall framework for the entire range of deprivation-reducing activities required.

5. Next steps in the philosophy of need

The conference clearly showed that the concept of need has a very wide contribution to make to philosophy. It can help us to understand rationality, human action and human nature, and it can help us to gain a richer understanding of the history of philosophy, as well as suggesting political priorities that need urgent attention. Wide-ranging discussions at the conference also threw up some potentially interesting further lines of enquiry, some of which I sketch briefly here.

The question of how the concepts of logical and metaphysical necessity are related to the concept of need in political philosophy may reward further study. One possibility, suggested by the treatment of necessities in Aristotle's philosophy, and by Garrett Thomson's statement that 'in using the term "need", we exploit the notion of natural necessity so as to force our hand practically' (p. 177), is that there may be a close logical connection between the different notions of necessity. How is the necessity in 'a triangle must have three sides' different from that in 'a human being needs water'? One difference might be that since the entities referred to in statements of logical necessity are abstract entities, they exist (if they do) necessarily, which is to say, the necessary conditions for their being, i.e. their needs, are necessarily met. The triangle absolutely must have three sides; the human being can struggle on for quite a while without water.

In the light of these outstanding general philosophical questions about necessity, the question of the nature of the necessity of good actions compared with the necessity of need seems pressing. When I need food, I must eat in a very strong sense. The 'must' of much needs-meeting behaviour seems very hard, but how hard is it, compared to the musts of logical and metaphysical necessity? When you need food, lack it, I have it, know you lack it, and I am in a position to give it to you, I 'must' give you food in quite a strong sense, too. But how strong, exactly? Many philosophers want the must of moral obligation to be very hard indeed, to be absolute. But if the moral must is so hard, if it absolutely compels me (*qua* moral and rational being—the compulsion is not 'causal', of course), is this not in tension with another philosophical conviction almost as dearly held, that good actions must be un-coerced?[18]

The issue of the proper place of need in human life may reward further exploration in the philosophies of mind and action, as well as in political philosophy. Meeting needs is something that must be done, and some philosophers for that reason have jibbed at making it morally required. Whilst needs-meeting can be done happily, creatively and caringly, people do often resent what they have to do. Leisure is then represented, as in Aristotle, as life beyond necessity. But we know from the political realities of the west, that being freed from necessity into leisure is not an unqualified benefit. Leisured people get bored, get depressed,

---

[18] Thanks to Geraldine Coggins for pointing out this tension in the idea of a needs-based morality.

over-eat, over-consume and act wastefully, perversely or confusedly in other ways.

Communities where leisure is epidemic urgently need philosophers to return to this topic, and tell us what it is about leisure that is beneficial, whether the benefits can be had without the harm, and how we might frame policies that foster meaningful leisure. Reflection may well reveal that the whole philosophical project of making the human good leisurely is misconceived, and that this can be shown a priori. In which case the right moral and political response will be to forget about fostering beneficial leisure, and concentrate on cultivating better attitudes to necessary work.

The association between need and humiliation promises several other themes in the philosophy of need which would reward further exploration. Human neediness, incapacity, dependency, vulnerability, patiency, suffering, helplessness, victimhood—all are facts of life. These are not just regrettable facts that would be eliminated under ideal conditions, as Aristotle and others suggest, but deep facts, all highly determinative of the people we are. There are signs that these ideas are beginning to be investigated, in large part thanks to the work of philosophers mapping the moral landscape of women's lives, which characteristically involve a great deal of subjection and a great deal of needs-meeting.[19] The 'underside' of subjectivity and agency that is

---

[19] See for example E. F. Kittay, *Love's Labour* (London: Routledge, 1999) and A. MacIntyre, *Dependent Rational Animals* (London: Duckworth, 1999).

subjectedness and patiency shapes what our second nature can be, shapes our grasp of the world and our place in it.

Further study of these ideas might help bring to light some features of our conception of ourselves, and deal with the moral issues they raise. An example might be how important safety is to us. We are motivated to deny our dependency, our vulnerability as contingent beings to our needs not being met, because we need to think of ourselves as safe. This idea of the safe self may be something we cannot get away from—a sense of safety is necessary for a functional identity as a human being.[20] But our instinctive desire to build safety into our very concept of self makes us vulnerable to certain vices. The vice of excess here is the perversion of safety into a mad denial of vulnerability, of the kind we see in the denial of neediness claimed to character-ise the 'free rational male'. The vice of defect here is the perversion of safety into a mad insistence on the reality of dangers so overwhelming that they can be used to justify the most extremely violent defences (think of the present War on Terror), the most absolute exclusions of threats (think of the wall in Palestine/Israel, or the immigration policies of wealthy countries), and the most extreme accumulations of resources and other goods as buffers against lack.

[20] Compelling arguments are offered for this claim in Judith Herman, *Trauma and Recovery* (London: Pandora, 1992).

1 An Idea We Cannot Do Without: What Difference Will It Make (eg. to Moral, Political and Environmental Philosophy) to Recognize and Put to Use a Substantial Conception of Need?

DAVID WIGGINS

1.

1. Conferences on the subject of need are lamentably rare. All the more honour then for this one to the Royal Institute of Philosophy (an organisation long dedicated to saving philosophy's better self from its worse), to the Philosophy Department at Durham, and to Soran Reader, the organizer and editor.

2. Someone asked me recently what first made me think it was important for philosophy to secure for itself a substantial and serious idea of *needing* and of *thing vitally needed*. What made it seem imperative to safeguard these categorizations from conceptual and rhetorical degradation? What suggested that there was a problem here?[1]

---

[1] I expressed doubts about starting a conference paper by drawing on personal memory in the way in which I shall. But the organizers reassured me that this was all right. So now we are stuck with this. In

The answer lay in my case outside formal philosophy. As almost everyone does before theory or dogma
crowds in, I knew the notion of need intimately. I had even
had to think about it, because, early in my working life, it
had been a part of my duty as a civil servant, when working
as an assistant principal in a section of the Colonial Office
that was dedicated to 'Colonial Welfare and Development',
to apply the notion. But there, as in the colonial territories
where various schemes were conceived and proposed to us
as falling under these heads, everyone knew in practice what
need meant, knew a need from a mere desire, and knew a
vital need from a need that was less than that.

The first real intimation that these obvious distinctions could not be taken for granted at the level of policy, or
even of common sense, came later and from elsewhere. It came
with the experience of hearing (in 1966 or 1967 at latest) the
arguments advanced by the LCC/London County Council
(shortly thereafter to become the GLC/Greater London
Council) for building across the close-knit urban and social
fabric of London a system of urban motorways. These arguments, fully endorsed by Labour and Conservative alike,

the paper given at Durham, as in this version, the text overlaps
(especially at §§ 8–14) with my book *Ethics: Twelve Lectures on Moral
Philosophy*, 2006 with Penguin UK and Harvard University Press. I am
grateful to these publishers for permission to reuse this material.
Dorothy Edgington helped me find words for my rough first thoughts
concerning the indispensability of the concept of need to any
convincing explication of the Precautionary Principle. See IV. All the
mistakes that have developed in the time since we had our conversation
are of course mine.

purported to justify the Council's (and the Ministry of Transport's) plans for Ringway One, Ringway Two and Ringway Three, all to be enclosed within a Ringway Four, outside London (now actually built and renamed the M25).[2]

3. What were these arguments? What was wrong with them? The economic version of the LCC's/GLC's argument, an argument loosely based on the so-called London Transportation Study, was that implementing these road-schemes 'would show a 20% return on the investment'. This figure was arrived at by taking the 'net [then] present value' of time-savings on the journeys which the Study projected drivers would make and setting that total against the 'net [then] present costs' of land acquisition, resettlement and construction. Translating all that out of the findings of the 'new science of cost-benefit analysis' and back into the categories of ordinary life, one might have said that, on one side, there was that which was described at the time (see, for example, *The Times*, 7 Jan 1969) as the 'prize of leisure and affluence: mobility' (represented by minutes or

---

[2] For more on these matters, see Stephen Plowden, *Towns Against Traffic* (Deutsch 1972), chapter 7. Plowden's book, given its date, could not say what was going to happen. For the record, let me say. In the run-up to the election of 1973, Labour, who won, were forced to make so many concessions to independent and oppositional groups that, when they gained office, they had to abandon the north and south sections of Ringway One. Ringways Two and Three now correspond to large roads, not quite on the scale projected. A qualified victory for the vital need-concept perhaps, which has gained ground or held its ground within the thinking of moderation and restraint. Even now it has impinged very little however on official or economic modes of thinking.

hours saved over various routes multiplied by the projected number of motorized trips along those routes). On the other side, one might have said, there stood not simply the destruction of 20,000 urban dwellings; not simply the almost certain diminution (experience showed) of facilities accessible to those too young or too old (or too green) to drive (for a mobile society is not the same as one with good general access to facilities); but the annihilation or degradation of many times more than 20,000 established niches for ordinary citizens to inhabit.[3] These were places in which ordinary human lives of passable urban contentment were already being lived, and in which it was possible to satisfy after some fashion a huge variety of familiar human needs. The disvalue of the destruction was swamped, however, by the simple numerosity of a vast sum of time savings for persons driving motor-vehicles. The ordinary politics of human weal and woe were being upstaged by a pseudo-science which was itself the plaything of commercial interests so placed that they contrived the whole direction and tendency of almost all the then current so-called research in transport matters. (You will say that I am cynical if I assert that things have not changed very much since then. So I leave that as a question: how much have they changed?)

4. In what I say about this, try to hear me as prescinding (as now I shall) from the role that I took on thereafter of active political opponent, a person occasionally

---

[3] Also, if that were not bad enough, a consequential 40% increase of traffic on densely inhabited secondary roads, an increase deducible from the Transportation Study itself.

invited in the nineteen seventies to speak at transport conferences—but invited only for him to represent or typify there the more conversable and soft-spoken version of the protester mentality. In recognition of your hearing me as prescinding from that mentality, I shall try to confine myself rigorously to strictly conceptual points that reasonable opponents ought to have treated as deserving of a proper answer. (Ought, even if they only rarely did so.)

The philosophical question was this. What was to be made of the fact that the evaluation of schemes such as this—and they are not confined to transport—makes no separate demarcation of the 'costs' that relate specifically to the deprivation of things seriously or vitally needed? What was to be made of the fact that nothing in the business of evaluation signals that what is at issue is the total transformation of the lives of a significant class of people (present and future) whose vital interests are to be sacrificed to the end of creating large quantities of some less important supposed benefit for a supposedly much larger (if not always or necessarily wholly disjoint) class of people?

The failure to make any separate demarcation under the heading of vital need is at least a failure of description.[4]

---

[4] In a way, it has been recognised as such by some studies. But so far the habitual response has been to compensate for it in (hit or miss) fashion, e.g. to multiply by some arbitrary factor any benefits or costs that accrue to the lowest income groups. Anything to avoid confronting questions of theory or principle or issues of commensurability or the possibility that the whole conceptual basis of some study already in progress is simply a shambles.

Since the times I am speaking of, it may be that some sense of this failure has encouraged closer description and has directed better efforts of quantification. But my impression is that the conceptual point still goes more or less unrecognized. Apart from the quantitative failing and the non-recognition of vital need *as* vital need, there is a further point here that you will instantly recognize as a variant on something that troubled Tocqueville and John Stuart Mill.[5] In the process of appreciation that ensues *after* the description and quantification are done, and in the judgment that a scheme represents such and such a return on the investment, there is nothing to prevent the mass of a majority's relatively unimportant interests from swamping the smaller totality of the vital needs of the minority. What was the philosophy of deliberative democracy to make of the fact that, over and over again, democratic procedures approve—and then in their planning procedures they institutionalize—modes of reasoning that hold in contempt the very sentiments of solidarity (solidarity surely owed to the putative victims of planning) which one might have supposed lay at the root of democracy itself?

5. How then is philosophy to mark, to bring out and to insist upon that which is so special about needing?

---

[5] Among the most important cases of the possibility which troubled Tocqueville and Mill is the case of a majority's outvoting a minority on an issue that mattered vitally only to the minority. For these issues, see Mill's *Considerations on Representative Government*, Chapter Seven.

The first task is for philosophy to find articulate expression for our easy intuitive understanding of the difference between the denial of fulfilment to vital needs as such and the denial of fulfilment to desires that do not correspond to vital needs. After the LCC/GLC proposals established for me the interest and urgency of the ideas of need and vital need, I was wondering where, philosophically speaking, to go next, when a friend who is now a consultant at the Portman Clinic and was then en route to train as a child psychotherapist and a psychoanalyst, drew my attention to a remark in G.E.M. Anscombe's article, 'Modern Moral Philosophy' (*Philosophy* 1958):

> To say that [an animate creature] needs [such and such] environment is not to say, for example, that you want it to have that environment, but that it won't flourish unless it has it.

The claim was a striking one. The *Oxford English Dictionary* seemed to suggest, however, that the need was a modal idea. Aristotle to the rescue then. I proposed that we collate with the 'unless' in Anscombe the passage in Book Five of the *Metaphysics* where Aristotle isolates a sense of 'necessary' as follows:

> [The necessary denotes a thing] without which it is impossible to live (as one cannot live without breathing and nourishment) or without which it is not possible for the good to exist or to come to be or for bad to be discarded or got rid of—as for example drinking medicine is necessary so as not to be ill or sailing to Aegina so as to get money. (1015a20 following).

44

Once this point was reached (and other philosophers I did not know of had surely pursued similar trains of thought), there were choices to make about how to marry up these ideas and how to relate to one another the purely instrumental sense of 'need', as in Aristotle's case of needing to sail to Aegina in order to get money (which it seemed best to elucidate first), and the serious, putatively quasi-categorical sense that Miss Anscombe was concerned with.[6]

Here is one theoretical choice. Transpose 'x needs to sail to Aegina to get' money into 'Necessarily [as of now, in present circumstances], unless x sails to Aegina, x will not get money', and contrapose that into 'Necessarily [as of now, etc.], if x gets money, then x sails to Aegina'. This gets us as far as a purely instrumental sense of 'need', a sense which leaves it entirely open whether x's getting money is an all-important or more or less dispensable end. If we want to say that it is all-important, then that must be made further explicit. Still less then have we reached anything that is remotely analogous to a categorical imperative. Suppose, however, that we now supply to the antecedent of such a conditional something whose coming to pass we think is somehow indispensable or unforsakeable. Then we can reach closer to that which Miss Anscombe intended.[7] For

---

[6] Categorical in a sense that contrasts with hypothetical. For the analogy with Kant's conceptions of the categorical and hypothetical imperatives, see G. Thompson *Needs* (Routledge, London 1989).

[7] I omit some details about time and the *t* variable deployed in the citation from the work referred to in note 8 below. See the reprint of my 'Claims of Need' (originally published in *Morality and Objectivity*

we can bring together now the instrumental sense and the quasi-categorical sense which may attach to the bare 'need' claim we encounter in natural language.

This is what I attempted in a version that I put in front of bemused planners, transport economists and men from the Ministry, at a seminar in Reading in 1979:[8]

Using the schema:

Necessarily at t (if _____ then.),

we can define [quasi-categorical or absolute] need in terms of instrumental need. We arrive at the case of [quasi-categorical] need and the special and central sense of the word, if we supply to the antecedent of the foregoing schema something that is *itself* unforsakeably needed, or is instrumentally needed for something unforsakeable (or instrumentally needed for something that is instrumentally needed for something unforsakeably needed):

Necessarily at t (if _____ (which is unforsakeable) is to be, then . . .)

ed. T. Honderich, Routledge, London, 1985) in *Needs, Values, Truth* (CUP 2002 third edition, amended) pages 7–8 with note. At note 10 on page 7 of that chapter are recorded many anticipations of these thoughts and explorations, by writers such as J. Feinberg, D. Miller, D. Richards, Alan White and others.

[8] David Wiggins, 'Public rationality, needs and what needs are relative to' in Peter Hall and David Bannister (eds.) *Transport and Public Policy*, London, Mansell, 1981. See also David Wiggins and Sira Dermen, 'Needs, Need, Needing', *Journal of Medical Ethics*, vol. 13, 1987, pp. 61–68.

If so much is correct, if this is a plausible reading of there being an absolute need that ..., then we can make sense of the further idea that sometimes the unforsakeable end will be unspecified but rather assumed in the context, and the whole antecedent be suppressed. Here, moreover, we can reconstruct the thing which is so often intended (whether truly or falsely) by an absolute or categorical need claim.[9] Take the same schema that gives us the instrumental needs-claim but prefix to it the words 'there is an unforsakeable end e such that', while supplying 'e comes to pass' to the '____' clause that forms the antecedent of the conditional schema. Thus we obtain 'There is an unforsakeable end e such that necessarily [as of t] if e comes to pass then ...' In other words, it is impossible [as of t] for a certain unforsakeable end e to come to pass unless ... According to this proposal, the absolute or quasi-categorical 'need' has a sense of its own which it acquires by further conditions being adjoined to the conditions of truth for the simple instrumental schema.

6. There were further decisions to make about how to understand the unforsakeable. In her own work on need,

---

[9] At this point, there is confusion to be guarded against. One point is that the analysis of all 'needs' sentences involves a conditional or hypothetical sentence 'if then ____'. Another quite different point is that, among needs sentences, some have an *overall* force or meaning that is not absolute, thus being in *that* quasi-Kantian sense hypothetical; but others have a force or meaning that is *in the quasi-Kantian sense* categorical or non-hypothetical, a force that is owed to the unforsakeability of a certain end. See note 6.

the friend I mentioned, Sira Dermen, soldiered on with Anscombe's 'flourish' formulation; whereas I myself was more drawn to Aristotle's words 'that without which it is impossible to live'. I tried to understand things needed in the absolute or categorical sense of 'need' as things without which the subject in question will be seriously harmed or else (in so far as s/he lives on) will live a life that is vitally impaired.

Another question about things needed related to the consequent of the complete conditional which lies within the scope of the 'necessarily' that governs the rest of our original schema. What sort of thing is to be supplied to the gap '. . .' holding a place for the obtaining of that 'without which [some unforsakeable end] will not come to pass'? As in the antecedent '___' specifying the unforsakeable end, it is very important that at '.' a place is being held for a sentence or open sentence *with a verb*. It follows that, even where, within '. . .', a grammatical object (such as 'nourishment') is given in construction with the verb, it is still important to determine what this verb or verb-phrase is. Only on occasion, moreover, is a simple 'have' or 'possess' the verb in question. Need-theorists have distorted and gravely damaged their conception of the subject by not stressing that, as often as not, when we put the ordinary English back together again and 'need' reappears in construction with 'to' + infinitive, the verb or verb-phrase may be 'to produce (for oneself) the object y', 'to reclaim y', 'to be at liberty to make x or buy y or grow x', or whatever. The choice of verb or verb-phrase is very important and important in ways that are

entirely accessible to a needs-theorist. If the always senten-
tial form of needs claims had been consistently and carefully
emphasized, moreover, there would have been far less cause
for the 'Capability Theory', advocated by Amartya Sen and
his allies and associates, to be seen as a rival to 'Needs
Theory'.[10] The concerns of these theories are entirely con-
sonant—though I do myself think that the needs framework
is better sustained by the ordinary significations of the words
of natural language. As correctly stated, it is well placed to
accommodate the important moral and political ideas that
capabilities theory has emphasized.

7. Explaining matters in the kind of terms I have
been recalling, I started in the later 1970s to bother philosophers I knew to take the notion of need more seriously.
I urged among others Richard Hare, Ronald Dworkin,
Thomas Nagel, Bernard Williams (who I noticed had used
the notion himself in connexion with medical needs) and
John Mackie (who was very sympathetic in principle) to give
some separate acknowledgement to needing as such. But
even after I had responded to some of the things that friends
and colleagues said back to me, and even after I had offered
a typology of needs, distinguishing the question of a need's
badness or gravity, of its entrenchedness, of its basicness and
of its substitutability, and I had defined vital needs in terms

[10] I share in the blame for this. In *Needs, Values, Truth* op. cit. I should
have said that 'have' was only a place-holder for the right verb. Nor did
I point out that *sometimes* the '. . .' clause, unlike the '____' clause,
contains no overt reference to the person(s) having the need, as in 'the
islanders badly needed the colonists to leave'.

of such categories as these, the philosophical impact still seemed to be negligible. Anyone else who has tried to champion the *need*-concept will probably have had the same experience. There must be something dangerous or subversive in what one is suggesting.

But how can it be dangerous? In the case where an animate creature, human or animal, depends and vitally depends on the condition ... holding, where this is a matter of the creature's getting access to such and such or so and so, it must be equally bad for the purposes of philosophy and the purposes of life for us to see its/her/his efforts to secure the condition's satisfaction as the pursuit of just any old desire. Vital needs (I suggested) were, in divers senses I had further explicated, *grave, deeply entrenched* and *scarcely substitutable*. They were things that mattered extremely. Precisely on the strength of that, I advocated something I called the Limitation Principle as a restraint upon aggregative reasoning. According to this, it counts as *unjust* to sacrifice the truly vital needs of one citizen to the aim of meeting the mere desires of some larger number. (See *Needs, Values, Truth*, p. 319 following.) I know of no response to this claim. (Unless the new rhetoric of rights is supposed to furnish a response. But there could be no quicker way than the simple equation of *need* with *right* to complete the degradation of the serious idea of a right—unless, of course, the right in question is simply the right to have one's plight *considered or taken into account*. But that sends us back to where we were: what is to be made of the fact that such and such a policy threatens citizen x's vital interests?)

When someone gets round to attacking or questioning Limitation Principles of the kind I was mooting or engages seriously with ideas of solidarity that give support to them, it will be time to celebrate some new acknowledgement of the philosophical importance of the idea of need— and time to celebrate the realization that, when an idea is as well established in the language as *need* and *vital need* are, there will be all sorts of purposes that the idea serves, purposes that it may be hard for humanity to fulfil without making use of the idea. Meanwhile, let theorists of need try to hold their ground.

8. In the time that remains I turn to moral and political philosophy themselves and try to show in more detail how the idea of need ought to have mattered there. I seek to show this by reference to the writings of Richard Hare and of John Rawls. If they had allowed more scope to *need* and *vital need*, then, given the large influence of each, this might even have come to impinge not only on philosophy but on public policy. Who knows? Finally, towards the end, I shall point to one other place where the notion of need appears to be indispensable to us both theoretically and practically, namely in connexion with ideas of safety and risk that seem to underlie the so-called *Precautionary Principle.*

2.

9. According to Hare, you will remember, if someone is to venture into the business of making a moral judgment about

some situation, then this judgment commits the person to making a *similar* judgment about any situation which is *relevantly similar*.[11] The commitment is one of 'logic' and of practical reasonableness. Thus anyone who makes a judgement about what he ought to do in a given situation is committed to prescind from the identities of person and determine his own proper line of conduct by reference to the special rationality of *generalised prudence*.

Hare begins by modelling generalized prudence upon *individual prudence*—that is upon ordinary prudence that is corrigible by reference to fact or logic and is rational with respect to the deliberator's own interests and/or preferences. In the second instance, Hare goes on to explain the universalizing rationality that morality proper requires by thinking of it as prudence with respect to *all* interests and/or preferences. Hare's contention (you will remember) is that the only way in which generalised prudence can give its proper due to each preference or interest while seeking to do the best for all collectively is for such prudence to proportion whatever it awards to each interest to the strength of that preference – as rationally adjusted, if necessary.[12] This last is called the principle of equal interests, and Hare contends that it is equivalent for all relevant purposes to classical

---

[11] See, for instance, *Moral Thinking*, Oxford 1982 and all the studies that led up to it.

[12] You might suggest that it should be proportioned to the degree of importance of the interest, but this distinction does not figure in the construction.

Utilitarianism.[13] In this way, classical Utilitarianism graduates to the status of a rational requirement.

This construction of Hare's is familiar and invites a
wide variety of commentaries. The only thing I want to
attend to here is Hare's conceptions of individual deliberation and of prudence, namely the part of the whole business
that he sums up in a principle which has come to be called
the *prudential principle*. The *prudential principle* advises me,
other things being equal, to try to maximise the satisfaction
of preferences – my own preferences and any others that
I care about.

Even here, at the outset, I think a doubt arises. Is
'maximize the satisfaction of my preferences' really the thing
a rational deliberator (even an entirely self-interested
rational deliberator) actually intends in practising individual
prudence? Surely a rational deliberator asks himself constantly not so much *how to maximise* his preference-
satisfaction but *what to prefer*, or *what preferences to persist
in*? Indeed, one might think that he will be foolish not to
interest himself always in the question *what really matters
here? what does a person such as I am (and such as I aspire to
be) vitally need?* If Hare's object is to show what makes
choices rational, then it is a pity for him to begin from so

---

[13] To get an exact fit with Utilitarianism, it has to be all right to suppose
that there is no mismatch between the strength of a (rationally
corrected) desire and the efficiency with which it can turn into the
effective satisfaction of desire any benefits the universalizer's choice of
maxim may award to it. Unluckily, such an assumption is not generally
true (see here my *Needs, Values, Truth*, page 86, *ad finem*).

miserably attenuated a conception of the ordinary rationality of ordinary first-person deliberation.

10. What difference would it make to recognise the indispensability to deliberation of the question 'what do I need?' Well, if a practitioner of generalised prudence were challenged to have regard for the idea of vital need or he embarked on marking among desires the special significance of vital needs, then he would have to begin by looking again at the idea's basis in individual prudence. In that place he would have to notice the key role that is played by the idea of need in clearing away a whole mass of unimportant desires or preferences and in the establishment of priorities. In Hare's framework, he would then have to transpose this observation to generalised prudence. With or without further modifications of Hare's method, the result might have some claim to be a new post-Harean version of universal prescriptivism. But it would not be utilitarianism. It would be closer to a position once espoused by Leibniz in a passage that is cited by John O'Neill:

> Virtue is the habit of acting according to wisdom . . .
> Wisdom is the science of felicity [and] is that which must
> be studied above all things . . . Justice is charity or a habit
> of loving conformed to wisdom. Thus when one is
> inclined to justice, one tries to procure good for
> everybody, so far as one can, reasonably, but in
> proportion to the needs and merits of each.[14]

---

[14] See Leibniz's note, 'Felicity', as translated in P. Riley ed. *Leibniz: Political Writings* (Cambridge: Cambridge University Press, 1988).

Such Leibnizian wisdom is only a few steps from the noble non-partisan political ideal of William Beveridge, a participative ideal that the capability theorist can as readily salute as the needs-theorist. (Indeed there is no disagreement.)

3.

11. Next I shall venture to say something about John Rawls. As a comment on Rawls's system, what I say may be unfair (though that is not the intention). But independently of fairness to Rawls, I think the comment will pay its own way as an argument for the indispensability of the need concept.

As you know, Rawls models his conception of justice on the findings of a group of free and equal persons who are to exercise ordinary prudence in debating with one another under a veil of ignorance the conditions of fruitful cooperation in a well-ordered society whose other members they formally represent. This veil of ignorance is to prevent the deliberators from knowing anything about the part it will fall to each of them to play in this society. It deprives each deliberator of all knowledge of the content of his/her own particular conception of the good, *except* to the extent that deliberators can work out this conception by thinking of themselves as free and equal deliberators or by reflecting that there are some good things, namely the *primary goods*, that anyone will want whatever else they want (certain rights, liberties, opportunities, powers, income, wealth). These primary goods are the basis for the rest of the construction.

In deference to Rawls's adaptability and persistence, I shall attach the comment I want to make here to a relatively recent summation by Rawls himself of his own position, a summation he revised for publication in *Political Liberalism* (1993):

> A conception of justice must incorporate an ideal form for the basic structure in the light of which the accumulated results of ongoing social processes are to be limited and adjusted.
>
> Now in view of the special role of the basic structure, it is natural to ask the following question: by what principle can free and equal persons accept the fact that social and economic inequalities are deeply influenced by social fortune, and natural and historical happenstance. Since the parties regard themselves as such persons, the obvious starting point is for them to suppose that all social primary goods, including income and wealth, should be equal: everyone should have an equal share. But they must take organizational requirements and economic efficiency into account. Thus it is unreasonable to stop at equal division. The basic structure should allow organizational and economic inequalities so long as these improve everyone's situation, including that of the least advantaged, provided these inequalities are consistent with equal liberty and fair equality of opportunity. Because they start from equal shares, those who benefit least (taking equal division as the benchmark) have so to speak a veto. And thus the parties arrive at the difference principle. Here equal division is accepted as the benchmark because it reflects how people are situated when they are represented as free and equal moral

> persons. Among such persons, those who have gained more than others are to do so on terms that improve the situation of those who gained less. These intuitive considerations indicate why the difference principle is the appropriate criterion to govern social and economic inequalities ...
>
> Thus the main principles of justice, in particular the difference principle, apply to the main public principles and policies that regulate social and economic inequalities. They are used to adjust the system of entitlements and earnings and to balance the familiar everyday standards and precepts which this system employs.[15]

For the record, I set down here Rawls's two principles of justice in revised formulations that are coeval with the reprint:

a. Each person has an equal claim to a fully adequate scheme of equal basic rights and liberties, which scheme is compatible with the same scheme for all; and in this scheme the equal political liberties and only those liberties, are to be guaranteed their fair value.[16]

b. Social and economic inequalities are to satisfy two conditions: first, they are to be attached to positions and offices open to all under conditions of fair equality of opportunity; and second they are to be to the greatest benefit of the least advantaged members of society.

---

[15] J. Rawls, 'The Basic Structure as Subject', reprinted in Rawls, *Political Liberalism* (New York: Columbia University Press, 1993), see 281–3, from *American Philosophical Quarterly* 14 (April 1977).

[16] For 'fair value' see op. cit. *Political Liberalism*, 356–363.

12. Comment. The first question that Rawls has the deliberators ask in our citation is by what principle deliberators who are free and equal persons and know that they are free and equal can accept the fact that social and economic inequalities are deeply influenced by social fortune and natural/historical happenstance.[17] To one who is fully engaged with the need-concept, however, as well as sympathetic to the veil of ignorance device, it will seem strange that this should be the first question. Surely there is another and even more obvious question? Given that, *whatever* principles may be instituted by human beings to regulate the social and political spheres, the human world will always be replete with contingency, good luck, bad luck and the rest, one might have expected that most deliberators would prefer to ask this: what guarantees of what strength can be placed among the conditions of social cooperation in order to ensure that the worst of the bad luck anybody encounters will be alleviated by concerted social action? After all, the thing that affects and harms the dispossessed or destitute is not so much inequality as such as dire unsatisfied need. For simply as such, *inequalities* (e.g. of income or wealth) are not the kind of things that have to detract from the freedom or equality—or even the happiness—of the free and equal persons whom the deliberators represent. (Indeed the bare

[17] It assists in the interpretation of this question of Rawls's to collate it with a sentence from the same paper (p. 271 in the same reprint): 'what the theory of justice must regulate is the inequalities in life prospects between citizens that arise from social starting positions, natural advantages and historical contingencies'.

promise of equality as such will have a sinister ring if there is a chance that the thing promised should prove to be equality in immiseration.)

Suppose that we prefer the need-theorist's question.[18] In that case we shall expect the deliberators to go by a direct route against contingency or natural happenstance. We shall expect them to seek to invent principles precisely to counter its worst effects. If they do this then, given that what matters most is the removal of impediments to the life or happiness of cooperators, it would seem to be a reasonable condition for them to insist upon that the principles of cooperation should make explicit provision not only to buffer misfortune (deliberators might say) but to enshrine, in the spirit of maximin, certain well-considered principles relating to the vital needs of members of a well-ordered society, principles promoting their freedoms and their opportunities to make the best they can of their situation. On this basis, the deliberators might then go on to inquire what further safeguards need to be written into the principles of cooperation in order that public policies should

---

[18] One might wonder here whether there is something within Rawls's construction that makes Rawls's prefer to begin with his question. If there is not, and it is not clear that there is, then what else makes it the first? To judge from the wording of the question and the presence there of the words 'free and equal', an assumption is at work here about the connection between citizenly equality and equality of income and wealth, or equality of life chances. The assumption is momentous. It evidently determines the direction we see Rawls move in. Before taking the truth of the assumption to be obvious, compare Rawls's procedure with the rival idea that the needs theorist is seen proposing in the text.

be framed to protect cooperating members of the society from avoidable immiseration or personal disaster or any other avoidable thing that obstructs their active life within the society.

13. If the deliberators formulate principles of cooperation along these essentially ameliorative lines, and they chiefly concern themselves with the misfortunes or disabilities Rawls prefers to call 'social and economic inequalities or differences', this will surely lead them in the direction of a partly remedial and partly enabling conception of justice. Such a conception will be a proper celebration, a needs-theorist may say, of the citizenly equality that free and equal deliberators will seek to see implemented in due course. On the other hand, deliberators who prefer Rawls's question will be led to an altogether different conception of justice, and a different conception of equality.

Anyone who lacks all preconceptions in political philosophy, yet finds interesting and promising the idea of arriving at a substantive conception of justice by working out the principles that will condition the prospect of fruitful cooperation, will wonder at this point why on earth the notion of vital need does not figure in the text of either of Rawls's principles of justice. How can Rawls have supposed that the difference principle would do all the work of a principle relating to need as such?[19]

[19] Let me refer here to the illuminating treatment of this question given by Brian Barry in *The Liberal Theory of Justice* (Oxford: Clarendon Press, 1973), at pp. 54–55 and 115.

14. If you see any force in the sort of criticism I have been making of Rawls's mode of execution of his project, you may think there is another advantage in pursuing the foregoing line of criticism. The ordinary notion of 'need' is deeply imbedded in the language. There is a mass of inexplicit understanding for the semantics of the verb to draw upon. But how do things stand with our understanding of 'equal' as it occurs imbedded within our understanding of the 'inequalities' that Rawls addresses in the passage we began from? How well do we grasp this idea of 'equal'?

This is the point at which the idea of a contract seems to come into its own. Once we accept the contract idea, there will be a tendency for such a contract to be thought of as concluded *as if at some particular moment*— albeit a notional moment when there is as yet no history of the society that the contract is to make possible, no pattern of holdings, and no past events of any moral or social significance. Under *this* condition 'the obvious starting point [will be] . . . to suppose that all social primary goods, including income and wealth should be equal'.[20] Under such a starting point conception, it may well appear equally obvious how to construe the idea of all social primary goods being equally distributed. For if *from the outset* everyone has

---

[20] Here is a disobliging suggestion. Perhaps this obviousness ought to be compared with that of Laplace's notorious Principle of Indifference, to the effect that, in the case of complete ignorance, the *a priori* probability of a given proposition is 1/2. For the fate of this principle, cp. the discussion in J.M. Keynes, *A Treatise on Probability* (1921), Chapter IV *et passim*.

the same, then from the outset their shares are equal. And the identity of these shares entails the equality of the recipients. Yes. The trouble is though that this is not enough to give us any idea of what it amounts to *constitutively* to measure the equality or inequality of the distribution of social primary goods at a point (say) six notional months after the notional starting point. All that identity of shares can furnish is one sufficient condition of equality. If other dispositions of social primary goods besides identical ones are sufficient for equality between recipients, then what are the necessary conditions of equality in this sense?

These are not easy questions at all. There is evidently no vast fund of speakers' inexplicit knowledge that philosophy can draw upon to explicate this notion of equality. Contrast the situation with 'just' or 'free' or 'fair' or 'owed'—or with 'need'. Is it projected that the relevant sense of 'equal' should be a free construction of the theorist's mind? Is the thought that he is not so much to discover this sense as to invent it? But surely not everyone will be content with this prospect, unless they are already equality theorists.

At this point someone with a different take from Rawls on the problem of legitimacy (and much less patience perhaps with as-if-Platonic myth-making) might well protest that it is only the working out of the contractualist expectation that can oblige anyone to find better than rhetorical sense for a notion of equality that stands in no certain relation at all to 'equal' as 'equal' occurs in 'free and equal persons'. It is only *this* expectation that commits us to the possibility of a *metric* of social primary goods. But why was this philosophically compulsory? So far as fairness or allegiance is concerned, can we not make do with the notion of equal that figures in 'free and equal deliberators', leaving the other and supposedly connected sense to wither on the vine? Why is it not enough to use the notion of vital need to limit the gravity of the effects of contingency? And why not see the deliberators as debating, preferably from the starting point of some 'we' that they understand of free and equal citizens, *the conditions of perpetuating* or *renewing* or *improving* social cooperation in an ongoing society, whose exact details they know well enough, in a more selective amnesia doing duty for the thicker veil of ignorance operative in Rawls's original position? But then, on these terms, we are back with the same question as before: do we really have to start with the question that Rawls puts first in the passage I have quoted from him?

4.

15. These remarks about Hare and Rawls gesture at just some of the possibilities revealed by setting free the serious notion of need and giving it its independence. No wonder the distinguished philosophers whom I used to charge with their neglect of the notion of need mostly resisted my exhortations. The possibilities that I have been describing represent major disruptions. They are disruptive of certain sorts of theory. A further misgiving may have arisen from these friends' or colleagues' wondering whether the particular purposes for which I wanted the notions of need and vital need would prove to be of a greener hue than any that they

were sure they wanted at that time to be associated with. But this brings me to my last topic, which is the so-called Precautionary Principle, a principle often now appealed to in environmental contexts. My claim is that the pretheoretical appeal of this principle and its claim to attention can be much better understood when we position it in its relation to vital human need, as seriously understood.

16. The Precautionary Principle figures in the Maastricht Treaty, is incorporated in the draft (2003) for the European Constitution, and is present already in a large number of declarations, treaties and White Papers in which HMG has now (2003) involved itself. But what does it say? It is hard to find any canonical statement of the principle, but here, to be going on with, is one official utterance:

> In order to achieve sustainable development, policies must be based on the *precautionary principle*. Environmental measure must anticipate, prevent and attack the causes of environmental degradation. Where there are threats of serious or irreversible damage, lack of full scientific certainty should not be used as a reason for postponing measures to prevent environmental degradation.[21] *Bergen Ministerial Declaration*, May 1990.

---

[21] More cautiously, the White paper *The Common Inheritance (Cmnd Paper* 1200, September 1990): 'Government will be prepared to take precautionary action to limit the use of potentially dangerous materials or the spread of potential dangerous pollutants, even where scientific knowledge is not conclusive, if the balance of likely costs and benefits justifies it . . .'.

Such declarations, despite their vagueness, arouse opposition. But let us begin by trying to find some basis for them. What is it that appeals here to our rational intuitions?

The declaration cited cannot be derived immediately or directly from the received or standard framework for understanding risk. You could not deduce anything like the Bergen Declaration either from the orthodox idea that we should choose our environmental policies to maximise expected utility,[22] for instance, or from the more broadly utilitarian way of thinking that supports that idea. The precautionary outlook expressed in the Declaration commits us from the outset to take a certain attitude towards the relative importance of more or less assured (real or supposed) benefits to human beings and of possible (even if relatively improbably or relatively distant in time) damage to the environment.

---

[22] You calculate the expected utility of a policy in a given situation by assigning a probability and a utility to each possible outcome there, multiplying the probability together with the utility for each outcome and then taking the sum of these products. Expected utility theory, together with any constraints that it places upon rational choice under conditions of risk or of uncertainty, has its origins in philosophical utilitarianism, a theory which puts needs on a par with desires and, in many versions, discounts the future in ways that appear to offend against reason. Meanwhile, among its most sympathetic interpreters, the defects of the theory are now seen as lying with the monolithic generality of its aspirations. See for instance the temperate conclusions of John Gray's editorial *Introduction* in the Oxford World Classic edition (1991) of John Stuart Mill *On Liberty and Other Essays* (see especially page xxvi following). A conclusion one might draw from all this is that the way forward is not to replace expected utility by another theory with the same scope.

In a way of its own, it appears to intervene at the level of the valuation of different *kinds* of outcome. The Declaration seeks to associate reason itself with a *special* concern for the environment, and no such concern can be derived from expected utility theory taken just as it stands. In due course, I shall suggest that a more general idea is at work here. But, in advance of that, I remark that the Declaration suggests the possibility of an asymmetry or incommensurability—plausible in itself perhaps to the innocent intellect, but unknown to expected utility theory or the framework in which that is at home—between the evaluation of nearly certain large human benefits in the present and the evaluation of possible longer term threats to that which ultimately contains, conditions and circumscribes human life itself and is presupposed to the continuance of the economic order itself, namely threats to the earth. In so far as we want to understand the force of the precautionary demand, rather than to prepare to pour scorn upon it, the first thing we must do is to see the earth as that which, directly or indirectly, supplies all vital human needs.

17. Let me take that last thought a little further by citing a remarkable essay that is too rarely referred to but richly deserves at last to come into its own:

> There is no dearth of goals in the modern situation of unbounded powers clamouring for actualization, nor is there a dearth of means; what now claims our attention are the dangers lurking in the actualization of the goals and the uses of the means.
>
> The a priori object of an unconditional economic imperative is the continued possibility of the economic

system itself: not necessarily of the given system, but of a viable economy as such. This was hardly a consideration in former times. With all the ups and downs of capricious nature, the good old Earth could be trusted to endure and to regenerate the conditions for future life, even patiently to repair the follies of man. Modern technology has changed this radically. Thanks to it, we live in an era of enormous and largely irreversible consequences of human action, in an era of what I call the total and global impact of almost any of the courses we embark upon under the conditions of technological might; and we must anticipate that these courses, once set in motion, will run self-propelled to their extremes. In these circumstances, the otherwise abstract obligation to preserve for posterity the conditions necessary for an economy as such, turns into a fairly concrete principle for normative judgment i.e., for approval or rejection of policies. The a priori imperative whose positive form might be, 'Act so that the effects of your action are compossible with the permanence of an economic order,' is for purposes of critical application better expressed in the negative equivalent, 'Act so that the effects of your action are not destructive of the possibility of economic life in the future,' or simply, 'Do not compromise the conditions for an indefinite continuation of some viable economy.'[23]

There is much to admire here. Jonas not only anticipates the claim I have already made that, for purposes of practical reason, the name 'Earth' does not stand for just any old object

---

[23] H. Jonas, *Philosophical essays: from ancient creed to technological man* (Englewood Cliffs, N.J., Prentice-Hall, Inc., 1971). (See Part One, Essay 4, 'Socio-Economic Knowledge and Ignorance of Goals'.)

of reference. In effect, he subordinates every theory, not least any defensible version there may be of the theory of expected utility (together with corresponding attitudes towards uncertainty/risk), to a momentous normative claim, a claim purporting to be mandatory for any kind of practical thinking about matters economic or environmental that purports to transcend simple egoism. For Jonas' own formulations of this claim, see the citation. But here is another: in so far as we deliberate otherwise than alone or purely egoistically about the resources of the earth and in so far as we recognize the huge power that is at our collective command over its future, we have to ask ourselves what the constituency is within which and on behalf of which we shall think or speculate about these matters; if the earth's resources do not belong exclusively or specially to any one generation, *then we who deliberate here and now have no right to assume that any finite given number is the number of centuries during which there will be human beings on earth.* But this implies that, however far they lie in the future, we have no right to discount the resource needs of generations to come. Still less, one might think, have we any right to engage in activities that diminish the chances of there being such generations. These are quasi-procedural claims which condition the very idea of non-egoistic, rational deliberation about environmental questions.

18. So much for incipiently precautionary thinking. But what will one who prefers to start out from expected utility theory and the constraints which that theory places on deliberation under conditions of risk/uncertainty have to say about the Bergen declaration or similar statements? He will

say that he finds here attitudes and evaluations determined by a certain outlook—an outlook upon the future and future needs that is not impermissible in itself, but is only one outlook among others. The weightings proposed by the precautionary principle are the product, he will say, of one particular attitude of 'risk aversion', namely special aversion to risks to the environment. Such attitudes are not, however, to be credited to rationality as such. About the rationality of the aversion itself a utility theorist will take no stand.[24] Within the confines of expected utility, where given benefits and harms are treated symmetrically, there can be no question of his doing so. So far as he is concerned, only one concession is in sight here regarding the rationality of the precautionary principle. Sometimes paid-up expected utility theorists will point out that, if we act now on the simple basis of the best utilities and probabilities we can assign on the basis of poor information, then our actions may prove to have foreclosed all sorts of options one might have had in the future if one had acted with a stronger sense of the possibility of error in our present estimations of probability and utility.

So far as it goes, a precautionary theorist can, of course, agree with the last point.[25] But it doesn't go very far,

---

[24] Unless he is eager to confuse the attitude's not being required by the theory of rationality that he himself accepts with the attitude's being condemned by that theory as *irrational*. This type of confusion is of course far from unknown.

[25] Thus echoing, in effect, the advice that J.R. Lucas has repeatedly offered for a decade or two to public inquiries and public consultations: assess the cost of error.

he will say. It does not tell us how long to wait, or how to think about what to do in the meanwhile. It marks no special link between rationality and the care of the earth, even though the earth is that from which the needs of all future generations will have to be supplied. It does not engage with Jonas's point about the impropriety of discounting the future. And it does not direct us to differentiate between the satisfaction of desires that are relatively trivial (however strong or numerous they may be) and the fulfilment of vital needs.[26]

19. So much now for the first kind of complaint commonly brought against a precautionary principle, namely the complaint to the effect that it ought not to represent itself in the way that it does as a categorical demand of practical rationality. And so much for the line of reply. The second complaint will be that a principle of the kind that the precautionary theorist desires offers no rule of conduct and leads to no operational definition of sustainability in a policy or line of conduct. Putting the second complaint in my own words, I am tempted to paraphrase it as follows: as so far sketched, the principle offers no prescriptive rule of management in the light of which patterns of consumption and rates of depletion of environmental resources could ever be exactly choreographed to dance satisfactorily near—near but not over—the edge of the level

[26] A similar response needs to be made where a utility theorist reminds us of the law of diminishing marginal utility. That only directs us towards the earlier units of no matter what benefit. It does not discriminate between things desired and things needed.

at which we can leave our descendants with as large and as good a resource base as is available to us and bequeath them the same freedom as we have to make our own decisions about how to be, what to do, and how to live.[27]

My own inclination, despite this criticism, is to persist in the defence I have offered of the precautionary idea—both of its claim (à la Jonas) to be a constituent principle of reason and of the divers economic prescriptions that it suggests. In so far as it gives no operational 'rule' for sustainable development, I shall not refuse to regret that deficiency but, suspecting that some such deficiency is integral to the true conceptual and logical situation, I shall be much more eager to remark that it *does* direct us to search out the countless *sufficient* conditions for certain sorts of development to 'meet the needs of the present without compromising the ability of future generations to meet their own needs'.[28] Even now, we *could* arrange to live in such a way, I believe, and with something to spare. Not only that. It is a demand of public reason for us to try to do so, working simply on the basis of sufficient conditions of sustainability. If or when sustainability is more fully operationalized, (unless this turns into some further idiocy of targetry), that will enhance the clarity of the Bergen Declaration and its variants, provided that we remember constantly their

---

[27] Cp. Robert M. Solow, 'Sustainability: an economist's perspective' 1993, Washington D.C. Resources for the Future.
[28] These words I quote from the Brundtland Report (*Our Common Inheritance*, Oxford, 1987).

normative and conceptual provenance. No need though to wait for that enhancement.

20. It is hard not to compare the way in which the Bergen Declaration has so far fallen flat with the way in which philosophical campaigns have fallen flat on behalf of the concepts of need and vital need. The Bergen failure is only the public and practical enactment perhaps of the older but similar failure in philosophy. What lies at the root of these failures?

It is too soon to be sure. I note though that, from the nature of the case, our philosophical campaign offers no routine into which apprentices can be inducted, no game in which philosophical aspirants can be trained up to prove quasi-philosophical theorems. Maybe we are now at a point where philosophy prefers teachability or productivity over interestingness or truth. (Let nothing stand in the way of 'theory', not even the prior necessity for the orderly surveying of rough ground?)

Mutatis mutandis has a similar unwillingness to 'operationalize' appeared to disable the precautionary outlook? Here though, in this second case, I remark that the failure would not have been so great as it has been if the friends of precaution had better seen the great difficulties and dangers of incorporating into European law, statute or directive anything that resists general reduction to text or test. Nor would it have been so great if the friends and foes of green causes had seen that care for the earth really can leave space for economic development as discriminatingly conceived. Even if countless policies are excluded, all sorts of other policies, indefinitely many in fact, *can* meet the needs of the present without compromising the ability of future generations to meet their own needs. It is sad that, instead of humanity's doing something positive with the precautionary thought, what we have seen is a constant whittling away of the substance of all precautionary declarations[29]—out of fear, presumably, lest such declarations be turned into prohibition and prohibition obstruct developments that are still represented to us, sometimes mendaciously, as economic or technological imperatives. In so far as there really are any such imperatives, why do we suppose that all ways of fulfilling them, all ways without exception, will contravene the precautionary outlook? Consider the economic imperatives that might in a given context follow from Jonas.

21. Three reactions at least are possible to the present state of affairs. First, we can hold out more and more insistently for the full Brundtland definition that counts as sustainable only developments that meet the needs of the present without at all compromising the ability of future generations to meet their own needs. And then overnight, everyone must down tools, unless what they are doing is sustainable. Of course, this is madness.

---

[29] See Dieter Helm, 'The Assessment: Environmental Policy—Objectives, Instruments, and Institutions' *Oxford Review of Economic Policy*, **14**, No. 4 (1998). 'Almost any policy . . . can be claimed to be consistent with sustainability, since the definition has been stretched by governments to be sufficiently wide to be practically almost meaningless' (p. 17).

Secondly, we can rearrange our ideas to rejoice somehow in the dilution, as here:

> Sustainable development is a deliberately ambiguous concept; this is its strength. Its organizing focus is ecological and human—sensitive accounting, the application of a precautionary duty of care, and the scope for civic activism at a local level. This provides it with its distinctive role in the evolution of human and natural well being.[30]

There is a third and better thing we can do. Apart from looking immediately for schemes that counter the environmental degradation the Bergen Declaration proscribes (schemes that could perfectly well qualify as contributions to growth), we can first distinguish the task of understanding the 'sustainable' from the immediate tasks of prescription and proscription. If we preserve the conceptual purity of the idea of sustainability itself, then we shall be in a position to count a policy as strictly or absolutely sustainable if its implementation leaves behind it at least as large and good an environmental resource base as it itself inherits from its predecessors. On these terms, we can focus for some transitional period on the second best. We can interest ourselves actively in the comparatives 'more sustainable' and 'less sustainable' and prefer the *more* sustainable among the options open to us.[31] At the same time, however, we can

---

[30] T. O'Riordan and H. Voisey (eds.) *The Transition to Sustainability* (London: Earthscan Publications, 1998).

[31] Careful legislators, if only they will revert to the style of the English common law, might then try to formulate some general duty lying

prepare to implement as soon as possible a longer term resolve in favour of the absolutely sustainable. If, at the moment, relatively few policies possess this amiable property outright—and that is certainly the manifest appearance—then let us avow that and recognize how far our conduct falls short of the standard that Jonas proposed. Let us recognize also the sheer callousness and egoism (if we care nothing for our descendants) or else (if we do care about them) the utter recklessness of that which we have done and are still doing. Surely a course of action is reckless if there is some alternative to it that ministers to the vital needs of the present but creates less uncertainty with respect to satisfaction of the vital needs of the future. The point of the precautionary principle is that, taking up the rational point of view within the constraints Jonas proposes, it opposes itself to the reckless.[32]

upon this or that body or legal person to take such care as is in the circumstances possible to prefer the more sustainable over the less sustainable way of pursuing their legitimate objectives. The sense of such laws is of course to be determined gradually by reference to an emerging body of case law. As Aristotle says in his discussion of equity in *Nicomachean Ethics*, Book V, chapter 10, the subject matter of the practical is indefinite, unlimited, but susceptible in context of sufficient in context determination.

[32] If the reader really is at a loss for an example of the reckless, let me provide one. Human beings have only been releasing such things as pesticides, artificial fertilizers, herbicides, plasticizers and pharmaceuticals into the environment for about seventy or eighty years. In really serious quantities, we have only been doing this for half as long as that. In the life span of the human race this is a bare moment, the blink of an eye. Even if pregnant mothers on the Faroe Islands are now being warned not to eat too much of

22. However suddenly, I shall end with a quotation from the first page of Pushkin's *Queen of Spades* (inspired perhaps by the St. Petersburg paradox): "'Cards interest me very much," said Herman, "but I am not in a position to risk the necessary in the hope of acquiring the superfluous"'. In this declaration the needs theorist can say he finds the voice of reason speaking—deploying effortlessly the semantic-cum-logical resources that we need to incorporate within any conception of collective reason which can suffice for the consideration or reconsideration of policies that seem to sacrifice to the interests of the present the vital necessities of one huge portion of the rest of the enormous human

their traditional allowance of whale-meat, no doubt it is questionable how large or serious a *present* threat this constitutes to human beings in the present day. It is far more significant that already, a moment after the bare moment it has taken for us to start upon our dispersion of these substances into the oceans, there is scarcely a sea, however remote from human settlement, where fish do not already carry traces of these substances. If we can bring about so much in seventy years, what shall we have done in a hundred and seventy? Whatever reasonable safety threshold is set for bioaccumulation, it will take no more than two or three further moments in the history of mankind for present levels to be substantially exceeded. It will be hard for one who reflects on *this* to react with anything but relief to the information that, at the third conference on the North Sea, The Hague, March 1990, 'the participants adopted the following premises as a basis for their future work. They will continue to apply the *precautionary principle*, that is to take action to avoid potentially damaging impacts of substances that are persistent, toxic and liable to bioaccumulate even when there is no scientific evidence to prove a causal link between emissions and effects.' Did the participants keep to their resolve?

constituency on whose behalf we have now to deliberate environmental questions. Less and less are we now in a position to risk *that which is (or will be) necessary to human life* in the hope of acquiring the superfluous, i.e. that of which *we have no vital need.*

2   Needs and Global Justice

GILLIAN BROCK

In this paper I argue that needs are tremendously salient in developing any plausible account of global justice. I begin by sketching a normative thought experiment that models ideal deliberating conditions. I argue that under such conditions we would choose principles of justice that ensure we are well positioned to be able to meet our needs. Indeed, as the experiment aims to show, any plausible account of distributive justice must make space for the special significance of our needs. I go on to offer some empirical support for this view by looking at the important work of Frohlich and Oppenheimer. I then present an account of our basic needs that can meet a number of goals: for instance, it provides a robust theoretical account of basic needs which can enjoy widespread support, and it can also provide an adequate framework for designing policy about needs, and thus help us to discharge our global obligations. I then briefly discuss the relationship between basic needs and human rights, arguing why the basic needs standard is more fundamental than—and required by—the human rights approach. Finally, I tackle a few important sets of objections to my view, especially some objections concerning distributing our responsibilities for meeting needs.

1.   Global Justice: The Basic Framework

In this section I offer a systematic way of thinking through what global justice requires of us, a way which I believe can tackle a number of issues together, though here I focus on how it can supply us with an excellent framework for settling matters of global distributive justice. By discussing a normative thought experiment I show that global distributive justice requires, at the very least, that all are suitably positioned to enjoy the prospects for decent lives which, as I go on to show, is importantly cashed out in terms of meeting human needs.

I take my inspiration for the thought experiment from Rawls, though crucial details of my view are quite different from Rawls' account as should become quite clear soon enough. Rawlsian-style thought experiments are well suited to examining what an ideal world might require of us.[1] These thought experiments, when properly set up, are a good way of fleshing out what we can reasonably expect of one another in a way that avoids inappropriate partiality: if people do not know what positions they might find

---

[1] I say 'Rawlsian-style' rather than 'Rawlsian' since I think there is much of value in the method Rawls employs, but much less of value in the assumptions he makes and the conclusions he thereby endorses, as discussed in *The Law of Peoples* (Cambridge: Harvard University Press, 1999). Importantly, the method I describe provides a way we can try to help people think through what it would be reasonable to agree to in the choosing situation I go on to outline.

themselves in during the lottery of life, they will pay more attention to what would constitute fair arrangements.[2]

An easy way to enter the thought experiment is to imagine a global conference has been organised. You have been randomly selected to be a decision-making delegate to this conference. You are to participate in deciding what would be a fair framework for interactions and relations among the world's inhabitants. Though you have been invited to the decision-making forum, you do not know anything about what allegiances you have (or may have after the conference concludes), but you do know that whatever decisions are made at this conference will be binding ones.

It may turn out that you find you belong to a developing nation, occupy a territory with poor natural resources, belong to a generation which does not yet exist, and so forth. Given these sorts of possibilities, you are

---

[2] Many people raise questions of the following kinds when talk of social contracts is introduced: Is the contract supposed to be actual or hypothetical? If only hypothetical then why does a purely hypothetical contract have any binding force anyway? And if it has no binding force, then why adhere to it? I see talking in terms of social contracts as a way to specify what expectations various parties to the contract may reasonably have of each other: it is simply a way of fleshing out what those reasonable expectations might be. So, in answer to the questions listed: no, the contract developed assuming the ideal world presupposition is neither an actual contract nor a purely hypothetical one. It is a way to sift through what (actual) parties might reasonably expect of one another, by imagining a certain (hypothetical) choosing situation. Talking about social contracts is a way to talk about, and so uncover, the reasonable expectations people might have of one another (especially in situations of ongoing cooperation).

provided with reasons to care about what you would be prepared to tolerate in all these cases.

You can have access to any information you like about various subjects (such as, history, psychology, or economics), but so far as possible, very little (if any) information about subjects like the demographics of world population should be made available. The idea is that you should not have access to information which could lead you to deduce odds, since (for instance) if you know that over 1 billion of the 6 billion people alive today are Indian, some might be tempted to gamble that they are going to turn out to be Indian, and so try to ensure Indians get better treatment than others. I want to eliminate scope for this sort of gambling. I contend that if a rational individual does not know the odds, it is not rational to gamble (under at least certain conditions, especially the ones described). She will have to think more seriously about what the strains of commitment will really involve and what she will honestly be prepared to tolerate.

More positively, certain information will be made available to all delegates. This information pack includes material about our urgent global collective problems and how we will have to co-operate to solve them. Delegates will have information about various threats to peace and security, including threats we face as a result of the increasing number of people who have access to weapons (especially weapons of mass destruction), and the activities of terrorists and drug traffickers. Delegates will have information about various environmental threats we face, such as, the destruction of the ozone layer and the current state of knowledge about global warming. Information about threats to health such as the spread of highly infectious diseases will also be included. Some of this information will make clear that these problems have global reach and require global co-operation if they are to be resolved. Some of this material will also maintain that the people of the world are in a state of interdependence and mutual vulnerability, they rely on each other crucially if they are to achieve any reasonable level of peace, security, or well-being both now and in the future.[3]

The main issue delegates must entertain concerns what *basic* framework governing the world's inhabitants we can reasonably expect to agree on.[4] Delegates will be aware that all entitlements chosen will need to be financed and so generate obligations.[5] What is the minimum set of protections and entitlements we could reasonably be prepared to tolerate? What would be the minimum reasonable lot for people to agree to? Since delegates have no particular knowledge of how they will be positioned, who each will be once

[3] They will also have information about those who dissent from these common views.

[4] Here I do not mean what Rawls calls 'the basic structure' since there is anyhow so much confusion in Rawls's own account of what this is. (See, for instance, G. A. Cohen, *If You're an Egalitarian, How Come You're So Rich?* [Cambridge: Harvard University Press, 2000], especially 134–147.) Rather the basic framework covers the basic rules of interaction, both individual and institutional, governing human beings in the world.

[5] Delegates will be given detailed information about the resources available to finance provisions for currently existing generations. They will also be provided with our current state of knowledge concerning the rate at which resources may be used to ensure sustainability.

the conference adjourns, it would not be rational to agree to any arrangements that would be too unbearable, since they might end up having to occupy the position of such a person. More positively, delegates would find it reasonable for each person to be able to enjoy the prospects for a decent life and much discussion would be about the (minimum) content of such a life. I submit we would centre discussion towards the terms of agreement around at least two primary guidelines of roughly equal importance, namely, that everyone should enjoy *some* equal basic liberties, and everyone should be protected from certain real (or high probability) opportunities for serious harms.[6]

Reasonable people will care, at least minimally, about enjoying a *certain* level of freedom. Freedom may, of course, not be the only thing they care about and often they may not care about it very much when other issues are at stake about which they care more deeply. Nevertheless, reasonable people will care at least a little about enjoying *some* freedoms. Many kinds of freedoms will be of interest, but importantly, they would include freedom from assault or extreme coercion (such as slavery) and *some* basic freedoms governing movement, association, and speech. We need to be permitted to evaluate and revise the basic organising

---

[6] Perhaps someone may wonder whether there is only one important principle at issue here, the principle concerning protection from real opportunities for serious harms, since the freedoms highlighted are important because being deprived of them can lead to serious harm. I prefer my formulation because it brings into better view two key features that would be selected in the normative thought experiment.

ideas of our lives should we choose to do this. Delegates should recognise that it is possible they could find themselves in a society with whose major organising values, principles, and commitments they disagree. In such situations, it would be reasonable that some might want to have the scope to question and revise the values operative in the society, or at least a certain freedom to live their lives in accordance with values they find more congenial. Recognising this they would, therefore, endorse a certain freedom of dissent, conscience, and speech.[7]

---

[7] Delegates would want certain minimum guarantees about what counts as permissible treatment. Heading the list of guarantees we would choose would be guarantees against assault, torture, imprisonment without trial or sufficient warrant, extreme coercion of various kinds (such as slavery) and so forth. But as I have also suggested, it would be reasonable for them to add some freedoms governing dissent, conscience, speech, association, and movement.

Would this idea really need further justification? Perhaps someone might press for one, especially someone concerned with the idea that those not from liberal democracies might not see this emphasis on freedom as so important or even reasonable. So let me say more about why I think the level of attention I give to freedom can be expected to be universal. If you do not know anything about what sort of position you will occupy under the new arrangements, why would you allow some people to have more freedom of a very basic kind than others? Unless you agree that everyone should have equal basic freedom, you might end up (say) giving some people more basic freedom than you have: you might deny yourself the freedom to go about your business free from assault, though others enjoy this liberty. Given their lack of knowledge about their particular interests, contractors would be most rational in agreeing to equal basic liberties. Similarly, it would not be rational to agree to adopt (say) racist or sexist practices, or practices

84

In addition to caring about protecting freedom, rational decision-makers will also want protection from real opportunities for serious harms to which they would be vulnerable (and potentially powerless to resist) in certain cases. Under some kinds of arrangements there could be enormous opportunities to inflict harms. For instance, multinational corporations operating in unregulated market economies can threaten people's abilities to subsist in various ways, for instance, they can pollute so severely that they poison the soil and water such that crops are no longer able to grow properly, (or perhaps more controversially, they can control labour markets so that wages are set at or below bare subsistence level). In these kinds of cases people's abilities to subsist may be significantly undermined.

Indeed, people considering what arrangements to adopt would be vigilant to ensure that meeting their needs is within their reach and so importantly protected, since being unable to meet our basic needs must be one of the greatest harms that can ensue.[8] Reflecting on the gravity of such a harm in particular, more positively but in a similar vein, we would find it reasonable to have certain guaranteed minimal opportunities and those would be strongly coloured

that favour certain religions over others, since one may find oneself at the receiving end of such practices once the conference concludes. It would be more rational not to place constraints on one's liberties and opportunities, since it would be rational to have more rather than less freedom to pursue whatever your goals turn out to be.

[8] Indeed, what could be a more fundamental harm than being deprived of one's livelihood or the ability to eke out a livelihood for oneself and one's dependents?

by what is necessary to be enabled to meet our basic needs for ourselves.

Furthermore, delegates should consider the possibility that they are permanently disabled and they should also consider the actual periods of extreme dependence which naturally occur in the human life-cycle. Having contemplated these issues, delegates would want adequate protections to be guaranteed should the need arise. Delegates should be strongly motivated to choose not only that we ensure certain minimal opportunities to meet our needs ourselves are available, but also that persons should have adequate provisions to be assisted with need-satisfaction, should they not be in a position to meet their needs themselves.

So my claim is that the minimum package it would be reasonable to agree to in the ideal choosing situation I have identified is that we should all be adequately positioned to enjoy the prospects for a decent life, as fleshed out by what is necessary to be enabled to meet our basic needs and those of our dependents (but with provisions firmly in place for the permanently or temporarily disabled to be adequately cared for) and certain guarantees about basic freedom.[9] We would use this as a base-line and endorse

---

[9] I have suggested that a rough guiding principle we would choose is to have social and political arrangements that allow reasonable opportunities for us to be enabled to meet our basic needs. But wouldn't we want more? Would we find it reasonable to endorse something like a Global Difference Principle, or more substantive equality? As I go on to discuss in the next section, a needs-based principle is in fact most often chosen (in relevant experiments) and this for compelling reasons as we see.

social and political arrangements that can ensure and underwrite these important goods.

The minimum package endorsed will have implications for most spheres of human activity, especially economic activity and political organisation. For instance, economic activity must be sensitive to everyone's prospects for a decent life and regulations must be devised to ensure this. Extensive sets of rules would need to be outlined to make plain for all just what would constitute important threats to people's prospects for decent lives. Organisations that can monitor and enforce these rules must be established.

What sort of governance structure would we endorse? There are many kinds of arrangements we could choose but two key guiding principles would operate: we would want our vital interests (such as our ability to subsist) protected and it can be anticipated that we would want to retain as much control over affairs that directly affect us as is consistent with protection of those vital interests. Any governing authorities we endorse will have as a high priority that they are to protect our vital interests and the legitimacy of governing bodies will rest on their ability to do an adequate job of this. Mixed forms of governance might reasonably be chosen such that in some matters local bodies have complete control, in others—where protection of vital interests can only be secured if there is widespread co-operation across states—joint sovereignty might reasonably be chosen. At any rate, whatever governing structures we endorse would have as the central part of their mandate to protect people's vital interests, to ensure that people are so positioned that meeting their basic needs is within their reach and their basic liberties are protected.[10]

As discussed, delegates are aware that all entitlements chosen need to be funded and so generate financial obligations. Resources will need to be forthcoming to fund the arrangements that are chosen as minimally acceptable. We will need to address the issue of what counts as fair ownership of resources, but whatever account of fair ownership of resources we endorse, cannot be such that it effectively blocks funding reasonable arrangements necessary to underwrite the basic framework, since obligations to set up and do our part in supporting the basic framework are more fundamental.

---

[10] Questions about the kind of favouritism we may show to co-members of our group can only be addressed once there is commitment to the basic framework with all its protections. Assuming this is the case and we have a suitably well organised basic structure in which vital interests are protected, all have prospects for decent lives and as much control over those lives as is consistent with protection of vital interests, it may be permissible to favour other interests of compatriots and in other ways be partial to members of one's group in conferring further benefits, so long as this is not in conflict with provision of the basic agreed framework. Theoretically, at the very least, there is some permissible space for favouring our compatriots in certain matters, but the extent of the favouritism we may show must be governed by the commitment we all have to support the basic framework and does not include (for instance) favouring the non-basic interests of compatriots above more needy non-compatriots, since this would not be selected in the normative thought-experiment.

2. Empirical evidence for the view

A skeptic might complain that such arm-chair theorising is all well and good, but what evidence is there really that anything like what I suggest would be chosen, would *actually* be chosen? I am happy to report that there is quite a bit of encouraging evidence to support these claims. First of all, I talk about the work of Norman Frohlich and Joe Oppenheimer.

Frohlich and Oppenheimer argue that the key to understanding issues of distributive justice is choosing under conditions of impartiality (that is, where one must set aside certain particular interests we actually have which might well skew our judgments about fairness). They designed some experiments to set up conditions of impartiality so that they can assess what principles would be chosen and how stable these choices prove to be over time.[11] Imperfect information can generate ideal conditions for impartiality to operate, and so the experiments set up a situation in which subjects do not know what will be in their immediate self-interest, yet must choose, as a group, by which principle of distributive justice they will run their affairs. Frohlich and Oppenheimer repeated their experiments in different countries to ensure the results were generalizable. They were particularly interested to see whether Harsanyi's principle of maximising the average income or Rawls' idea of maximising the income for the

---

[11] Norman Frohlich and Joe Oppenheimer, *Choosing Justice: An Experimental Approach to Ethical Theory* (Berkeley and Los Angeles, California: University of California Press, 1992).

worst off would be chosen. They offered participants four principles, but allowed them also to choose any other they could think of.[12] The four principles were:

1. Maximising the floor income: 'The most just distribution of income is that which maximizes the floor (or lowest) income in the society'.[13]
2. Maximising the average income: 'The most just distribution of income is that which maximizes the average income in the society'.[14]
3. Maximising the average with a floor constraint of $____: 'The most just distribution of income is that which maximizes the average income only after a certain specified minimum income is guaranteed to everyone'.[15]
4. Maximising the average with a range constraint of $____: 'The most just distribution of income is that which attempts to maximize the average income only after guaranteeing that the difference between the poorest and the richest individuals (ie., the range of income) in the society is not greater than a specified amount'.[16]

Individual subjects then ranked which of these principles they preferred and how confident they felt about their rankings. For principles in which there is a dollar sign followed by a blank space, participants were asked to fill in the blank, if they chose that principle.

There were several stages to the experiments such as checking that participants understood all the principles, also

---

[12] Ibid., 201.   [13] Ibid., 35.   [14] Ibid.   [15] Ibid.   [16] Ibid.

that they understood that their selection would determine their income and that they would be randomly assigned to an income class. The participants also had to deliberate and decide as a group which principle they supported. After the group selection was made, subjects drew chits from a bag to get a distribution into an income category (low, middle, or high income). Later in the experiments they were given the chance to perform tasks to earn income and to have redistributive policies applied to see whether people were able to live with their choices.[17]

Unanimous agreement was reached on a single principle in all cases in which the experiments were run properly.[18] Interestingly, the principles chosen in the experiment do not support either Rawls' or Harsanyi's models. Indeed, there was almost no support for the Difference Principle—it was chosen in only about one percent of cases. It was certainly the least popular choice. By far the most popular choice in all countries was the principle with the guaranteed floor constraint: Around 78% chose the floor constraint principle, 12% chose to maximise the average income (Harsanyi's solution), 9% chose the range constraint principle, and 1% chose the Difference Principle (Rawls's choice). Overwhelmingly, groups 'wanted an income floor to be guaranteed to the worst-off individual. This floor was to act as a safety net for all individuals. But after this constraint was set, they wished to preserve incentives so as to maximise production and hence average income'.[19]

---

[17] The tasks consisted of correcting spelling mistakes.   [18] Ibid., 56–7.
[19] Ibid., 59.

What arguments were used for the floor-constraint principle? In just about all groups there was a concern that individuals not fall below some minimum level of income— *that they have enough to meet their basic needs.*[20] But concern was also raised about how to set the floor so that it didn't undermine incentives to work.[21] There was also tension expressed between 'the desire to preserve entitlements and to ensure that people at the bottom were not too badly off'.[22] Overall, three factors dominated the discussion: balancing people's basic needs with entitlements and incentives.[23]

---

[20] Typical of the points made on this issue were these two sets of comments:

1. 'I would like to see that everyone at least has the basic things. After that I don't really care. [If the floor is too low] . . . a lot of people are going to be starving, and they will be without shelter and housing' (Transcripts, 99).

2. 'If you have people that are really poor, . . . they have a tendency to just stay there because you know there isn't enough nutrition, they can't get an education, and all these kinds of things. But if you put it on a certain minimum, then they have a chance to get out of that situation. They have a chance.' (Transcripts, 72).

[21] Ibid., 61–62.   [22] Ibid., 63.

[23] Since there was such a high level of support for a floor-constraint principle, can we say the principle is a fair rule? Frohlich and Oppenheimer go on to extensive discussion to check whether various factors may have undermined the execution and design of the experiments and so what we can say about the results. They argue that the subjects are not so homogenous in values or background that the resulting choices simply reflect that homogeneity rather than universal preference (ibid., 74).

How stable are the choices when people must live with their decisions? Do the high producers feel they are not getting their due when part of what they earn is redistributed to others? Frohlich and Oppenheimer found continued firm support for the floor constraint principle and, in fact, confidence over the principle and productivity increased when people experienced the results of having their decisions implemented.[24] I return to some of these important findings later, but before leaving Frohlich and Oppenheimer's work, it is worth noting that their experiments have been repeated many times now in different contexts with similar results.[25]

They seem particularly concerned that they are not just reporting people's antecedent preferences. They show how the experiments did make a difference to participants' views, since their rankings, preferences and confidence levels all change during the experiments. After extensive analysis they conclude that 'the shifts in both preference and confidence are clear evidence of considerable movement caused by both the learning and decision phases' (ibid., 104).

[24] Ibid., 118.

[25] Rena de la Cruz-Dona and Alan Martina, *Diverse Groups Agreeing on a System of Justice in Distribution: Evidence from the Philippines* (Australia National University, Canberra: Mimeo, 2000); Michael Jackson and Peter Hill, 'A Fair Share,' *Journal of Theoretical Politics* 7 (1995), 69–179; Grzegorz Lissowkski, Tadeusz Tyszka and Wlodmierz Okrasa, 'Principles of Distributive Justice: Experiments in Poland and America,' *Journal of Conflict Resolution* 35 (1991), 98–119; Tatsuyoshi, Saijo, Shusuke Takahashi and Stephen Turnbull, 'Justice in Income Distribution: An Experimental Approach' Mimeo presented at the 1996 ISA, San Diego, April 18, 1996. Other experimental evidence for the salience of needs in issues in distributive justice can also be found in a host of other places, such as, Maya Bar-Hillel and Menahem Yaari,

Of course, there is some much more direct evidence that can be appealed to, in arguing that people *would* choose policies about helping people to meet their needs in any plausible account of global distributive justice: overwhelmingly, they do *in fact choose* such policies in relevant fora. A number of conferences have recently taken place, and attention to basic needs was very much a cornerstone of the policy recommendations that ensued.[26] Granted, these conferences took place in less than ideal circumstances, especially with respect to impartiality—delegates of course knew everything about their actual circumstances, interests, and other relevant information about their positionings. The fact that such conclusions followed without even imposing the relevant requirements of impartiality is further evidence of the power and the salience we attach to the concept of our basic needs.

'Judgements of distributive justice,' in Barbara Mellers and Jonathan Baron, *Psychological perspectives on justice: Theory and applications* (Cambridge: Cambridge University Press, 1993), 55–84; Helmut Lamm and Thomas Schwinger, 'Norms concerning Distributive Justice: Are Needs Taken into Consideration in Allocation Decisions?' *Social Psychology Quarterly* **43** (1980), 425–429; and David Miller, 'Distributive Justice: What the People Think,' *Ethics* **102** (1992), 555–593, especially, 570–576.

[26] Consider, for instance, the recommendations that were captured in the Earth Charter (eg Principle 9), and the Johannesburg Declaration on Sustainable Development (eg Principle 18). The general thrust of the Millennium Development Goals is also (arguably) an example of this focus.

3. Is any theoretically robust account available to match our ordinary intuitions about the relevance of our needs?

So far I have argued that global justice involves giving special attention to everyone's basic needs. I have argued that not only is this required by looking at theoretical arguments, but I have also offered strong empirical evidence for the view. In our deliberations about justice we do in fact give special weight to considerations of basic need.

According to my view of global justice, part of our obligations to all involve ensuring that they are adequately positioned with respect to meeting their basic needs. So we will need an account of basic needs which can enjoy widespread support across cultures, can be used in the actual world as a basis for policy, and can be specific enough that we can use it in evaluating whether we are making progress with respect to the needs meeting aspects of global justice. Is such an account forthcoming? Is any theoretically robust account available to match our ordinary intuitions about the relevance of our needs and yet determinate enough that we can use it in designing policy?

On my account, a need is basic if satisfying it is a necessary condition for human agency. I link my account of basic needs to agency for several reasons, for instance, the link emphasises that needs are important because of what they enable us to do (and doing things requires being able to act, or agency). The link also provides good leverage in arguing for our responsibilities to meet these needs for several key opponents of such policies, such as libertarians.[27] For now, I want to focus on how this link to agency helps us derive a list of our basic needs which can circumvent concerns about how an account of such needs could be sufficiently 'objective', non-arbitrary, and enjoy widespread cross-cultural support.

If basic needs are those things the satisfaction of which is necessary for human agency, by examining the prerequisites of human agency, of what being a human agent is like, we can derive a more specific list of such conditions, and so basic needs. For instance, by definition, to be an agent one must be able to deliberate and choose. In order to deliberate and choose one will need at least a certain amount of (1) physical and mental health, (2) sufficient security to be able to act, (3) a sufficient level of understanding of what one is choosing between, and (4) a certain amount of autonomy. Because of its important role in developing (and maintaining) (1)–(4), I also add a fifth basic need which underlines the importance of our social needs, namely, (5) decent social relations with at least some others.[28]

---

[27] For more on arguments targeting libertarians see (for instance) Gillian Brock, 'Is Redistribution to Help the Needy Unjust?', *Analysis* **55** (1995), 50–60, reprinted in *Necessary Goods: Our Responsibilities to Meet Others' Needs*, Gillian Brock (ed.) (Oxford: Rowman and Littlefield, 1998), 173–183.

[28] While I think we can derive the other conditions all conceptually, by thinking about the nature of human agency and what must be required for its development and the exercise of it, getting at this last need may be more a matter of looking at empirical evidence. There is a huge amount of empirical evidence that not meeting this need can

On my account, the basic needs themselves are constrained by the nature of human agency and so, are universal, though the ways in which they may be satisfied may vary. This is an important point: we need to distinguish between the needs themselves and the 'satisfiers', or what would satisfy them. On my view, the basic needs themselves are fixed by the preconditions for agency and so are universal, but even casual inspection confirms that the satisfiers are subject to enormous variation and this allows for much cross-cultural flexibility in how we may meet needs.

How can we attach such an account to measuring need-satisfaction in the actual world so that we can design policies and evaluate whether we are making progress with respect to meeting needs? A number of empirical measures are now widely used today to assess the meeting of needs which can give us figures for populations and hence cross-population comparisons, and here I draw substantially on the work of Len Doyal and Ian Gough.[29] To assess physical health we can use measures like life expectancy and mortality rates at specific ages, prevalence amongst children suffering from developmental deficiencies, percentage lacking access to safe water or sanitation, calories

significantly impair one's psychological health see, for instance, M. Kellmer-Pringle, *The Needs of Children*, 2nd edn (London: Hutchinson, 1980), M. Seligman, *Helplessness* (New York: Freeman, 1980, especially 137); George Brown and Tirril Harris, *Social Origins of Depression* (London: Tavistock, 1978); Raoul Naroll, *The Moral Order: an Introduction to the Human Situation* (Beverly Hills: Sage, 1983).

[29] Len Doyal and Ian Gough, *A Theory of Human Need* (Basingstoke: Macmillan Education Ltd, 1991).

consumption below WHO requirements, percentage in structures that do not protect against weather conditions typical in the area, percentage experiencing concentrations of pollutants greater than WHO standards, and percentage not immunised against various diseases. Similarly, for mental health we can use indicators that assess prevalence of various mental illnesses. To assess the second basic need, having sufficient security to be able to act, we can use measures such as homicide rates, percentages who are victims of state violence, war, crime, and so forth. To assess whether people have a sufficient level of understanding of what they are choosing between we can use indicators such as illiteracy, 'lack of attainment in mathematics, science and other near-universal basic skills,'[30] what Doyal and Gough refer to as 'lack of culturally relevant knowledges,'[31] and so forth. To assess levels of autonomy, a number of variables are relevant, certainly all of (1) – (3) already discussed, but some additional factors are important too, notably, the economic opportunities available to one which can be measured by unemployment levels, number of hours available for economic activity after other essential tasks (such as collecting safe water and fuel) are completed, illnesses and deaths related to the main lines of work available in the area, percentage in absolute poverty, and levels of state provisions for particular contingencies such as unemployment. For decent social relations with at least some others, we could use measures such as the percentage of children abandoned,

---

[30] Ibid., 190.   [31] Ibid.

abused, or neglected, and Doyal and Gough's measure of the percentage of people without close relationships.[32]

Summarising the key issues of this section, then, my account provides a theoretically robust model of our basic needs, which can be used in determining which central needs we must be concerned with in order to meet our obligations of global justice. It provides a solid framework that lends itself well to be a bridge to the empirical factors that should come under investigation for us to realise policies concerned with needs in the actual world.

4. What is the relationship between human rights and needs?

Someone might object that human rights is a better discourse for talking about our obligations of global justice, than discourse about human needs. There are a few reasons why such a view is inadequate. Most obviously, human rights discourse is not obviously better when talking about matters of global *distributive* justice, for instance, we don't see people *actually* talking this way in the relevant empirical evidence I referred to earlier. More interestingly, we might see why the human rights discourse is not better than talk of needs when we ask about the basic relationship between these two.

What is the relationship between human rights and needs? There are several possibilities. One is that they are

---

[32] Ibid.

just different kinds of standards addressing different issues: the human rights standard focuses on our reasonable entitlements and protections we are owed as human beings. By contrast, our human needs are what we require to function minimally well as the kinds of creatures we are. But even cursory inspection of these two descriptions should indicate that a knowledge of what our human needs are must be had before we can sensibly have a go at defining the entitlements that will be protected as human rights. In order to draw up a sensible list of our human rights we must have a sense of our basic needs.

This is a key aspect of the relationship between basic needs and human rights: we must have an account of our basic needs in order to draw up a sensible list of human rights. A needs-based account is thus more fundamental than a human rights account. It is necessary to drawing up a coherent and comprehensive list of our human rights. A plausible list of human rights must be informed by an account of human needs. A needs-centred account is more basic than—and so makes plausible—an account of human rights. Indeed, I submit we can explain all the human rights that are set out in the Universal Declaration of Human Rights in terms of my account of basic needs, a commitment to equality between persons, or clarification of the purposes of the document. I show this in Appendix 1. (See Appendix 1 for a detailed analysis of this claim for each article.) This explanatory power can be a consideration for favouring my account of basic needs over rivals, if they are not similarly potent.

Even fans of human rights should be keen on discourse about human needs, because it has a number of desirable features. First, as I have already suggested, it is necessary to any robust and theoretically defensible account of our human rights. Second, it is the more basic language that appeals to more people in the world. While talk about human rights is popular in some cultures, particularly in the West, it does not always enjoy good resonance in many others. In fact, many claim to see it as oppressive Western ideology deeply at odds with their own ways of thinking. Needs discourse, by contrast, is much more widely used in a greater range of cultures. An advantage of human needs discourse, then, is that it is much more usable to a wider range of people, and this may well appeal to even fans of human rights discourse. For those who despise talking about human rights, we can talk in terms of human needs (which anyhow undergird our concern for human rights), and many of the salient claims convert back easily enough into rights discourse.

5.   Some objections to my view

Here I consider some key objections to my view as so far presented, focusing particularly on objections concerning how to distribute our responsibilities for meeting needs.

Objection 1: Since I use a contractarian framework, even though needs are a crucial part of what I recommend as the global justice standard, doesn't my contractarian framework mean that all the work is being done by contractarianism and there is no power to the concept of need after all?

This objection is misguided for at least two reasons. First, though I do use a global justice framework that is contractarian, its contractarian features are only necessary as a heuristic for allowing us to set aside certain interests we actually have which may skew our judgments about fairness. Also, though it is contractarian, what is chosen is strongly needs-based. As I go on to argue, there are very good reasons why this is so: first, it resonates extraordinarily well with what we commonly believe about the power of needs and second, this is because the concept of basic needs in fact has enormous force.

Objection 2: Someone might object that, sure needs matter in considering issues of justice, but even more important is the balance between needs, entitlements, and incentives. The right balance would have attention to needs dropping out of an appropriate picture of justice.

One of the reasons I introduced the empirical evidence is to be able to address concerns of this kind. What we find when we examine the dialogue participants actually had, is that a balance was sought *and found* between the three central ideas. We could arrive at a reasoned view of the weight to give a commitment to meeting basic needs which does not thwart entitlement or dampen incentives. It is not the case that considerations of entitlements and incentives drowned out our appropriate concern with needs. As the empirical evidence shows, concern for needs is strong and robust even when we take these other factors into account. Another objection can be mounted along similar lines, as I discuss next.

Objection 3: Needs matter, but holding people responsible for their own decisions matters too. If people do nothing to help themselves, or if the governments of people do nothing for their own people, there is no reason why the burden should fall on others who have no connection with the needy.

What is the best way to distribute responsibility for meeting needs? Some will argue that persons should be responsible for meeting their own needs. If they are not able to do this, their compatriots and leaders in their country are responsible for designing and implementing policies and courses of action that will assist people to become self-sustaining with respect to their needs. If governments are not helping their people then if we have any responsibility here (and this is often doubted) it is to put pressure on those governments to help their people with the resources they need.[33]

What is wrong with this picture by which we parcel out responsibilities so neatly is that it ignores the fact that there are a variety of ways in which certain matters are significantly outside governments' control, in particular, the institutional framework within which our actions take place is often not something individuals or governments can easily unilaterally control. And this is a further reason why the normative thought experiment is a useful touchstone. We can check whether various features of the institutional framework are ones we would choose when suitably situated in conditions of impartiality (as discussed in the normative thought experiment). As an illustration of what I have in mind here, I want to say something about the enormous problem of corruption—a problem we could do much more to combat with more collective action.

Foreign aid, though desirable, is by no means necessary to finance improvements for the worst off. In many

---

[33] David Miller holds such a view in *On Nationality* (Oxford: Clarendon Press, 1995), see for instance 76–77.

cases, the revenue that would be derived simply from resource sales, if actually received and properly spent, would be more than enough to finance the necessary provisions for helping people to meet their needs.[34] This is especially clear if we look at the case of oil and the crippling corruption that sometimes surrounds its sale. Consider how, for instance, $1.4 billion in oil revenue disappeared in Angola in 2001, an amount equal to about a third of state revenue. A promising way to prevent such corruption is to ensure oil payments become more transparent. 'When oil companies bid for drilling rights in Europe's North Sea or the Gulf of Mexico, the size of their payments is public knowledge, as are the tax payments they later make once they have found oil and begun to report profits. But in developing countries such as Angola, Indonesia, Nigeria, and Azerbaijan, payments are often murky. This makes it hard to be sure that the money has been spent for the public good rather than for lining private pockets.'[35]

The oil companies could voluntarily fix this problem themselves. British Petroleum, for instance, has promised to make public details of payments in Angola. But not all oil companies are equally willing. The reluctant oil companies should of course be strongly encouraged to adopt a similar policy of transparency, but if they do not do this voluntarily, pressure can be brought to bear to ensure they are *required* to do this, for instance, it could be made a condition of oil companies' being able to list on major stock

---

[34] 'Oil and Corruption', *New Zealand Herald* editorial, 9th April, 2002, 10.
[35] Ibid.

exchanges (such as in New York or London) that they adopt the transparency practice.

The lessons we learn about the case of oil seem quite generalisable. More transparency in payments, and the flow of money to less developed countries more generally, would eliminate some of the ease with which corruption can flourish and ensure payments that are intended to benefit the citizens of a country actually do so.

What seems clear is that as a delegate to the hypothetical global conference outlined in the normative thought experiment you would not choose a world in which such corruption, such thwarting of basic needs, could flourish. When forced to set one's self-interest aside, allowing so much corruption to flourish would not be tolerated. We are collectively responsible for allowing our institutional framework to remain unmodified, though this responsibility might be quite unevenly distributed.

The fairest way to distribute responsibilities is to go back to the drawing board and first ensure that the rules governing the basic framework are fair ones. Then we should modify or set up relevant organisations that can make these rules as specific as they need to be to realise the general principles we endorsed in the normative thought experiment, and also can monitor compliance and sanction violators. Again, global organisations can usually best deal with those who suffer when violations occur rather than haphazardly leaving matters to whoever is about, such as, compatriots who are often not in a very good position to help themselves, let alone anyone else. As David Miller states, 'our overriding interest is to identify an agent who can remedy the deprivation or suffering that concerns us'.[36] If we have an overriding interest in relieving suffering, this would suggest that we set up global institutions that can manage to relieve suffering, and that we should all be forced to support them, if we are unwilling to do so voluntarily.

6. Conclusions

In this paper I argued that needs are extremely salient in developing any plausible account of global justice. I began by sketching a normative thought experiment that models ideal deliberating conditions. I argued that under such conditions we would choose principles of justice that ensure we are well positioned to be able to meet our needs, and as the experiment aims to show, any plausible account of distributive justice must make space for the special significance of our needs. I offered some empirical support for this view by looking at the important work of Frohlich and Oppenheimer. I then discussed my preferred account of our basic needs and showed how it can meet a number of goals: for instance, it provides a robust theoretical account of basic needs which can enjoy widespread support, and it can also provide an adequate framework for designing policy about needs, and thus help us to discharge our global obligations. I discussed the relationship between basic needs and human rights, arguing why the basic needs standard is more fundamental than—and required by—the human rights

[36] David Miller, 'Distributing Responsibilities', *The Journal of Political Philosophy* **9** (2001), 453–471.

approach. Finally, I responded to a few important sets of anticipated objections to my view, especially some objections concerning distributing our responsibilities for meeting needs.

Appendix 1

I claim that we can explain all the human rights that are set out in the Universal Declaration of Human Rights in terms of my account of basic needs, a commitment to equality between persons, or clarification of the purposes of the document. Here I list the articles and indicate how each can be relevantly explained.

For ease of reference, I number the needs as follows: (1) physical and mental health, (2) sufficient security to be able to act, (3) a sufficient level of understanding of what one is choosing between, (4) a certain amount of autonomy, and (5) decent social relations with at least some others.

Article 1: commitment to equality

Article 2: commitment to equality

Article 3: needs 1, 2, and 4

Article 4: need 4

Article 5: 1, 2, and 4

Article 6: equality

Article 7: equality

Article 8: equality

Article 9: need 4 and 2

Article 10: equality

Article 11: (articles 1 and 2): (legal) equality

Article 12: 1, 4, and 2

Article 13: (articles 1 and 2): can involve 1, 2, 3, 4, and 5 if we think about the reasons why people want freedom of movement

Article 14: (article 1): 1, 2, and 5

Article 14: (article 2): purposes of the document

Article 15: (article 1): equality and 2

Article 15: (article 2): equality, 2, and 4

Article 16: (article 1): 2, 4, 5, and equality

Article 16: (article 2): equality and 4

Article 16: (article 3): 5

Article 17: (articles 1 and 2): 2 and 4

Article 18: 2 and 4

Article 19: 2 and 4

Article 20: (article 1): 2, 4, and 5

Article 20: (article 2): 4

Article 21: (article 1): 4, equality

Article 21: (article 2): equality

Article 21: (article 3): equality and 4

Article 22: 1, 2, 3, 4, 5, and equality

Article 23: (article 1): to be relevantly self-sustaining as a needs-meeter (and so 1, 2, 3, 4, and 5)

Article 23: (article 2): equality

Article 23: (article 3): to be relevantly self-sustaining as a needs-meeter (and so 1, 2, 3, 4, and 5)

Article 23: (article 4): 1, 4, 2

Article 24: 1, 2, and 4

Article 25: (article 1): to be relevantly self-sustaining (where possible) as a needs-meeter (especially in meeting needs 1 and 2)

Article 25: (article 2): recognition of childhood (and early motherhood) as a special time of vulnerability with respect to meeting needs (and so 1, 2, 3, 4, and 5)

Article 26: (article 1): 3

Article 26: (article 2): 3, equality, and purposes of the document

Article 26: (article 3): 4, 5, and 1

Article 27: (article 1): 3, 4, and 5

Article 27: (article 2): 4 (especially autonomy in controlling the fruits of one's labours)

Article 28: clarification of the purposes of the document

Article 29: (article 1): 1, 2, and 5

Article 29: (article 2): equality and 2

Article 29: (article 3): clarification of the document's purpose

Article 30: clarification of the document's purpose

Note: in a sense, equality comes into the explanation of all these articles. I list it as part of the explanation only when its salience is specially relevant to explaining a particular article.

3 Need, Humiliation and Independence

JOHN O'NEILL

1. Needs, justice and community

The needs principle—that certain goods should be distributed according to need—has been central to much socialist and egalitarian thought. It is the principle which Marx famously takes to be that which is to govern the distribution of goods in the higher phase of communism. The principle is one that Marx himself took from the Blanquists. It had wider currency in the radical traditions of the nineteenth century. In the twentieth century it remained central to the mutualist form of socialism defended by Tawney and Titmuss. The principle underlay the development and justification of the modern welfare state—thus the National Health Service is still founded upon the idea that the distribution of medical resources should be determined by medical need, not by ability to pay. One source of the power of the needs principle lies in the fact that it appears to be both a principle of justice and a principle of community or social solidarity. As a principle of justice it is offered as a corrective to the particular forms of unequal distributions of goods that can result from market transactions, and as a principle of community or social solidarity as a corrective to the possessive individualism taken to be the corollary of a market order.

Recent discussion of the needs principle in political philosophy has focused on its status and defensibility as a principle of justice.[1] However, in much of the history of egalitarian thought, its role as a principle of community was at least as significant. This is clearest in the work of Marx in which its status as a principle of justice or equality is denied,[2] but its status as a principle of community is affirmed. Production and distribution according to need involves a direct concern for the well-being of other persons. It forms a bond of community between members of a society and confirms our social nature:

> In your use or enjoyment of my product, I would have the *immediate* satisfaction and knowledge that in my labour I had gratified a *human* need, i.e. that I had objectified *human nature* and hence procured an object corresponding to the need of another *human being.*
> I would have acted for you as the *mediator* between you and the species, thus I would be acknowledged by you as the complement to your own being.[3]

Market transactions on the other hand involve acting towards others not as ends in themselves, but as a means.

---

[1] See for example D. Miller, *Social Justice* (Oxford: Clarendon Press 1976), ch.4 and *Principles of Social Justice* (Cambridge, Mass.: Harvard University Press 1999) ch.10.

[2] K. Marx, Critique of the Gotha Programme in K. Marx and F. Engels *Selected Works* (London: Lawrence and Wishart, 1968). For a discussion see N. Geras, 'The Controversy about Marx and Justice' in *Literature of Revolution* (London: Verso, 1986).

[3] K. Marx, 'Excerpts from James Mill's Elements of Political Economy' in L. Colletti (ed.) *Early Writings* (Harmondsworth: Penguin, 1975), 277.

In market exchange we approach others as self-interested agents whose relations to each other are instrumental and impersonal: 'Man ... produces only in order to *have*. The object of his production is the objectification of his own *immediate* selfish needs ... I have produced for myself and not for you, just as you have produced for yourself and not for me'.[4] This emphasis on community and social solidarity is typical of defences of the needs principle in the wider currents of nineteenth century egalitarian thought.[5]

A similar line of thought underpins the appeal to need in the form of egalitarianism defended by writers such as Tawney and Titmuss, in which equality is defended as a condition of a particular kind of community. The ideal of equality is tied to the creation of a community in which certain forms of power, exploitation and humiliation are eliminated and solidarity and fellowship fostered and in which vices of character of which inequality is a constitutive

---

[4] Ibid.

[5] For example in the work Kropotkin, while the needs principle is taken to be a principle of justice (D. Miller, *Social Justice* (Oxford: Clarendon Press 1976) ch.7), it is primarily introduced as a principle of distribution that expresses relations of community. Organisations based on the principle 'to every man according to his needs', such as museums, libraries, parks, and schools are presented as examples of local communism that run counter the 'the current of Individualism' that is fostered by market society (P. Kropotkin, *The Conquest of Bread* (London: Chapman Hall 1906), 33–35). So also are the variety of associations of mutual aid through which individuals respond directly to the needs of their fellows, such as the guild, the trade union, village communities, life-boat associations (P. Kropotkin, *Mutual Aid: A Factor of Evolution* (Boston: Porter Sargent, 1955) chs.6–8).

condition—such as dependence, servility, sycophancy, arrogance and snobbery—are overcome.[6] The needs principle is sometimes offered as a principle that fosters such a community. It is particularly evident in the work of Titmuss, informing his account of the central institutions for the distribution of social welfare. Non-market institutions providing welfare services on the basis of need are taken to create bonds of social solidarity in modern societies which market economies would otherwise undermine. Thus for example the following account of his 'institutional-redistributive model of social welfare':

> It sees social welfare as a basic integrated institution in society providing both universal and selective services outside the market on the principle of need. Universal services, available without distinction of class, colour, sex or religion, can perform functions which foster and promote attitudes and behaviour directed towards the values of social solidarity, altruism, toleration and accountability.[7]

Titmuss's influential account of the gift relationship belongs to this model of social welfare.

---

[6] See for example R. Tawney, *Equality* (London: Unwin 1964), pp.40–44 and passim. For a discussion see D. Miller, 'Equality and Justice' *Ratio (new series)*, **10**, 1997, pp.222–237 and J. O'Neill, 'Chekov and the Egalitarian' *Ratio (new series)* **14**, 2001, 165–170.

[7] R. Titmuss, 'Developing Social Policy in Conditions of Rapid Change: the Role of Social Welfare' in B. Abel-Smith and K. Titmuss (eds.) *The Philosophy of Welfare: Selected Writings of Richard M. Titmuss* (London: Allen and Unwin, 1987) 263.

In this paper I will be concerned primarily with the defensibility of the needs principle as a principle of community or social solidarity, rather than as a principle of justice.[8] Why might the needs principle be thought problematic as an account of social relations? One stark formulation of possible problems is to be found not in criticisms of the needs principle but in one of the early statements of the principle. While the principle of distribution according to need has been at the centre of one strand of modern egalitarian thought it has a much older lineage. It appears in the *Acts of the Apostles* iv.35 as the principle of distribution among the early Christian communities. In virtue of its place in the *Acts* it had a continuing influence in Christian thought in particular as a basis for the monastic community. One formulation of that principle is to be found in Rule of St. Benedict which is presented in Bettenson's *Documents of the Christian Church* as follows:

---

[8] It might be objected that distinguishing the needs principle as a principle of justice from its role in promoting a well-constituted community is somewhat artificial. One reason for thinking distribution according to needs is constitutive of a good community is that it is a condition of justice within a community. However, there are I think good reasons for analytically separating the two. A just society need not necessarily be one marked by strong bonds of community, and it may be that considerations of the quality of our social relations entail that sometimes we depart from strict justice. See J. Wolff, 'Fairness, Respect and the Egalitarian Ethos', *Philosophy and Public Affairs*, **27**, 1998, pp.97–122 and J. O'Neill, 'Chekov and the Egalitarian' *Ratio (new series)* **14**, 2001, pp.165–170. Likewise, questions of the adequacy of the needs principle as a principle of community raise different considerations from those concerned with justice.

As it is written: 'It was divided among them singly, according as each had need' [Acts iv. 35]: whereby we do not say – far from it – that there should be respect of persons, but a consideration for infirmities. Wherefore he who needs less, let him thank God and not be grieved; but he who needs more, let him be humiliated on account of his weakness, and not made proud on account of the indulgence that is shown to him.[9]

Now this may be a bad translation.[10] However, it is a translation that captures a real potential difficulty in the needs principle, that at least in certain circumstances to make a needs claim can be a source of humiliation. To appeal to others on the basis of need or to distribute goods on the basis of need can be inconsistent with the demands of dignity and the respect of persons.

Versions of this Benedictine problem are to be found in more recent debates both among defenders and critics of the needs principle. Among its defenders, one version appears in the recognition that in certain conditions

[9] Rule of St. Benedict, XXXIV in H. Bettenson (ed.), *Documents of the Christian Church* (London: Oxford University Press, 1963), p.167.
[10] Other translations have 'show humility' in place of the rather more blunt phrase 'be humiliated'. There are also complications about the term 'respect of persons' which since Kant has a particular meaning which differs from older usages. The denial of 'respect of persons', can be traced back to *Ephesians* 6.9. The standard gloss on the denial is that it is required by justice: 'a just judge regards causes, not persons'. To give respect to persons is to grant a person some good in virtue of who they are—because they are that particular person—not in virtue of their qualities which renders that good their due (Aquinas *Summa Theologica* IIa-IIae 63).

distribution according to need, for example through means-tested benefits, is a source of social stigma and humiliation; hence the concern with the conditions in which redistribution of wealth can be made consistent with the dignity of the needy.[11] Among critics, other versions of the problem form part of a wider set of worries about collectivist models of community.[12] Those models of community are criticised for being insufficiently alive to the loss of individual autonomy and independence which some forms of community can involve. Objections invoke a family of concepts associated with dignity and independence—autonomy, self-sufficiency, social standing, social worth. While the appeal to needs is *prima facie* constitutive of relations of care within a society, it is open to objections concerning its compatibility with the autonomy and independence of individuals in modern societies. Correspondingly, needs based criticisms of the market fail to recognise the ways in which markets foster independence and autonomy.

In recent discussion such scepticism about the appeal to needs in the distribution of goods is expressed in concerns about paternalism or authoritarianism. To appeal to needs is to appeal to the existence of necessary conditions for a person to live a flourishing life or realise some basic

[11] R. Titmuss, 'Universal and Selective Social Services' in B. Abel-Smith and K. Titmuss (eds.) *The Philosophy of Welfare: Selected Writings of Richard M. Titmuss* (London: Allen and Unwin, 1987).

[12] R. Keat, 'Individualism and Community in Socialist Thought' in J. Mepham and D.-H. Ruben (eds.) *Issues in Marxist Philosophy*, Vol IV, (Brighton: Harvester Press, 1981).

capacities for human functioning.[13] As such a needs principle is normally taken to involve a commitment to some form of objectivity about human flourishing that allows for some distance between what a person believes is good for her and what is good for her. In the background to a number of criticisms of the needs principle is the worry that this feature of needs-claims forms the basis for a paternalist or authoritarian practice. Some sets of experts are able to judge for an actor what is in her interests. Paternalism can be local, where the doctor or social worker determines his patients' or clients' needs without reference to their account of their good. It can be global, where at a political level at worst it leads to 'a dictatorship over needs' in which the state imposes upon citizens its particular conception of their needs according to its particular contested account of the good life.[14] In virtue of these features the needs principle is incompatible with a recognition of the autonomy of persons, with their capacity to formulate their own conceptions of a good life and make choices according to that conception. It is inconsistent with what Harsanyi calls the principle of Preference Autonomy: 'The principle that, in deciding what is good and what is bad for a given individual, the ultimate criteria can only be his own wants and his own

---

[13] I assume here that the needs principle concerns categorical or non-instrumental needs. See D. Wiggins, 'Claims of Need' in *Needs, Values, Truth* (Oxford: Blackwell, 1991).

[14] F. Fehér, A. Heller and G. Márkus, *Dictatorship over Needs: An Analysis of Soviet Societies* (Oxford: Blackwell, 1983).

preferences.'[15] In contrast, a market economy since it is directly responsive to the preferences of individuals through their expression of willingness to pay for a good is consistent with the autonomy of individuals. A market order responsive to the wants of individuals is to be preferred to a social and political order that is responsive to their needs.

This line of argument is not compelling. That there are real dangers in appeals to needs leading to objectionable paternalistic or authoritarian practices is undeniable. However, nothing in the needs principle as such requires a commitment to the forms of authoritarianism that form the proper object of liberal criticisms, nor is the issue of objectivity as such at issue. A needs principle may involve a commitment to some form of objectivism about human flourishing or well-being. However that commitment is consistent with a commitment to autonomy. The objectivist can recognise that the capacities to deliberate about the ends of life and make choices on the basis of such deliberations are basic human capacities and their exercise is part of what makes for a flourishing human life. Hence, a theory of need can recognise there are educational, cultural and material conditions for the development and exercise of those capacities and a principle of need can insist upon their proper distribution. Insofar as preferences expressed in markets are themselves formed by rational deliberation, they presuppose that those prior conditions have been met. Autonomy

---

[15] J. Harsanyi, 'Morality and the Theory of Rational Behaviour' in A. Sen and B. Williams (eds.) *Utilitarianism and Beyond* (Cambridge: Cambridge University Press, 1982) 55.

requires individuals who have the capacities to exercise rational judgements and choices and those capacities require non-market domains of informal and formal education, and material, cultural, familial and working conditions that develop the capacity for self-determination. Given these non-market conditions for the development of the capacities for rational deliberation in the formation of preference, the market cannot of itself provide a reliable basis for the distribution of resources.[16] Moreover, an objectivist account of human well-being does not entail that what people want is irrelevant to their well-being. It is consistent with an endorsement constraint on what makes a person's life go well. One cannot improve an individual's life by supplying resources that are by some objective criterion valuable to the individual, but which are not recognised and accepted as such by that individual.[17] However, that endorsement as a necessary condition of a good life does not entail that it is sufficient. That people are unhappy if they do not get what they want does not entail that they are happy if they do.

The objectivity of needs-claims in itself does not render the appeal to needs inconsistent with autonomy. There are, however, lines of argument around the consistency of the appeal to needs with a proper recognition of the independence and self-sufficiency of individuals which are distinct from these recent concerns with the objectivity of

[16] For a discussion see C. Macleod, *Liberalism, Justice, and Markets: A Critique of Liberal Equality* (Oxford: Clarendon Press, 1998).
[17] R. Dworkin, 'In Defence of Equality', *Social Philosophy and Policy*, **1**, 1983 pp.24–40.

needs-claims. One powerful line of argument is to be found in the work of Adam Smith. Smith's argument appeals to the Stoic values of independence and self-sufficiency and the potential conflict of those values with appeals to necessities in public life. It is Smith's line of argument that will be my central concern in this paper.

2.   Needs, benevolence and independence

At the centre of Smith's defence of commercial society is the appeal to the values of self-sufficiency and social independence: 'Nothing tends so much to corrupt and enervate and debase the mind as dependency, and nothing gives such noble and generous notions of probity as freedom and independency. Commerce is one great preventative of this custom.'[18] However, while the conditions for social independence stand at the heart of Smith's account, he also clearly recognises that human beings are vulnerable beings who are dependent on each other and indeed that society flourishes when members attend to the needs of others:

> All the members of human society stand in need of each others assistance, and are likewise exposed to mutual injuries. Where the necessary assistance is reciprocally afforded from love, from gratitude, from friendship, and esteem, the society flourishes and is happy. All the different members of it are bound together by agreeable

[18] A. Smith, *Lectures on Jurisprudence* (Indianapolis: Liberty Press 1982), vi.6.

bonds of love and affection, and are, as it were, drawn to one common centre of mutual good offices.[19]

However, while in *The Theory of Moral Sentiments* Smith allows that society flourishes in such conditions of mutual benevolence, Smith goes on to make a number of qualifications to that claim. First, there are limits to the degree to which such bonds of benevolence can extend to the wider assembly of strangers that makes up society. Individuals' partiality to themselves and to the local communities to which they belong render beneficence too weak to act as a basis for wider community. Individuals show partiality to themselves: 'the misery of one, who is merely their fellow-creature, is of so little importance to them in comparison of what they feel for themselves'.[20] In his echo of Hume's famous example, if an individual loses his little finger he will not sleep, whereas he can still sleep soundly following the news of a disaster that kills millions of strangers in China.[21] Individuals show partiality to the local communities of families and friends to whom they are directly related.[22] Benevolence cannot be expected to extend to or be extended from the wider 'assembly of strangers' with whom our lives are related.[23] Secondly, such bonds of reciprocal beneficence are not a necessary condition of society. Specifically, through market exchange, individuals who are

[19] A. Smith, *The Theory of Moral Sentiments* (Indianapolis: Liberty Press, 1982), II.ii.3.1 p.85.
[20] Op.cit., II.ii 3.4, p.86.   [21] Op.cit., III.3.4, pp.136–7.
[22] Op.cit., VI.ii.1.   [23] Op.cit., I.i.4.9.

not directly motivated by concern for each other's needs can still serve each others' necessities.

> Society may subsist among different men, as among different merchants, from a sense of its utility, without any mutual love or affection; and though no man in it should owe any obligation, or be bound in gratitude to any other, it may still be upheld by a mercenary exchange of good offices according to an agreed valuation.[24]

The market order thus described does not exist in a moral vacuum. Rules and sentiments of justice governing negative responsibilities to avoid harming others are a necessary condition for a social order. However positive sentiments of beneficence are not necessary conditions for society.

Smith's claim that through market exchange individuals can meet each other's needs without benevolence is expressed more famously in the much-quoted passage from *The Wealth of Nations*:

> It is not from the benevolence of the butcher, the brewer, or the baker that we expect our dinner, but from their regard to their own interest. We address ourselves, not to their humanity but to their self-love, and never talk to them of our own necessities but of their advantages.[25]

In this passage in *The Wealth of Nations*, however, claims about the limits of benevolence are supplemented by a distinct claim concerning the problems with the status of

[24] Op.cit., II.ii 3.2, 86.

[25] A. Smith, *An Inquiry into the Nature and Causes of the Wealth of Nations* (Indianapolis: Liberty Press, 1981), I.II.2.

the person who is the object of an act of beneficence, with the forms of social dependence it is engenders. To make an appeal on the basis of one's own need, to talk of 'our own necessities', and hence to call on the benevolence of others, is to render oneself dependent on others: 'Nobody but a beggar chooses to depend chiefly upon the benevolence of his fellow-citizens.'[26] Smith is not claiming here that we should never appeal on the basis of our necessities to the benevolence of others or their humanity. However to 'chiefly' make such appeals is not consistent with one's independence as an agent. The direct appeal to need renders me dependent on the gift of others. In this respect the request that calls upon need contrasts with a demand made upon a person's interest or self-love which in contrast are consistent with one's independence. To appeal to their advantage is to approach others as an independent agent among other independent agents. The argument here for commercial society turns not merely on the negative point that market exchange is consistent with limited benevolence. It is rather the positive point that by stripping away reliance on the gift of others, the market fosters social independence. Commercial society realises the Stoic virtues of independence and self-sufficiency: 'Every man, as the Stoics used to say, is first and principally recommended to his own care; and every man is certainly, in every respect, fitter and abler to take care of himself than of any other person.'[27]

---

[26] Ibid.   [27] A. Smith, *The Theory of Moral Sentiments* VI.ii.1.1.

This claim that commercial society fosters the virtues of independence is central to Smith's account of the achievements of commercial society over pre-modern societies. In commercial society, through exchange and the division of labour, the labourer is no longer personally dependent on the wealthy. Markets free us from the forms of dependency that the gift in pre-commercial economies involves. In pre-commercial society the 'rustic hospitality' of the large property owner serves as a means by which the wealthy exercised power and the poor were rendered dependent: '[The great proprietor] is at all times ... surrounded with a multitude of retainers and dependants, who, having no equivalent to give in return for their maintenance, but being fed entirely by his bounty, must obey him ... Before the extension of commerce and manufacture in Europe, the hospitality of the rich, and the great, from the sovereign down to the smallest baron, exceeded everything which in the present times we can easily form a notion of.'[28] In commercial society ties of personal dependence are broken. The interdependence of individuals is disassociated from personal dependence. Since the income of each worker is not tied to that of any particular individual, the ties that the rich previously exercised over their workers are broken. 'Though [the wealthy person] contributes, therefore, to the maintenance of them all, they are all more or less independent of him, because generally they can all be maintained without him.'[29]

[28] A. Smith, *An Inquiry into the Nature and Causes of the Wealth of Nations* III.IV.5–6.

[29] Op.cit., III.IV.11.

124

Central to Smith's defence of commercial society is a concern with the conditions in which particular virtues of independence can be sustained and vices of servility avoided. The division of labour mediated by exchange relations is taken to allow the combination of the interdependence of individuals through the division of labour in the production of the necessities and luxuries of life with social independence. A person's fate is no longer dependent on others. Smith recognises that this is partial. Social recognition in commercial society still follows wealth and vanity is the prime mover of economic growth.[30] And as I shall show below, for Smith this entails self-delusion about the extent of our self-sufficiency. However, in contrast to pre-commercial society, it is taken to offer social independence to actors in the market place. By appealing to each other as self-interested agents, we sustain our independence. Appealing to each other as agents in need of each other's benevolence cannot sustain that independence.

In Smith's argument one can see the embryo of a reply to Marx's criticisms of commercial society and his defence of the forms of community based on direct appeals to need. The argument would run that while market exchange is instrumental, it does not follow that it is simply a matter of treating others as means and not ends. Rather, through market relations we recognise others as independent agents of standing, towards whom we act neither as benefactor nor as dependent. Agents are recommended to

---

[30] Smith, *The Theory of Moral Sentiments*, I.iii.2.1, p.50.

their own care and we mutually recognise each other as individuals who are best able to care for themselves. Marx's claim that in commercial society individuals care primarily for their own needs and not those of others is not a failing of markets, but a virtue. In market society there is a recognition of mutual independence. It is rather a society organised directly around meeting the claims of need that render individuals problematically dependent upon each other and fails to properly acknowledge their capacities to care primarily for their own lives.[31]

Now clearly there is much in Smith's argument the egalitarian can accept, in particular that there is something objectionable in the forms of dependency in pre-commercial

---

[31] This line of defence of commercial society finds expression in a different idiom in Hegel's account of civil society. Through contract individuals recognise each other as independent rights holders, as individuals of standing. Correspondingly, the direct alleviation of poverty by welfare payments from public sources of income or the wealthy leads to a dependency that is incompatible with the principle of civil society: 'the needy would receive subsistence directly, not by means of their work, and this would violate the principle of civil society and the feeling of individual independence and self-respect in its individual members' (G. Hegel, *Philosophy of Right* (London: Oxford University Press 1967), paragraph 245). The difficulty for Hegel is that poverty is also taken to be an inevitable consequence of the workings of civil society. Central to Hegel's solution is alleviation of poverty through corporations based on particular skills, where membership of the association already confirms an individual's standing (Op.cit., para. 253A). The problem with the solution, as Hegel recognises, is that those who are most vulnerable to poverty, unskilled day labourers, are excluded from corporations (Op.cit., para. 252A).

society. Marx, for example, joins Smith in praising commercial society for rescuing individuals from personal dependence that existed in pre-commercial society. Typical is the following comment from the *Grundrisse*: 'in the money relation, in the developed system of exchange ... the ties of personal dependence ... are in fact exploded, ripped up ... and individuals *seem* independent ...'[32] What Marx rejects in the kind of view presented by Smith is the form of independence that individuals realise in modern market societies. It is 'an independence which is at bottom merely an illusion'.[33] There are two components to Marx's argument. First, personal dependence is replaced by what Marx calls 'objective dependency',[34] their dependency on the impersonal workings of market society, and for the worker while he is not dependent on any particular capitalist, he must sell his labour power to some capitalist. Full independence requires social relations being brought under the 'communal control' of individuals.[35] Second, Marx repeats the theme that this form of independence cannot adequately express individuals' social nature. The independence achieved by the money relation is 'more properly called

[32] K. Marx, *Grundrisse* (Harmondsworth: Penguin, 1973) 163.

[33] Ibid.

[34] A variation on this theme is to be found in the work of Kant: '[M]oney makes one independent, one gains respect by the possession of it; one has worth, needs no one and depends on no one. But in making us independent of others, money in the long run makes us dependent on itself; it frees us from others in order to enslave us.' (Kant, *Lectures on Ethics* (London: Methuen, 1979), 177).

[35] K. Marx, Op.cit., 162.

indifference'.[36] The needs principle shorn of its relation to personal dependence is taken to be the basis for a wider community. Those two claims are independent. There are grounds for scepticism about Marx's claim about the possibility of bringing all social relations under conscious communal control. There are epistemological limits to any such project.[37] However, the second claim may still have independent force. Marx's own specific arguments on independence and community have been examined in detail elsewhere and I will not pursue them further here.[38] Rather I will draw on a larger tradition of egalitarian argument about the forms of independence or self-sufficiency fostered by market exchange. As we shall see, Smith himself argues that commercial society is founded upon a fortuitous self-deception about self-sufficiency. The nature of that deception and a wider related set of misconceptions about autonomy I explore in sections 5 and 6. I want however to begin by considering in the next section some prior issues about the relation between benevolence, justice and need.

---

[36] Op.cit., 163.

[37] I discuss this further in J. O'Neill, *The Market: Ethics, Knowledge and Politics* (London: Routledge 1998), ch.10.

[38] See C. Gould, *Marx's Social Ontology: Individuality and Community in Marx's Theory of Social Reality* (Cambridge, Mass.: MIT Press, 1978), R. Keat, 'Individualism and Community in Socialist Thought' in J. Mepham and D.-H. Ruben (eds.) *Issues in Marxist Philosophy*, Vol IV, (Brighton: Harvester Press 1981) and D. Archard, 'The Marxist Ethic of Self-Realisation: Individuality and Community' in J. Evans (ed.) *Moral Philosophy and Contemporary Problems* (Cambridge: Cambridge University Press, 1988).

3. Impersonality, rights and justice

Smith's arguments on independence in commercial society turn on assertions about the relation between claims of need and benevolence, the limits of benevolence in a world of strangers, and the conflicts between calls on the benevolence of others and personal independence. One response to the arguments might be to break the first link between claims of need and benevolence. Consider the following illustration of the possible conflict between need and dignity from Ignatieff's *The Needs of Strangers*:

> I came upon one old man once doing his shopping alone, weighed down in a queue at a potato stall and nearly fainting from tiredness. I made him sit down in a pub while I did the rest of his shopping. But if he needed help, he certainly didn't want it. He was clinging on to his life, grasping for breath, but he stared straight ahead when we talked and his fingers could not be pried from his burdens.[39]

The old man does not want help since it potentially robs him of his independence and dignity. He doesn't require the charity of others.

The moral that Ignatieff wants to draw from the tale, however, is not that we should reject the distribution of goods according to need. It is rather that claims of need are not to be addressed by personal benevolence and gift. The virtue of the welfare state is that it transforms needs into rights and entitlements satisfied by bureaucratic means.

---

[39] M. Ignatieff, *The Needs of Strangers* (London: Hogarth Press 1990).

> [The old] have needs, and because they live within the welfare state, these needs confer entitlements—rights—to the resources of people like me ... The mediated quality of the relationship seems necessary to both of us. They are dependent on the state, not upon me, and we are both glad of it. Yet I am also aware of how this mediation walls us off from each other.[40]

Through the pension book the old receive benefits without dependency on the gift of particular persons. It grants some form of personal independence: 'The bureaucratic transfer of income among strangers has freed each of us for the enslavement of gift relations.'[41] However while the satisfaction of need through impersonal bureaucratic means sustains social independence, it also undermines solidarity, the direct response to needs of others: 'Yet if the welfare state does serve the needs of freedom, it does not serve the needs of solidarity. We remain a society of strangers.'[42] To call upon impersonal institutions to distribute according to entitlements appears to rob the principle of distribution according to need of its power as a form of social solidarity.

Ignatieff's line of argument breaks the link between needs-claims and personal dependence. However, it does so by breaking the link between needs and social solidarity. How compelling is Ignatieff's argument? There are two components to the argument. One is institutional. The welfare state realises personal independence by distributing goods through impersonal bureaucratic means which cut us off from direct concern with others. It is unclear to me

[40] Op.cit., 9–10.   [41] Op.cit., 18.   [42] Op.cit., 18.

that relations between strangers that remove claims of need from personal gift-relations need be of that kind. There are a variety of different institutional forms which can mediate between strangers and which can have different effects on social solidarity. Some distributions according to need among strangers might foster solidarity. Titmuss argues plausibly for example that blood donation might have that nature.[43]

The second component to Ignatieff's argument concerns the relation between needs-claims and rights and entitlements. The expression of needs-claims as rights-claims does promise to break the link between claims of need and calls upon benevolence. Rights-claims turn moral requests into moral demands. To make a claim on the benevolence of agents is to make a moral request. It is to place power in the hands of the benefactor. To claim a right or entitlement is to make a demand that appeals not to the benevolence or charity of agents, but rather to what is required of them. To express needs-claims in the form of rights is thus to put the power in the hands of the recipient of a needs claim. Hence, the transformation of needs-claims into rights-claims renders needs-claims consistent with an agent's affirmation of her independence. However, again it might be argued that while this serves the needs of justice, it does not serve the needs of solidarity. The translation of needs into rights threatens to undermine the forms of direct

---

[43] R. Titmuss, *The Gift Relationship* (London: Allen and Unwin, 1970) and D. Archard, 'Selling Yourself: Titmuss's Argument against a Market in Blood,' *The Journal of Ethics*, **6**, 2002, 87–103.

solidarity involved in response to needs.[44] If responding to needs-claims is only a matter of respecting rights, then it belongs to the Kantian sphere of impersonal and impartial duties, not to the sphere of the sentiments. If it is granted that sentiments of benevolence cannot be extended into the sphere of strangers, and that in meeting claims of need we have to rely simply on rights, then the needs principle can no longer be understood as a principle of community. If one's concern is purely with justice then this is not a problem. The needs principle as a principle of justice takes need out of the sphere of benevolence and charity. It does so however to the detriment of the needs principle as a principle of social solidarity. Indeed it might be argued that the source of the attraction of the needs principle, that it is a principle of both justice and solidarity, is also a source of instability. The demands pull in opposite directions.

The obvious response to that argument is to deny the Kantian assumptions about justice on which it is based. Justice need not be understood as a cold virtue that takes us into the sphere of impersonal duties. Justice is not just a matter of laws and duties, but also of the passions, and to be moved by

---

[44] The thought that it might be is central to some of Simone Weil's scepticism about rights and to 'the shrill nagging of claims and counter-claims' that she took the language of rights to engender. Hence the following comment: 'to place rights at the centre of social conflicts is to inhibit any possible impulse of charity on both sides ...' (S. Weil, 'On Human Personality' in D. McLellan, *Simone Weil* (London: Macmillan 1989), p.280). For a discussion of Weil's arguments see P. Winch, *Simone Weil: 'The Just Balance'* (Cambridge: Cambridge University Press, 1989), ch.14.

sentiments of justice is to be moved directly by the condition of those who are the victims of injustice. Solidarity can be and often is based on the passions of justice. Indeed this response might be thought to be broadly consistent with Smith's view of justice. For Smith, justice is also a matter of the sentiments. However, as far as the needs principle is concerned a clear inconsistency with Smith's views remains. While Smith rejects an impersonal view of justice he holds that sentiments of justice, unlike those of beneficence, are not concerned with meeting the needs of others. Benevolence and justice differ in their object and related sentiment: sentiments of benevolence are based in the 'sympathetic gratitude' a spectator feels for actions that aim at some positive good; sentiments of justice are based in the 'sympathetic resentment' that a spectator feels for actions that are hurtful of others and are deserving of punishment.[45] While negative duties to avoid harm to others are morally required of us and can be enforced, positive duties to do some positive good are not requirements and are not enforceable in the same way.[46] Acting directly to meet the needs of others falls under those positive duties. Negative duties to avoid harm to others are a necessary condition for a social order. No society can exist without the rules and sentiments of justice. However, commercial society makes possible a social order that can survive without sentiments of beneficence that aim at some positive good for others.[47]

[45] A. Smith, *The Theory of Moral Sentiments*, II.ii.1–2.

[46] Op.cit., II.ii.3.

[47] The claim is one about which there are good grounds for scepticism. Market relations themselves require a background of social relations of

Smith's account of the moral psychology of justice, has two components, an account of the basis of sentiments of justice in the emotions of sympathetic resentment, and an account of the proper scope of those emotions. One response to Smith's account might be to reject the first component and enlarge the scope of the sentiments of justice. Emotions such as compassion or pity also come within the sphere of justice. One might indeed deny there is a real distinction between justice and benevolence and with Leibniz take justice to be the charity of the wise.[48] There are, however, considerations that suggest that Smith's account of the moral psychology of justice as being specifically related to emotions such as resentment or anger might have something right about it. A response to injustice, say involving some terrible injury visited upon a person, may involve not just anger or resentment on behalf of the injured person, but also benevolent emotions of compassion and pity. However, the object of those benevolent emotions are the condition of the person, not the fact of injustice. A person who suffers the same injuries but from accidental

---

positive regard. As MacIntyre notes, if one's butcher has a heart attack before one, the response 'Ah! Not in a position to sell me my meat today I see' (MacIntyre, *Rational Dependent Animals* (London: Duckworth 1999), 117) would not just be improper, it would make the workings of a market society itself impossible.

[48] 'Justice is charity a habit of loving conformed to wisdom. Thus when one is inclined to justice, one tries to procure the good of everybody ... in proportion to the needs and merits of each' (Leibniz, 'Felicity' in P. Riley (ed.) *Political Writings* (Cambridge: Cambridge University Press, 1988) 83).

causes will still be a proper object of compassion and pity, but anger and resentment will no longer be appropriate responses to their situation. The emotions of sympathetic resentment and anger are specific responses to the injustice. Benevolent emotions are a response to a person's needs, not to injustice as such. So would go one plausible line of reply on behalf of Smith.

A second response to Smith would be to enlarge not the sentiments of justice, but rather the proper scope of those particular sentiments that Smith takes to be constitutive of justice. The emotions of sympathetic resentment or anger include among their proper objects not just harms consequent on the intentional actions by individuals, but wider conditions of neediness. One might for example take the forms of neediness in the world that are consequent on avoidable structural conditions to be themselves the proper object of sympathetic resentment. Or again in the case of a person accidentally injured, while sympathetic resentment or anger might not be appropriate to the condition as such, it can be appropriate with regard to failure by specific individuals or public bodies to assist that person. Correspondingly, the sentiments of justice can govern positive duties to meet certain needs. Sentiments of justice can include positive regard for the needs of others. They can and do form bonds of social solidarity with others including strangers. This response closes something of the possible gap between the needs principle as an account of justice and an account of community. The promise of the needs principle as I noted at the outset might lie in its combining the two. However, what of the positive concerns of benevolence? In the next section I will argue that even if we reject this account of the passions of justice, there are grounds for questioning the assumption that being an object of benevolence entails a loss of social independence.

4.   Equality, community and vulnerability

To make a needs-claim is to acknowledge one's dependence on others. However, is it the case that it necessarily involves a loss of social independence, or correspondingly a failure of standing? A feature of Smith's examples of benevolence and pre-commercial gift economies and the dependence that is taken to follow from them is that they take place against the background of large asymmetries of wealth and vulnerabilities. There is in the history of the egalitarian tradition of political thought a position that reverses this argument, that insists that a background of a rough equality in vulnerabilities is a condition of a community based on needs. Part of the thought behind this is to be found in the following passage from Rousseau:

> Why have kings no pity on their people? Because they never expect to be ordinary men. Why are the rich so hard on the poor? Because they have no fear of becoming poor. Why do the nobles look down upon the people? Because a nobleman will never be a commoner ... So do not train your pupil to look down from the height of his glory upon the sufferings of the unfortunate, the labours of the wretched, and do not hope to teach him to pity them as long as he considers them as far removed from himself. Make him clearly thoroughly aware of the fact

that the fate of these unhappy persons may one day be his own, that his feet are standing on the edge of an abyss, into which he may be plunged at any moment by a thousand unexpected irresistible misfortunes.[49]

Rousseau in this passage defends a strong claim about the emotions of compassion—that 'we never pity another's woes unless we may suffer in like manner ourselves'.[50] That claim that the belief that a like calamity could befall oneself is constitutive of the emotion of pity is one that is found often in the philosophical tradition. Thus Aristotle offers the following characterisation:

> Pity may be defined as a feeling of pain caused by the sight of some evil, destructive or painful, which befalls one who does not deserve it, and which we might expect to befall ourselves or some friend of ours, and moreover to befall us soon.[51]

Hobbes makes a similar claim:

> *Griefe*, for the Calamity of another, is PITTY; and ariseth from the imagination that the like calamity may befall himselfe; and therefore is called also COMPASSION, and in the phrase of this present time a FELLOW-FEELING.[52]

[49] J. J. Rousseau, *Emile*, B. Foxley (trans.) (Dent: London, 1911), book IV, 185.
[50] Ibid.
[51] Aristotle, *Rhetoric*, W. Roberts (trans.) (Clarendon Press: Oxford, 1946), II.8 85b12ff.
[52] T. Hobbes, *Leviathan* (Harmondsworth: Penguin, 1968), I.6 126.

137

However, while our belief in the possibility of calamity may foster emotions of pity or compassion, it is far from clear that the belief is a necessary condition for the emotion. On the conditions for the possibility of sympathetic emotion Smith is I think right to deny the necessity of the thought that the some condition could befall oneself: 'A man may sympathize with a woman in child-bed; though it is impossible that he should conceive of himself as suffering her pains in his own proper person and character'.[53] It is possible to feel pity or compassion for persons in situations one could not possibly fall into. There are epistemic limits on fellow-feelings in such cases: imagination is not a substitute for the direct experience of a particular condition for which one feels fellow-feeling. However, the possibility of compassion or pity as such is not ruled out. Similarly to return to Rousseau's example, while kings, the rich, and nobleman may seldom feel pity for those in a subordinate position, it is possible for them to do so.

What is true, however, is that an equality of vulnerabilities—the real possibility that like calamities might fall on agents—transforms the social meaning of the attitude, in particular for the person who is its object. A condition of equality removes the possible condescension that follows inequalities in vulnerabilities. There is a difference between expressions of pity or benevolence within an inegalitarian society and that within a society in which as Rousseau puts it 'tomorrow, any one may himself be in the same position as

---

[53] A. Smith, *The Theory of Moral Sentiments*, VII.iii.1.4.

the one he assists is in today'.[54] In conditions of equality the emotion can be understood as an expression of solidarity or fellow feeling, where the standing of individuals is recognised to be equal. In conditions of inequality it cannot be thus understood—and hence its problematic status as a possible expression of charity. The benefactor does 'look down from the height of his glory upon the sufferings of the unfortunate', and the recipient finds themselves an object of a sympathetic gaze from above.

The principle of distribution of needs in the socialist tradition came out of a particular practical experience within working class communities in which the expression of fellow feeling in this sense was central. As Tawney and Titmuss have noted, a particular mutualist model of equality grew out of the experience of mutual aid in conditions of common vulnerabilities that marked the early history of working class movements.[55] Mutual assistance on the basis of needs took place on the basis of an awareness of a background of equality of vulnerabilities. Certainly something of this kind finds formal expression in the rules of the trade-unions and friendly societies of the eighteenth and nineteenth centuries. Consider for example the following from the Rules of the Sociable Society in Newcastle, 1812:

[54] J. -J. Rousseau, *Emile* p.185.
[55] R. Tawney, *Equality* (London: Unwin, 1964), 40ff and R. Titmuss, 'Social Welfare and the Art of Giving' in B. Abel-Smith and K. Titmuss (eds.) *The Philosophy of Welfare: Selected Writings of Richard M. Titmuss*, 122.

> We, the members of this society, taking into our serious consideration, that man is formed a social being . . . in continual need of mutual assistance and support; and having interwoven in our constitutions those humans and sympathetic affections which we always feel at the distress of our fellow creatures.[56]

Or again consider the introduction to the Rules and Orders of the Honourable Society of Workington February 2nd, 1792:

> When we look upon mankind as being subject to an innumerable train of evils and calamities, resulting either from pain or sickness, or the infirmities of old age, which render them unable to procure even a scanty subsistence, when at the same time they are made capable of the noblest friendship, common prudence induces us so to form ourselves into society, that the insupportable condition of the individual may, by the mutual assistance and support of the whole, become tolerable.

Such societies had clear limitations as organisations to meet common needs. They were limited in the scope of those they included and existed within a wider context of large inequalities of wealth which carried real inequalities in vulnerability. However, in the local communities of vulnerability which they formed, they expressed a central theme taken up in a wider tradition of egalitarian thought, that the existence and recognition of common vulnerability to evil and calamity

---

[56] Cited in E. P. Thompson, *The Making of the English Working Class* (Penguin: Harmondsworth, 1968), 461; see chapter 12 for a discussion of this tradition.

robs the fact of dependency of its potentially humiliating condition.

5. Autonomy, self-sufficiency and independence

The egalitarian response to the problems of the possible conflicts between claims of need and social independence is founded upon a claim about the limits of self-sufficiency. Rousseau's individuals always stand on the edge of an abyss: misfortune can always befall us. The association of mutual aid start from the 'innumerable train of evils and calamities' to which individuals' lives are subject. This recognition of the real limits of self-sufficiency and of our dependence on others is not as such inconsistent with a modest account of the ideal of social self-sufficiency. Indeed Smith's account of self-sufficiency looks on first reading to offer a suitably modest account of the ideal. A feature of Smith's version of the Stoic ideal of self-sufficiency and social independence which marks it off from many more recent accounts of those values lies in its acknowledgement of our dependence on others. It is true that the assertion 'every man, as the Stoics used to say, is first and principally recommended to his own care'[57] invites the response that on entering the world we are first recommended to the care of others on whom we are dependent. However this is an observation that Smith himself goes on to make: 'In the natural state of things ... the

---

[57] A. Smith, *The Theory of Moral Sentiments*, VI.ii.1.1.

existence of the child, for some time after it comes into the world, depends altogether upon the care of the parent'.[58]

In saying we are first recommended to our own care, Smith's claim is that as adults who have matured from such states of early dependency, the primary responsibility for our well-being is ourselves. In making that claim Smith as we noted earlier is well aware that this responsibility can only be discharged against the background of dependence on others: 'All the members of human society stand in need of each others assistance, and are likewise exposed to mutual injuries.'[59] Finally, Smith stresses that wealth and power do not protect individuals from the vulnerabilities of illness, old age and death to which we are all subject:

> In the languor of disease and the weariness of old age, the pleasures of the vain and empty distinctions of greatness disappear ... Power and riches appear then to be, what they are, enormous and operose machines contrived to produce a few trifling conveniences to the body, consisting of springs the most nice and delicate, which must be kept in order with the most anxious attention ... They keep off the summer shower, not the winter storm, but leave him always as much, and sometimes more exposed than before, to anxiety, to fear, and to sorrow; to diseases, to danger, and to death.[60]

The account of self-sufficiency which Smith holds we can realistically expect to achieve looks and indeed is a modest

---

[58] Op.cit., VI.ii.1.3.　　[59] Op.cit., II.ii.3.1.　　[60] Op.cit., IV.1.8.

one and indeed may seem to echo the remarks of Rousseau or the documents of early mutual aid associations.

However, Smith gives a twist to this account of social independence. He goes on to argue that while this 'splenetic philosophy' might be true, it is not the account of self-sufficiency that actors in commercial society themselves must assume. The development of commercial society itself requires self-deception about the limits of our self-sufficiency:

> agreeable aspect ... The pleasures of wealth and greatness ... strike the imagination as something grand and beautiful and noble, of which the attainment is well worth all the toil an anxiety which we are so apt to bestow upon it ... It is this deception which rouses and keeps in continual motion the industry of mankind.[61]

It is in this context that the well-known metaphor of the invisible hand appears in *The Theory of Moral Sentiments* to refer to the indirect and unintended link between the self-deception of the rich, 'their natural selfishness and rapacity' in the pursuit of 'vain and insatiable desires' and 'the distribution of the necessaries of life' across the whole population and hence the general improvement of the condition of the poor through the encouragement of commerce and industry.[62] Smith himself raises doubts about the corruption of character that is a consequence of that self-deception.[63] And

[61] Op.cit., IV.1.9–10.
[62] Op.cit., IV.1.10; cf. Smith, *An Inquiry into the Nature and Causes of the Wealth of Nations* III.iv.17 and IV.ii.9.
[63] A. Smith, *The Theory of Moral Sentiments*, I.iii.3.1.

there are questions of the empirical adequacy of this claim about the link between this self-deception and the general improvement of conditions for all. But over and above this, the self-deception issues in a misconception about the nature of self-sufficiency which is fostered by commercial society.

Amongst defenders of market economies, and indeed many of its critics, there is a general tendency to immodest characterisations of the values of independence, self-sufficiency and autonomy.[64] Consider the way in which autonomy is characterised through a series of one-dimensional contrasts between autonomous and non-autonomous persons: autonomy is a virtue that is defined in opposition to one vice—heteronomy. The autonomous person who displays self-authorship in the sense that her judgement and choices are her own, who is able to rely on her own capacities of thought and decision, is contrasted with the person who displays excessive dependence on the authority of others, who is acquiescent to the judgements and choices of others. The autonomous person who determines in some significant way her own character is contrasted with the heteronomous individual whose identity is defined in terms of some pre-given or other-determined role or character. These vices of heteronomy are vices. However, the simple contrast of autonomy with heteronomy is liable to blind one to other vices which equally undermine autonomy. To use the Aristotelian terminology, the virtues of the

[64] J. O'Neill, *The Market: Ethics, Knowledge and Politics* (London: Routledge, 1998), chs.5–7.

autonomous character need to be contrasted not only with vices of deficiency, but also those of excess.

Self-authorship can take the excessively individualistic form which fails to acknowledge necessary dependence on others: the resulting self-conceit is as much opposed to autonomy as excessive dependence. Benson makes the point thus:

> The virtue of autonomy is a mean state of character with regard to reliance on one's own powers in acting, choosing and forming opinions. The deficiency is termed heteronomy, and there are many terms which may be used to describe the heteronomous person, some of which suggest specific forms of the vice: credulous, gullible, compliant, passive, submissive, overdependent, servile. For the vice of excess there is no name in common use, but solipsism might do, or arrogant self-sufficiency.[65]

The existence of these vices often goes unrecognised. Worse, a feature of much recent discussion of the concept of autonomy, especially in discussions of the relation of markets and autonomy, is that the concept is given an elaboration which celebrates not the virtues of autonomy but these vices. The vices of arrogant self-sufficiency are presented as virtues. The post-modern celebration of the self who plays with identity is perhaps the starkest example. However something of it can be found in the widespread assumption made in many defences of market society noted earlier, that the

[65] J. Benson, 'Who is the Autonomous Man?' *Philosophy* **58**, 1983.

ultimate criteria for determining what is good and what is bad for an individual are that person's wants and preferences. The principle expresses a strong conception of autonomy according to which to be autonomous not only requires being the author of one's own projects but also of the standards by which they should be judged. This romantic image of autonomy expresses not a virtue but a vice. The existence of authoritative standards that are independent of the preferences of individuals is a condition of education within a variety of practices that are a condition of autonomy. The very capacity to rationally reflect upon one's own projects that is constitutive of autonomy relies on the acceptance of such standards.[66]

Smith's core account of self-sufficiency does not display the vices of arrogant self-sufficiency. However, the assumptions of radical self-sufficiency that he takes to be required by commercial society do display those vices. Its obverse is the social invisibility of the networks of care and support that sustain the apparently self-sufficient actors of market society, in particular the rich and powerful. There are good reasons to prefer the egalitarian line of thought that begins from that modest account of self-sufficiency, from what Smith calls 'splenetic philosophy', that starts from our vulnerabilities and the degree to which such vulnerabilities render us dependent on others. A good social order needs to start not from the denial of common vulnerabilities but an

[66] See J. O'Neill, *The Market: Ethics, Knowledge and Politics* ch.7 and R. Keat, *Cultural Goods and the Limits of the Market* (Basingstoke: Macmillan, 2000).

acknowledgement of their existence. Self-deception about the limits of self-sufficiency and the extent of our neediness is not a proper basis for public policy that is concerned to foster proper autonomy and social independence. While there can be contingent conflicts between some needs-claims, in particular social conditions of inequality and social independence, there is no necessary conflict between neediness and autonomy. The acknowledgement of our dependence on others, both physical and social, need not be in conflict with a proper understanding of the virtues of the autonomous person.

4 Needs and Ethics in Ancient Philosophy

CHRISTOPHER ROWE

1. Aristotle

What I propose to do in this short paper is to outline two different approaches to needs in Greek philosophy. The first is the reasonably familiar approach used by Aristotle, and, in some moods, by Plato; the second is a rather less well-known approach which can with some justice be associated with Socrates, and/or Plato when he is not in an Aristotelian mood (if I may so put it)—and also the Stoics, who seem to have picked up some distinctly Socratic ways of thinking. The Aristotelian line, if not necessarily familiar *as* Aristotle's, will be familiar just insofar as it gives some degree of that recognition to needs that most moderns would suppose the idea should be given. What I am calling the Socratic line, by contrast, appears to leave no room for the idea of needs at all (or at least, that will be my way of putting it for now; I shall need a rather different formulation later on). It is this second, 'Socratic', approach that primarily interests me, not least because it is non-standard.

But first the Aristotelian perspective. I quote from a recent review of a book on the philosophy of mind:[1]

---

[1] Review by Stephen Mulhall of O. Flanagan, *The Problem of the Soul: Two Visions of Mind and How to Reconcile Them* (London: Basic Books, 2003), in *The London Review of Books* 25/17, [11 September 2003], p.29.

Virtue theories understand human beings as members of a species who flourish in distinctively communal forms of life; given the right upbringing and circumstances, individual fulfilment and communal wellbeing are mutually supporting. However, it is central to any Aristotelian conception of human beings that they can pervert and, at the limit, destroy their capacity to flourish; they can develop vicious character traits that remove any chance of fulfilling their own nature and threaten the social fabric which makes possible the flourishing of others. Such people are a moral danger to themselves and those around them; by destroying their own humanity, they might plausibly be thought to have placed themselves beyond the moral pale—beyond the right to respect, or just treatment.

Hence, virtue theory lacks any way of grounding the thought that no human being, however evil their deeds and however foul their character, should be denied our unconditional respect or be treated as vermin, having forfeited all right to justice. Conversely, it cannot make sense of the thought that people in severe and ineradicable affliction, who appear to have lost all that gives life meaning, should be fully our moral equals. In other words, naturalistic morality is blind to the thought that every individual human being is inalienably precious—precisely the moral perspective on humanity that is centrally articulated in Western culture through its religious traditions, and their conception of human beings as having or being souls.

The way the author concludes here is unsurprising, given the context: a review, by some sort of non-materialist, of a book advancing a materialist theory of the mind. Nor am I myself at all inclined to share the reviewer's own preferred conception of a human being ('as having or being a soul'). Nonetheless I find the passage useful in the present context, of a discussion of *need*, insofar as the author raises questions about the implications of the Aristotelian conception of humanity, in terms of the active fulfilment of certain higher-level functions, for those who are prevented, for one reason or another, from fulfilling those functions.

The position is, of course, much worse for Aristotle than the reviewer admits (or has reason to admit). Aristotle is perfectly happy to accept that some people are in fact only incidentally human: that is, those who are, on his account, natural slaves, capable of taking orders but not of conceiving their own initiatives. Such people are, as he beautifully puts it, 'living tools', differing from ordinary common-or-garden tools just to the extent that they happen to be alive; and differing from donkeys or dogs just insofar as they can understand more, and are more versatile. (The masters of slaves can be their friends, insofar as slaves *are* human; not insofar as they are slaves.) Aristotle feels no need to apologise for this way of seeing things: he defends slavery largely, it seems, as part of an ongoing philosophical debate, in which the debate matters more than the unfortunate parts of its subject-matter, i.e. the slaves. What is more, the basic position articulated in his discussion of slavery comes to inform his account of the best sort of society at the end of the *Politics*. Here, he makes a sharp distinction between the *parts* of society, or a city-state, and its *necessary conditions*, the things without which the society cannot come about; and among those necessary conditions, along with—for example—food, the crafts, arms, and wealth will be certain groups of *people*: for example, farmers, and craftsmen. 'Nor should those who are citizens [and so parts of the city] be farmers,' Aristotle says. 'For leisure is needed, both for the development of virtue/excellence and for political actions' (*Politics* VII.9).

The position is clear: the fulfilment of the basic needs of the community (which I take it is what Aristotle has in mind in talking about the *hôn ouk aneu*, the necessary conditions that he contrasts with the 'parts' of a community or city) is *presupposed* by the idea of human flourishing and excellence; to the extent, even, that those who provide for the community's needs become merely an aspect of those needs. Providing for the community's needs will leave no time for those who do the providing (the farmers, the craftsmen, and so on) to perform those specific activities which would otherwise qualify them for membership of the community proper: the activities that belong to a *citizen*, as a member of the citizen-body. (In *absolutely* ideal circumstances the providers might be people who even lacked the qualities necessary for citizenship; but Aristotle is a little vague about how exactly these qualities are to be measured.) Individual farmers or craftsmen, in this supposedly ideal set-up, might be legally distinguishable from slaves, but they would be functionally indistinguishable. And as in the case of slaves, the question must arise as to just how different such people—the ones who service the true community—would be, in Aristotle's view, from the domestic animals living in, and servicing, that same community. The answer seems to be: not very different. It is not just the vicious—those with 'vicious character traits'—or

the suffering—'people in severe and ineradicable affliction'—
that Aristotle refuses to treat as 'inalienably precious'; by
implication, he will treat the majority of the population in
the same way. What is distinctive of humanity, for Aristotle,
is *rational activity* of one kind or another (whether scientific
or political), and anyone who is prevented for any reason at
all from making such activity a part of his life—for Aristotle is
talking exclusively about men—thereby becomes less than
human. Our basic needs we share with animals, some of
which are even moderately political, or rather social; anyone
who does no more, as Aristotle sees it, than fulfilling his own,
and his family's, basic needs—or, indeed, anyone who spends
his time fulfilling the basic needs of *others*—is to that (considerable) extent sub-human.

Whether the virtue-theorist *must* take such a line is
of course another question, which lies beyond the immediate
brief of this paper. Nor do I have space to discuss exactly
how the Aristotelian theory will fare in what Aristotle himself recognises is the real world: a world in which all communities are emphatically non-ideal, being predominantly
either oligarchies or democracies, and in which, by and
large, farmers, craftsmen, rowers in the fleet, factory-
workers, anyone you can name will *actually* be involved in
living some kind of rational, social, even political life.
I suppose the short answer to the second question—how
the Aristotelian theory will fare in the real world, as opposed
to an allegedly ideal one—is that in the context of political
reality, the Aristotelian theory might do a lot better, by our
lights. We may also note, incidentally, that in such a non-
ideal context, the notion of 'basic needs' will have to change

radically: to include, for example, not the kind of wealth to enable an individual to live a life of Aristotelian leisure, but a rather more modest income. But in all of that, beyond noticing that there are certain things that are needed *just for survival*,[2] Aristotle has no interest at all.

2.   Socrates

I now turn to the contrasting, 'Socratic', approach, which—at least by implication—ends up without a specific concept of *need* at all; or rather, which runs needs together with *desires* (though that will turn out to be pretty much the same thing). The larger context for this 'Socratic' position is that so far rather little understood set of ideas often labelled as 'Socratic intellectualism', which we find being variously explored and used in a number of Plato's dialogues (and then positively rejected in others: notably, the *Republic*[3]). Two excerpts from one of these dialogues, the *Lysis*, appear in the appendix to the present paper, mainly to provide some sort of indication of the sort of text the *Lysis* is: a text that includes some of Plato's densest, and most elusive, writing.[4]

---

[2] Cf. Aristotle, *Metaphysics* 5, 1015a20–26 (quoted by David Wiggins, *Needs, Values, Truth* [3rd edn] (Oxford: Blackwell, 1998), 25).

[3] I refer here to the arguments in Book IV that introduce *parts of the soul*, and specifically *irrational* parts that can—as it were—trump reason. (The point of 'intellectualism' is that it is the state of our intellect, our beliefs, that determines the quality of our actions; for, so the theory claims, we all share the same motivation: the desire for our own good.)

[4] The excerpts will be far from fully intelligible as they stand, torn from their dialectical context; but some general tendencies of Socrates'

I start with a convenient summing-up of Socratic intellectualism by C.C.W. Taylor (though it seems to me at least potentially misleading on some points, it gives an admirably clear sketch of the general outline of the theory):

> The basis of the theory is the combination of the conception of goodness as that property which guarantees overall success in life with the substantive thesis that what in fact guarantees that success is knowledge of what is best for the agent. This in turn rests on a single comprehensive theory of human motivation, namely, that the agent's conception of what is overall best for him or herself (i.e. what best promotes *eudaimonia*, overall success in life) is sufficient to motivate action with a view to its own realization. This motivation involves desire as well as belief; Socrates maintains (*Meno* 77C, 78B) that everyone desires good things, which in context has to be interpreted as the strong thesis that the desire for good is a standing motive, which requires to be focused in one direction or another via a conception of the overall good. Given that focus, desire is locked onto the target which is picked out by the conception, without the possibility of interference by conflicting desires. Hence all that is required for correct conduct is the correct focus, which has to be a correct conception of the agent's overall good.[5]

argument will certainly emerge even from a superficial reading (see below). For a full account of that argument, and theory, of the *Lysis*, see Terry Penner and Christopher Rowe, *Plato's Lysis* (Cambridge: Cambridge University Press, 2005).

[5] *A Very Short Introduction to Socrates* (Oxford: Oxford University Press, 1998), 62–3.

One clarification: 'correct' conduct is simply—no more than—conduct, action, that in fact leads to the best overall result for the agent. There is no *moral* good involved in the theory, just the good of the agent, though Socrates' ideas about just what *is* good for the agent in fact take us back a long way towards the sorts of behaviour one might expect to find recommended in any halfway decent sort of moral theory; not surprisingly, this has often led interpreters to misinterpret Socrates as being a sort of pre-Kantian.

But this is not the part of the theory that is most important in the present context. What we need to look at in this context is the Socratic account of desire. What Socrates says—Plato's Socrates, in certain Platonic dialogues, and *maybe* the historical Socrates too—is that all desire is for the good. That he means to be taken *au pied de la lettre*: that is, he is saying that no one ever desires bad things, only good things. Every human being has the same basic desires, or desire; the only important difference between individual human beings, that is, the only important difference relevant to our actions, lies in our *beliefs*. What we do on any occasion is determined by the current state of our beliefs; that is, by our beliefs about what will contribute most, now, to our overall good, starting from where we are now.

Here, though, I need to be more specific. In the extract from Taylor just quoted, desire was said to be 'locked on to the target ... picked out by the conception [sc. that one currently holds of the overall good]': this seems to be right so far as it goes, but it misses out the proper emphasis on one point—that the Socratic view sees us as permanently 'locked on' to *the real good*. Aristotle seems to recognise this as Socrates' view, though he himself dismisses it, as para-doxical, and indeed plainly false. But Socrates was evidently quite serious (again, whether this is just Plato's Socrates, in some dialogues, or the real Socrates): we are all permanently oriented towards, focussed on, hard-wired for, the real good. How can that be, asks Aristotle; are we then to suppose that we didn't after all want what we wanted, if what we went for was actually *bad*?[6] (What then made us go for it?) This objection exposes the fundamental problem that the Socratic theory might seem to have, of explaining why it is that we frequently do go for things that, by the theory, we don't want—because they are not good, and we only want what is (really) good; for after all, if our actions are not explained by wanting, or desiring, what makes us go for them? There is, I believe, a satisfactory answer to that question, even though Plato's Socrates does not fully articu-late it. But however that may be, the immediate point for the present context is that when Socrates claims that all human desire is for the good, he means, not that all human desire is for the *apparent* good, or for what *we happen to think* good, but that all human desire is for what *is, really and truly*, good. For why should we want anything that is bad? (Socrates is a psychological egoist; so that question answers itself. There is no way we *could* want anything bad.)[7]

---

[6] See especially *Nicomachean Ethics* III.4, 1113a 17–19.

[7] David Wiggins doubted, in discussion at the conference, whether Socrates could really be a psychological egoist. It is true that Socrates is not recommending selfishness; after all, he is in favour of friendship, wishing and doing good to others, not harming or doing injustice to

Now one consequence of this position is that, notoriously, there can be no conflict between reason and desire. This is the famous Socratic dictum 'No man does wrong willingly'; which is to say that, if anyone goes wrong, it is not willingly (intentionally, deliberately: *hekôn* in Greek), but only through ignorance. That of course presupposes the falsity of the Aristotelian view that akratic actions[8] are voluntary (that is, the actions Aristotle calls akratic), but I see no reason to quarrel with it for that reason. Socrates is not about to deny that one can feel a powerful thirst, or hunger, or whatever it may be; what he does deny is that one can feel, as we characteristically put it, *overpoweringly* thirsty or hungry, or *overpoweringly* lustful, or whatever, so that we eat, or drink, or go to bed with someone against our better judgement—with irrational desire, in the form of hunger, thirst, or lust, in the driving seat. That conjures up a nice picture, in view of Plato's picture in the *Phaedrus* of the irrational parts of the soul as the horses to reason's

---

anyone, and so on (see further below). But somehow or other such attitudes are combined with, and thought of as justified by, a theory which says that each of us always and only desires *our own* good (see the first of the two passages from the *Lysis* in the appendix below; the passage gives a flavour of the general approach to 'friendship'— conceived in an extraordinarily wide sense: see n.11 below—adopted by the Socrates of the dialogue). For a detailed treatment of how the Socratic theory pulls this off, see Penner and Rowe, *Plato's Lysis* (n.4 above).

[8] That is, actions stemming from *akrasia*—traditionally, and disastrously, translated as 'weakness of will' (disastrously, because Aristotle neither has nor has any need for a concept of the 'will').

charioteer: when the black horse of appetite gets out of control, it as it were climbs into the chariot and pushes the charioteer out of the way. But such a picture is an emphatically *non*-Socratic picture: there are no irrational parts to the soul in Socrates' conception, since the very notion of 'parts' depends on the idea of conflict, at the level of action. Particular desires feed into one's deliberation, so that 'I'm feeling particularly hungry', and so on, will form part of the background to a particular action; but desires, on the Socratic view, have no power to *overturn* rational judgements, in the sense of causing action contrary to what reason has judged. More generally, there are no such things as irrational desires that can cause actions just by themselves.

Whatever else we may say about the theory in question, it is evidently a thoroughly *humane* theory; specifically in that it resolutely sets itself against the view that we ever behave *just by instinct*, or as a result of *conditioning*, like Pavlov's dogs. We are, through and through, rational, and whatever we do, voluntarily, is a matter of rational decision; we do it because it seems to us, overall, the best thing to do. To which most people, like Aristotle, react with derision: how obviously contrary to observable fact![9] That seems to me[10] too hasty a reaction; but this is not the occasion to enter into that particular debate. I shall restrict myself instead to considering the consequences of the ('Socratic') theory I have just sketched for the subject of the present conference: the 'philosophy of need'.

[9] See Aristotle, *Nicomachean Ethics* VII.2, 1145b21–8.
[10] For reasons that are spelled out in *Plato's Lysis* (n.4 above).

I start from the claim that *all desire is for the good.* Once again, I stress that this is to be taken absolutely literally (*'au pied de la lettre'*). So *absolutely all* desires are for the good. The idea surfaces, though it may be quite difficult to see it at once, in the second of the two passages from the *Lysis* in the appendix;[11] it also surfaces in the *Republic*—only to be rejected. Socrates considers, and rejects, the view that hunger and thirst are for *good* food, *good* drink: no, he now says, hunger is just desire for *food*, thirst just desire for *drink*, and if the desire is strong enough, it will have you eating and drinking the sorts of things, or in the sorts of quantities, that you really think you shouldn't.[12] Now what this *Republic* passage is rejecting is precisely the view proposed by the *Lysis*—that *even* what we might call irrational desires, and what the Socrates of Book IV of the *Republic* calls, irrational desires, are in truth desires *for the good*. For, again, the claim is that *all* desire is for the good.

In order to understand how this might work, take the Stoic claim that all living creatures begin by desiring what tends towards their own self-preservation.[13] (The

---

[11] That is, just insofar as hunger, thirst, and other basic desires (*epithumiai*) surface in a context in which Socrates is attempting to give an account of all 'friendship' (*philia*)—which, as become unmistakable by this stage of the dialogue, is intended to include all an every kind of love, desire, or want. ('Good', 'bad', and 'neither good nor bad' desires, as the passage calls them, are those that have good, bad, or neither good nor bad outcomes.)

[12] *Republic* IV, 437B-439D.

[13] For the most recent account of Stoic (and other) theory in this area, see now Keimpe Algra, 'The mechanism of social appropriation and its

Stoics seem to have taken over much of Socratic ethical theory—much more than is usually supposed; so it is particularly appropriate to use their ideas as a way of understanding how Socrates might have gone.) If what the Stoics claim is true, then clearly what animals desire is what *actually* tends towards their self-preservation, or promotes their survival, not just what *might* but in fact *won't*. Sometimes they will get what they want; sometimes they will fail to get it —which just goes to show that they needed more discrimination. One of the things that distinguishes human from other animals is that as they grow older, they begin to have an ampler, more expansive perspective on what is *their own*, which brings with it a correspondingly ampler, as it were more generous set of desires. The process is called *oikeiôsis*, literally 'making one's own'[14]: it starts with one's family, then extends to one's associates and friends, citizens, and then, in the ideal case, to the whole of humanity.[15] What brings the process about is the development of *rationality*: one *comes to see* that what 'belongs', is *oikeion*, to one, and so is the proper object of one's concerns, is in principle close to being limitless. In the ideal case, the individual would acquire complete rationality, complete knowledge; he or she would become a sage.

role in Hellenistic ethics', in *Oxford Studies in Ancient Philosophy* 25 (2003), 265–96.

[14] This is the 'appropriation' in Algra's title (see preceding note).

[15] Cf. the notion of 'what belongs to us' (*to oikeion*) at the end of the second *Lysis* passage; this notion is in fact fundamental to the argument of the whole dialogue.

But what is of interest in all of this, in the present context, is the next step, which is to say that it is *wisdom itself* that is the goal of human existence. Virtue or excellence is what matters; but virtue or excellence, for the Stoics, *is* wisdom. This takes us straight back to Socrates again, since he says the same. The important point here is that if only wisdom or virtue is a good, nothing else is good—that is, as Socrates says, nothing else is good 'in itself', or 'for its own sake', or *truly* good. So, if all human desire is for the good, all human desire is for wisdom. Another bizarre-looking claim, one might say, but what it is saying is perfectly intelligible. What Socrates is saying is that absolutely nothing else, apart from wisdom, can be counted on to give you what you want, i.e. good or happiness. Take any action you like, any thing you like, and you will be able to say truthfully of it that, taken by itself, or better, in conjunction with the whole possible range of sets of circumstances that might surround it in a given case, it *might* turn out well, but then it *might* also turn out badly, or neither well nor badly.[16]

This helps us to understand what the Stoics said about supposed goods like health, wealth, high office (the ancients' lists of 'goods'—apparently desirable things— would have been pretty much the same as ours): that it is just plain wrong to call them *goods*, because everything depends on the circumstances; and what is more, circumstances can always change. Wisdom alone is the one secure possession, because it will reliably tell you how to extract the

---

[16] As with hunger, thirst, etc., in the second *Lysis* passage in the appendix below (cf. n.11 above).

maximum good from every situation. Even life itself, say the Stoics, is not a *good*, though it's a 'preferred' thing, and death is a 'dispreferred' thing: in normal circumstances, we would *expect* to be going for what preserves our lives—but don't put your money on it, the Stoics say; there will be times when it will be the wise thing to make a swift exit. And this is, essentially, the Socratic position. There is absolutely *nothing* that is always desirable (apart from wisdom or knowledge): not life, not food or drink, or sex, or anything else you could think of. Or, in other words, there is always a judgement to be made about whether anything is to be taken or rejected, even—in principle—at the most basic level.[17]

One can see easily enough where this is headed. On the sort of Socratic view I have been describing, there will be no room for any notion of *needs* at all. There are only *things that we might generally be said to need if the circumstances dictate it, if it's good for me to go on living and breathing*, and so on. Or rather, perhaps, it might be better to say that all *desires* get swallowed up into the category of needs (so that talk about desire for the good[18] is easily translated into talk about need and what is useful, for fulfilling need); for if needs are, roughly, those 'requirements' whose non-fulfilment will harm me, that will be something that is true

[17] This is not to suggest that Stoic and Socratic theories were identical; for one thing, the Stoics' approach is much more ascetic, more paradoxical even than Socrates' (so that they—or at any rate early Stoics—put an absolute ban on calling things other than virtue/knowledge 'good', which Socrates did not).

[18] As e.g. in the first *Lysis* passage in the appendix below.

of all Socratic *desires*, all Socratic desires being for the good.[19] And actually, desires as contrasted with needs have been got rid of, in the Socratic scheme, already: that is, if desires are understood as being for what we think good, the apparent good, or, to quote David Wiggins, if' "desire" ... is ... an intentional verb'.[20] Socrates wants to say that there are no such desires. Let us be clear about this: Socrates will not even allow that we want bad things *under certain descriptions*—as in David Wiggins's example of the oyster:

> If I want to have x and $x = y$, then I do not necessarily want to have y. If I want to eat that oyster, and that oyster is the oyster that will consign me to oblivion, it doesn't follow that I want to eat the oyster that will consign me to oblivion.[21]

What *Socrates* wants to say is that—provided that it is not the best thing for me to be consigned to oblivion—I do not want that oyster at all, under any description or none. Nor do I think that this is a simple mistake, which Socrates could have avoided if he had been born late enough to read Frege; it

---

[19] See the exchange at the end of the second *Lysis* passage in the appendix; though this fragment will be especially in need of commentary, to show where Socrates has come from and where he is going. ('But', I said, 'what desires, desires whatever it's lacking. Isn't that so?' 'Yes.' 'And what is lacking, in that case, is friend of whatever it's lacking?' 'It seems so to me.' 'And what becomes lacking is whatever has something taken away from it.' 'Of course.' 'It's what belongs to us (*to oikeion*), then, that's actually the object of passion and friendship and desire, as it appears, Menexenus and Lysis.')

[20] *Needs, Values, Truth*, 6.   [21] Ibid.

is more complicated than that. Socrates, and Plato too, even after he has passed beyond his Socratic period, in effect set up in permanent, anticipatory competition with Frege—not just in challenging what would have been, even in the fifth and fourth centuries BC, a standard view of desire, but in terms of the very metaphysical assumptions which ground that challenge. Or, if this seems too large a claim, I shall just assert my view that merely chanting excerpts from Frege against Socrates and Plato here would not be an adequate response.[22]

I propose to end here, with what is essentially a promissory note, and leaving things rather in the air. My purpose, however, has been the very limited one of expounding a particular, and pretty distinctive, position— the one I have labelled 'Socratic'—that flourished for some considerable time in the ancient world, both Greek and Roman, though it has since been almost forgotten; a position, moreover, that I think has considerable intrinsic interest. As a socialist, and social democrat, I myself shall always find it indispensable to go on talking about needs, and basic needs, and distinguishing needs from mere desires. But that is not the same thing as saying that I can, yet, make proper philosophical sense of any such distinction: not for the normal sorts of reasons, but because I feel the allure of the Socratic picture that has (true) desires actually collapsing into needs—which as I understand it would be to drive a

---

[22] For a full response, see Penner and Rowe, *Plato's Lysis* (n.4 above), especially Part II.

coach and horses through any normal modern notion of needs whatsoever.

Appendix: two passages from Plato's *Lysis*

a.   Plato, *Lysis* 215A3–C2

. . .'But in that case [Socrates is speaking] the like person isn't friend to his like; but the good to the good, to the extent that he's good and not to the extent that he's like, could he be a friend?'

'Perhaps.'

'But what about this: wouldn't the good person, to the extent that he's good, to that extent be sufficient for himself?'

'Yes.'

'But the one who's sufficient wouldn't be needing anything, to the extent that he's sufficient.'

'No question about it.'

'But the sort of person who doesn't need a thing wouldn't prize a thing either.'

'No, he wouldn't.'

'And what he didn't prize, he wouldn't love either.' 'Certainly not.'

'But if someone doesn't love, he isn't a friend.' 'It doesn't appear so.'

'How then on our account will the good be friends to the good at all, if they're not going to miss each other when they're away from each other (since they're sufficient for themselves even when they're apart), and they're also going to have no need for each other when they *are* both there? People in *that* sort of situation—what's going to bring it about that they make much of each other?'

'Nothing,' he said.

'But they wouldn't be friends if they didn't make much of each other.'

'True' . . .

b.   Plato, *Lysis* 220E6–221E5

... 'Good heavens ['By Zeus!'],' I [Socrates]said, 'if bad disappears, will there no longer even be any being hungry, or being thirsty, or anything else of that sort? Or will there be hunger, if indeed there are human beings and the other sorts of living creatures, but not hunger that is *harmful*? And so with thirst, and the other sorts of desires—there will be these desires, but they won't be bad, given that bad will have disappeared? Or is it ridiculous to ask 'What, I wonder, will there be or not be under those circumstances?'? For who knows the answer? This much in any case we do know, that even as things are it is possible to be hungry and to be harmed, and possible too to be hungry and to be benefited. Isn't that so?'

'Yes, absolutely.'

'Then it's possible also to be thirsty and to desire any of the other things of this sort and sometimes to desire them beneficially, sometimes harmfully, and sometimes neither?'

'Yes, very much so.'

'Then if bad things disappear, the sorts of things that actually aren't bad—why does it belong to them to disappear along with the bad?'

'It doesn't at all.'

'In that case there will be the neither good nor bad desires even if bad things disappear.'

'It appears so.'

'Is it possible, then, for a person desiring and feeling passion for the thing he desires and feels passion for not to love?'

'Doesn't seem so to me.'

'In that case even if bad things had disappeared, it seems, there will be some things that are friends.'

'Yes.'

'There wouldn't be, if the bad really were cause of a thing's being a friend—one thing wouldn't be a friend to another, if that had disappeared. For once a cause has disappeared I imagine it would be impossible for that thing of which this cause was cause still to be there.'

'What you say is correct.'

'Well then, hasn't it been agreed by us that the friend loves something, and because of something; and didn't we think, at *that* point, that it was because of the bad that the neither good nor bad loved the good?'

'True.'

'But now, it seems, another sort of cause of loving and being loved is appearing.'

'It does seem so.'

'So is it in fact the case, as we were saying just now, that desire is cause of friendship, and that what desires is friend to that thing it desires and at such time that it desires it, and that what we were previously saying being a friend was, was some kind of nonsense, like a poem that's been badly put together?'

'Quite likely.'

'But', I said, 'what desires, desires whatever it's lacking. Isn't that so?'

'Yes.'

'And what is lacking, in that case, is friend of whatever it's lacking?'

'It seems so to me.'

'And what becomes lacking is whatever has something taken away from it.'

'Of course.'

'It's what belongs to us (*to oikeion*), then, that's actually the object of passion and friendship and desire, as it appears, Menexenus and Lysis.'

The two of them assented ...

5   Aristotle on Necessities and Needs

SORAN READER

Aristotle's account of human needs is valuable because it
describes the connections between logical, metaphysical, physical, human and ethical necessities. But Aristotle
does not fully draw out the implications of the account of
necessity for needs and virtue. The proper Aristotelian conclusion is that, far from being an inferior activity fit only for
slaves, meeting needs is the first part of Aristotelian virtue.

1.   Aristotle on Necessity

The core concept of necessity, for Aristotle as for us, is of
'that which cannot be otherwise'. This concept plays a useful
role in all sorts of different contexts. We say 'it must be'
about things we must do in order to achieve our ends, things
we must do because something or someone requires it,
things that must be the case because something else is the
case, things we must believe if we believe the things we
already do. We might experiment with metaphysical applications of this idea of what cannot be otherwise, as when we
say 'there must be a God', or 'good must triumph over evil',
or 'there must be a reason for this'. Once you start to look,
necessities are everywhere. Aristotle took this homely notion
of necessity for granted. He talks in the *Prior Analytics*, for

168

example, of the way that some things belong to others 'necessarily' (29b29–32a17), and he does not distinguish between 'logical' necessity and 'metaphysical' or 'physical' necessity. For Aristotle, speaking in metaphysical terms, if something is a man, it must be an animal; just so speaking in logical terms, the concept 'animal' belongs to the concept 'man' necessarily. The purpose of logical deduction is then just to 'make the [metaphysical, physical or conceptual] necessity evident' (*Prior Analytics* 24b19).[1] Many modern philosophers are squeamish about the concept, and throw the baby of necessity out with the bathwater of teleology, limiting themselves to the *de dicto* necessities of conceptual definitions.[2] But outside the ivory tower, homely talk of necessities continues. In this paper, I will take for granted, as Aristotle did, that the idea of necessity is a useful, even a necessary one.

Aristotle treats the topic in most detail at *Metaphysics* 1015a15-b20. He begins with the primary sense of the necessary, which he gives as 'that which cannot be

---

[1] References in this paper are by the Bekker line numbers, and quotations are from the translations gathered in Jonathan Barnes' *Complete Works of Aristotle* (Princeton: Princeton University Press, 1985). There is an argument to be had about whether modern philosophers should really use 'original' Greek texts, but this paper is not the place for it. I have relied on translators. (I could cite Aristotle in support of this approach: translation is the kind of necessity Aristotle thought we should delegate, because it is instrumental, cannot be desired for itself, and is distant from the life-enhancing end of doing the philosophy.)

[2] See for example B. van Fraassen, 'The Only Necessity is Verbal Necessity', *Journal of Philosophy* 74 (Feb 1977), 71–85.

otherwise'. 'Somehow derivable' from this primary sense are four further senses in which something can be necessary. The first sense is of being required for life or existence. The second is of being required to achieve a good or avoid an evil. The third is of being coerced against will or nature. And the fourth is of being logically compelled, as in demonstration. All four of these senses of necessity are hypothetical, in the sense that they are requirements *if* something is to be: life or existence, good or avoidance of evil, conformity to an external force which might be resisted, conformity to the norms of reason. Aristotle then distinguishes a final sense of necessity which is not hypothetical or dependent, but is 'absolute' or 'independent'. An absolute necessity, he says, must be simple, partless, eternal and unmovable.

The idea of absolute or simple necessity intrigues Aristotle, and is mentioned at several points in the corpus. He identifies two absolute necessities: eternal cyclical motion in *Generation and Corruption*, and God at *Metaphysics* 1015b20 and *XII*, *Nicomachean Ethics X* and *De Anima III*. At *Generation and Corruption II* §11 337b1ff Aristotle discusses eternal cyclical motion. In contingent processes of coming to be and passing away, the earlier stage is required for the later to happen, but it does not make the later stage necessary. Aristotle uses the example of house-building: the foundations are required for the house, but do not make it necessary that the house will come to be. For the later stage to be necessitated by the earlier stage, 'it must be always in its coming to be' (337b35). Only in eternal cyclical motion is this condition satisfied: the later stage is always coming to be in the form of the earlier stage, so that we can say that the earlier stage necessitates the later, and the later stage then necessitates the next 'earlier' stage.

Aristotle's example—disconcerting because we now know that it is not an example of circular motion at all—is the motion of the fixed stars. But he also uses a better example, the eternal cyclical motion of a biological species. As the chicken 'is always in its coming to be', the egg, so the egg is always in its coming to be, the chicken. The stages of a biological cycle necessitate those that follow them. Aristotle also believes that there is a necessarily existing being. The existence of this being depends on nothing else. The absolutely necessary being Aristotle has in mind at 1015a15-b20 is God, described in greater detail in *Metaphysics XII*. God is the unmoved mover that must exist, given that being and movement exist. God is the necessary condition of everything else, complete in itself, perfectly active yet perfectly immobile, self-sufficient and requiring nothing. Aristotle's God is immaterial, and consists of 'thought thinking itself', or the perfect, eternal infinite activity of contemplation. Far from being philosophically arbitrary and religiously motivated, the properties Aristotle attributes to God—life and thought—are necessities of God's functioning, itself necessitated by the world in which God moves. At 1072b11 Aristotle says that God's necessity is part of God's glory: 'the first mover, then, of necessity exists; and in so far as it is necessary, it is good'.

Any necessity that is not absolute, is hypothetical. Hypothetical necessities are those things which must be if something which might not be, is to be. Aristotle distinguishes between three kinds of being or happening: those which are from necessity, those which are for the most part, and those which are by chance (see e.g. *On Interpretation* 19a7–22; *Topics* 112a1; *Physics* 196b10; *Generation and Corruption* 337b10ff; *Metaphysics* 1025a15 and 1064b30ff). The middle category, of things which are for the most part, encompasses things due to nature, custom, habit, reason or choice. Things in the second two categories, those which happen for the most part or by chance, are contingencies. Arguably, contingencies that happen by chance do not have necessities, and cannot be predicted, understood or explained as such. But things in the middle category certainly do have necessities, and can be predicted, understood and explained for the most part and with reasonable accuracy. For Aristotle the phenomena of human life fall into the second category, of contingencies which happen for the most part, which have necessities and can be predicted, understood and explained for the most part.

At *Physics II* §9 (199b34ff), Aristotle discusses the necessities of natural or artefactual things coming to be, and argues that they are only hypothetically necessary. An end or, 'the "for the sake of something" is found in events that happen by nature or as the result of thought' (1065a27). The necessities of such things are hypothetical in the sense that: *if* we are to have/there is to be a certain thing (which is contingent), *then* we must have/there must be these things. He says 'the necessary in nature is what we call by the name of matter', and emphasises that things are not strictly caused by their necessary requirements or matter, but rather come about for their ends, which are the true causes.

Aristotle also allows that 'in the definition too there are some parts that stand as matter': if one defines something a certain way, it can be the case that this cannot be unless something else is a certain way, which in turn has a concrete material requirement. His example is sawing. If sawing is defined as a certain kind of dividing, this is only possible with a saw with a certain kind of teeth, which is only possible with iron. Here it looks as though the necessities of anything—object or concept—are what must be presupposed for it to be. So for a house we must first have building materials: although these don't furnish the identity of the house, or cause it, they are necessary in the sense that without them there would be no house. And so also for the concept triangle we must presuppose the number three and the idea of a straight line: although these don't furnish the identity of a triangle, or cause it, there would be no triangle without them.

This common treatment of hypothetical physical necessity and hypothetical conceptual or logical necessity reinforces how for Aristotle, logical and physical necessities work in the same way. Like some modern philosophers Aristotle is 'an essentialist' who believes in '*de re* necessities'.[3] But where for modern essentialists only natural kinds have essences, for Aristotle any concept must have necessary conditions for its application to things, and these conditions are the essence of the thing under its identity as a bearer of that concept. Thus the citizen has an 'essence' or 'necessities' as much as the biological species. To be a citizen

---

[3] See for example Saul Kripke, *Naming and Necessity* (Oxford: Blackwell, 1980) or David Wiggins, *Sameness and Substance Renewed* (Cambridge: Cambridge University Press, 2001).

is to be a member of a state trained to be able both to rule and to obey (*Politics III* §§1–5); if I satisfy those necessary conditions, they are my essence as a citizen, and will be the foundation of some of the things I do by nature, habit, custom, choice or reason, and the full, final and necessitating cause of the things I do just as and for the sake of being a citizen (stand for office, vote, lounge at the common tables, row in the navy, etc.). The distinction between 'natural' kinds and 'social' or even 'essentially contestable' concepts would have struck Aristotle as contrived and unhelpful, I suspect. Each concept or kind is determined by different necessities, some biological, some social, some linguistic or historical. But once the necessities are determined, the way they feature in explaining things coming under the concept is exactly the same.

Aristotle distinguishes the necessities of contingent things from their complete causes, and he also argues that only some of these necessities are properly to be considered parts of the things for which they are necessary. At *Politics VII* §8 he discusses the necessities of the state, and argues that only some of them are proper parts of the state. Just as the builder is necessary for the house, but is not a part of it, so, Aristotle argues, property is necessary for the state, but is not a part of it (1328a30–35). What, then, makes a necessity a proper part? Aristotle seems to believe that a proper part of the whole is one which plays a role in the highest characteristic functioning(s) of the whole, and enables that whole to be self-sufficient. This argument relies on Aristotelian assumptions about the identity of complex, active things: the identity is given by the 'highest' part, so that my identity is given by my mind, rather than by my vegetative or appetitive soul. Aristotle identifies food, arts, arms, revenue, worship, and a power of deciding what is in the public interest and what is just in men's dealings with one another, as the necessities of the state (1328b6–14). These necessities in turn show what functions are required in the state: farming, artisanal crafts, warcraft, trade, priesthood and judicial functions are all needed. Warcraft, political and priestly functions are the necessities that Aristotle judges to be proper parts of the state. Farming, arts and crafts, trade and labour are the necessities that Aristotle judges fail to be proper parts of the state.

Although the necessities of contingent things are not sufficient to cause them, they contribute significantly to their being. Thus, for Aristotle, the necessities of human life contribute significantly to the existence of the state. The state for Aristotle arises naturally out of human existence needs, as follows:

> The family is the association established by nature for the supply of men's everyday needs. [. . .] When several families are united, and the association aims at something more than the supply of daily needs, the first society to be formed is the village. [. . .] When several villages are united in a single complete, community, large enough to be nearly or quite self-sufficing, the state comes into existence, originating in the bare needs of life, and continuing in existence for the sake of a good life. (1252b13–30).

For Aristotle, then, the state first arises out of human necessities. But from its origins in human needs, the state naturally develops beyond necessity. It develops to form a framework which is necessary to enable human beings to seek human goods which the provision of necessities cannot bring about, but can only make possible.

2. Aristotle on Human Needs

There is no doubt that Aristotle thought of the needs of contingent beings as necessities. 'That which must be if something is to exist or to live' is the first sense of necessity Aristotle gives at *Metaphysics* 1015a15. The human need for food in order to exist or live is a clear example, and the point is made repeatedly: 'no man can live well, or indeed live at all, unless he is provided with necessaries' (*Politics* 1253b35) and 'the perfect state cannot exist without a due supply of the means of life' (1325b35). There can be no human life unless these needs are met—even the contemplative life, which is the highest, most God-like life for man, and which has fewer and simpler practical requirements than other excellent ways of life, still depends on bodily needs being met: 'for our nature is not self-sufficient for the purpose of contemplation, but our body must also be healthy and must have food and other attention' (*Nicomachean Ethics* 1378b33).

Such necessities for life or existence are arguably less hypothetical or dependent than the second sense of necessity at *Metaphysics* 1015a15-b20, of 'that which must be if some good is to be achieved or evil avoided'. The achieving of a good or avoiding of an evil is a highly contingent matter—one may perfectly rationally choose not to pursue the good this time, or to tolerate the evil. But life and existence are less contingent. I cannot so readily rationally choose not to bother to exist. I might, in some extreme and rare situation, judge it would be better if my life ended (I had completed my life's tasks, say, or the future was objectively intolerable, or I owed my life as atonement for some crime). But for any existing thing, even when its existence is a contingent matter, its achievement of good and avoidance of evil will necessarily be less necessary for it, than its existence. The necessities that depend on my existence are thus closer to being absolute than the necessities that depend on my pursuit of a good.[4]

But however close the life or existence needs of human beings may come to being absolute, Aristotle nevertheless holds that most of them are not true parts of the lives for which they are necessities (1328a30–35). 'Farmers [who "will be of necessity slaves or barbarian country people" (1329a26)], artisans, tradesmen and labourers of all kinds are necessary to the existence of states, but the parts of the state are the warriors and councillors' (1329a35–9). Food, craft and trade are not proper parts of human life. These necessities merely exist for the sake of human life, as 'the art of the builder exists for the sake of the house' (1328a33).[5] Arts, craft and trade are 'ignoble and inimical to excellence';

[4] One might want to argue further, that existence needs are also closer to being absolute than the other two kinds of necessity mentioned in the *Metaphysics*: the necessity of coercion, or the necessity of following a certain form of reasoning.

[5] There may seem to be two questions here: is needs-meeting a proper part of the life of the individual, or is it a proper part of the state? But for Aristotle, as for Plato, these two questions come together: 'the same life is best for each individual, and for states and for mankind collectively' (1325b31; see also b14–32).

farming and labour, although morally sound and politically beneficial (1318b12) leave no leisure for politics. Aristotle argues that these mere necessities which are not true parts, should be the task of 'slaves or barbarian country people'. In every state, there must be some 'necessary people', who 'are either slaves who minister to the wants of individuals, or mechanics and labourers who are the servants of the community' (1278a8). Help is at hand, because on Aristotle's view, conveniently, people exist who are ideally suited to these necessary tasks, to whom they can therefore be rationally and justly delegated: natural slaves make good needs-meeters, because they 'have no deliberative faculty at all' (1260a12), and women do also, because although they have a deliberative faculty, 'it is without authority' (1260a13).

Aristotle takes meeting human life-needs to be ignoble, because it is only indispensable, not good in itself and so not choosable for its own sake (1332a9). Spending time meeting such needs is thought to be inimical to excellence, because it encroaches into the leisure essential for virtue. Those involved in meeting needs, like women in the household, farmers and labourers on the land, traders in the marketplace and artisans in the workshop, have no leisure, and leisure is required for political activity (1269a34; 1273a25; 1278a8ff; 1291b27). Meeting these needs also cultivates slavish skills, blunts the skills of virtue, and blurs the distinction between them (1277a33–b7). There are natural slaves, women and barbarian country people who are suited to these functions by nature, but the excellent human being is 'useless for hard work, but useful for political life in the arts both of war and peace' (1254b30).

178

It is worth considering how Aristotle conceives of the roles of the two kinds of necessary people, women and natural slaves, differently. Both are necessary to free the excellent human beings for higher activities. But where slaves are necessary for the state, women are necessary for the family and the household. A natural slave is a human being who 'participates in reason enough to apprehend, but not to have' (1254b22). To a modern sensibility, Aristotle's claim that some people are natural slaves appears offensively elitist and exploitative. But Aristotle's account of natural slavery may be more intuitive than he is given credit for. It is his treatment of women, rather than slaves, that should worry us. Women are necessities of the family and the household, which are themselves prior necessities of the state. Woman comes, in Aristotle's quote from Hesiod (1252a12) after the house, but before the ox (the 'poor man's slave') and the plough. For Aristotle, women have a deliberative faculty, but one 'without authority'. By this Aristotle meant what was in his time the plain truth: women were able to make perfectly good practical judgements (since they have a deliberative faculty), but they had absolutely no power to implement those decisions, either by commanding others to do their bidding, or by enacting their judgements through free actions of their own. Aristotle offers no good arguments for why women should be thus subject to male authority. Indeed, when he says women have a deliberative faculty, he implies such subjection will be both irrational and unjust.

Aristotle offers two weak arguments: first, he maintains that women are 'naturally weaker', and 'more fearful' than men, and men should rule them because of this, just as men should rule natural slaves because they lack a deliberative faculty. We can reject this argument because its premises are false. Second, Aristotle maintains women's subjection is necessary. Plato is sometimes praised for proposing that in his ideal state women should be educated alongside men for the same roles, including the elite role of Guardian. But this praise fails to notice a sinister aspect of the proposal, which bothered Aristotle. In Plato's state, it was envisaged less that women would be free, than that they would be held in common. Socrates assumes men are better than women at everything ('we need not trouble ourselves with exceptions like cooking and weaving', he says). Aristotle attacks Socrates' proposals, but not because they are insulting to women. Aristotle's worry has to do with what is necessary for human social life to be possible:

> If Socrates makes the women common, and retains private property, the men will see to the fields, but who will see to the house? ... It is absurd to argue from the analogy of animals that men and women should follow the same pursuits, for animals have not to manage a household. (1264b1–6)

Aristotle here argues in terms of necessities: human beings must live in families, families must have households, men must work in the fields, so women must see to the house. It could not be otherwise. Aristotle shares Plato's assumption that women do everything less well, but he thinks a partnership between the sexes is necessary for that most fundamental form of human life, a family living in a shared household.

Woman's supposed 'weakness' and 'fearfulness' then conveniently suit her to being subjected to leisurely male authority, and to the tasks and virtues of preserving the household. Aristotle's objection to Plato, then, was not that women deserve better than to be held as common sexual and reproductive chattel by men, but that men and the state need women to take care of family homes. This patriarchal worry is still with us: if women go out to work, politic, create and play, who will provide the necessary comforts of home? Aristotle's arguments are weak, because in place of some genuine justification for giving those who attend to public necessities command over those who attend to private ones, Aristotle offers only the sexist myth that women are weak and fearful.

Although he fully acknowledges their necessity, Aristotle despises private and public needs equally. He envisages a state in which women meet needs in the home, and slaves and barbarians meet needs on the land, in the market and in the workshop, while citizens rise above them: 'in a well-ordered state the citizens should have leisure and not have to provide for their daily wants' (1269a34). Distinguished from slaves and paid workers, citizens are defined as literally 'free men', men in whose lives necessities do not feature, but are all met by others: 'our definition of the excellence of a citizen will not apply to every citizen, nor to every free man as such, but only to those who are freed from necessary services' (1278a5–14). The function of these citizens—the highest possible function for a human being (see *Nicomachean Ethics X*)—is to enjoy the life of virtue, political activity and contemplation that their leisure, freed of the drudgery of meeting needs, makes possible. The good citizen ought not to learn the crafts of inferiors, because 'if they habitually practise them there will cease to be a distinction between master and slave' (1277a35).

But Aristotle does take some necessities to be proper parts of human life: the necessities of war, politics and religion. Warriors fulfil the necessity of 'maintaining authority both against disobedient subjects and against external assailants' (1328b7). Councillors fulfil the necessity of making political judgement, or 'deciding what is for the public interest, and what is just in men's dealings with one another' (1328b14), and priests fulfil the necessity of organising the honouring of the gods (1329a30). Aristotle offers two arguments for claiming that these necessities are proper parts. The first is that, unlike the other necessities which are 'inimical to excellence', they are apt for the expression of excellence, because they are the highest functionings of human life (recall that the identity or nature of a life is given by the highest thing in it). Because they are among our 'highest' functions, warcraft, politics and religion are apt to embody human excellence. The second is that, unlike the other necessities which are 'ignoble', these necessities are good in themselves and choosable for their own sake:

> [Some things] are good only because we cannot do without them—it would be better that neither individuals nor states should need anything of the sort—but actions which aim at honour and advantage are absolutely the best. The conditional action is only the choice of a lesser evil; whereas these are the foundation and creation of good. A good man may make the best even of poverty

and disease, and the other ills of life; but he can only attain happiness under the opposite conditions. [...] This makes men fancy that external goods are the cause of happiness, yet we might as well say that a brilliant performance on the lyre was to be attributed to the instrument and not to the skill of the performer. (1332a12–26)

Aristotle here holds that the activities of the warrior, councillor and priest 'aim at honour and advantage', and 'are the foundation and creation of good', whereas the activities of the slave, tradesman, artisan and labourer are simply those we cannot do without, and it would be better if we did not need anything of the sort. Such activities do not involve intrinsic goods. The view Aristotle appears to be urging here, is that a human life in which there was no need for war, political judgement and worship would be an impoverished life; whereas a human life in which there was no need for eating and drinking, or arts and crafts, or trade, or work, would be an enriched and improved one—perhaps because we would have so much more leisure to devote to war, politics and worship.

Aristotle offers reasonably detailed and interesting arguments for his claim that needs and needs-meeting are not proper parts of an excellent human life, whether of the individual or of the state. But was he right? In the following sections I will argue that Aristotle was wrong. Needs are proper parts of human life. Meeting needs is noble, and is expressive of human excellence. Far from encroaching on leisure, needs, as the 'matter' of human life, give leisure a content it could not have without them. Meeting needs involves and cultivates skills which complement other virtues and do not undermine them or blur the distinction between them. And excellent people should meet needs rather than leaving that to other people because that is the only form of self-sufficiency contingent beings like ourselves can coherently aspire to, and because meeting needs is no easier, and so no better suited to inferiors, than any other characteristically human activity.

3. Internal Tensions in Aristotle's View of Needs

In this section I will argue that the reasons Aristotle gives for holding that the 'grand' necessities of warcraft, politics and religion are proper parts of human life while the 'ordinary' necessities of food-provision, arts and crafts, trade and work are not, are inadequate. Second, I will argue that the Aristotelian virtuous person will, as a matter of necessity, recognise and take themselves to be obliged to meet many human-life needs, not just those of war, politics and religion.

a. Which Necessities can be Parts of Human Life?

Aristotle distinguishes between necessities that he takes to be true parts of human life (warcraft, political judgement and worship), and necessities that exist merely for the sake of it but are not organic parts of it (farming, arts and crafts, trade and labour). As a convenient shorthand, from now on I will refer to the former as 'grand' and the latter as 'ordinary' necessities. Why should we accept Aristotle's view that

184

ordinary necessities are not proper parts of human life? What is it about fighting that makes it apt to express human excellence, where cultivating and supplying food or other essential goods is not? What is it about deciding what is for the public interest, rather than, say, deciding what your child or your mother now most needs, that makes it apt to express excellence? What is it about arbitration in public disputes that makes it noble and excellent, rather than merely indispensable? What is it about worship?

By the criteria Aristotle himself uses to determine whether a human life is a good one, we might question whether a life without the ordinary necessities of food, art and craft, labour, work and trade would be better than a life that contained these things. We can cite examples to show that ordinary necessities can provide plenty of opportunity for the exercise of judgement and the expression of human excellence. A farmer has to judge what to farm, how much, with whose help and when. He has to watch over his crop, tend it, harvest it, and market it. All of these activities can be done well or badly, as part of human life well lived or mindless of their noble role. They can be done in a leisurely way, with thought and for the sake of the good, or they can be done rapidly and carelessly.

It might be objected that Aristotle precisely denies that trade, work, labour, craft, art, food preparation and care-work can be leisurely activities, rather than destroying leisure. His vision of the activities of the 'necessary people' is one of unrelieved, exhausting and mind-numbing toil. But this begs the question. If war, politics and religion can fill leisure without destroying it, why can a reasonable amount of

185

manual labour or care-work not do the same? Having to dig potatoes for eighteen hours a day seven days a week may, indeed, unfit me for thought or happiness. But why should having to dig enough potatoes to feed my community, with the help of every able-bodied member of that community, do so? Might a bit of toil not, in fact, enhance my ability to think and to enjoy life? Aristotle shows an inkling of this possibility in *Politics VII* 15, where he notices how leisure, the supposed highest good and end of all activity, once it is achieved very easily tends to corrupt people, inclining them to hubris, decadent, wanton, outrageous behaviour (1334a11-b5).

Aristotle seems to have mistaken a fact about excessive quantity of any activity for an intrinsic quality specific to activities of a particular type. Too much labour, work, care etc. is of course destructive of leisure. But just as we can think, fight, administer justice and worship mindfully and happily, so we can farm, or labour, or nurture, or trade, mindfully and happily, as rational human beings. We can do any of these things in an alienated, reluctant way, with contempt and in a spirit of resentment that it is necessary at all. An Aristotelian outlook is one which makes the concept of life and its characteristic activities irreducible, basic and central. Such an outlook surely obliges us to embrace and accept the natural parts of our life—which is what all these necessities are—and to do them as well as possible, using as fully as possible that rational capacity which is the highest thing in us.

If we can question whether Aristotle is right to claim that ordinary needs-meetings are ignoble, we can also question whether the grand needs-meetings he does favour, of

186

warcraft, politics and worship, themselves rightly should be taken to be proper parts of human life, manifestations of 'leisure' and 'man's higher functions', rather than encroachments. Warcraft is full of opportunities for meaningless and destructive activity, and it gets in the way of the leisurely activities of contemplation and friendship at least as much as farming, or having to obtain, prepare and serve food does. Politics, too, is full of posturing, jockeying for position, ineffectual and poorly focused debate, and it, too, can easily hinder rather than help the activities of contemplation and friendship that human beings most value. The same goes for worship. Anyone who has heard a bit about some fruitless trench warfare, or an interminable court-case or a tedious sermon, will quickly confirm that there is nothing about war, politics or religion as such that makes them immune to the perils Aristotle attributes to 'necessary activities' alone.

It is at least as plausible that the ordinary necessities of nourishment, creation, labour and trade may enhance human life and provide opportunities for excellence, as it is that the grand necessities of war, politics and religion may do so. Even if we think of the good life as Aristotle does, as comprising only the highest activities done as part of leisure, without busy-ness or toil, there is no good Aristotelian reason to think that the activities of farming, arts and crafts, work and trade cannot be proper parts of that life.

b.   Does the Virtuous Man meet Needs?

The Aristotelian good man is portrayed as someone who does not meet ordinary needs. But can this be right, given all

Aristotle says about the good man? Could there be an Aristotelian good man who did not know what human life needs are? Could there be a good man who did not know what to do about such needs? Could there be a good man who did not actually by their own efforts meet such needs, in themselves or in others, when they encountered them? I think not. On the first point, Aristotle implies in the *Politics* that the good man need not know what ordinary necessities are. But if, as Aristotle commonly recognises, ordinary necessities comprise some of the 'matter' of human life, which must be there if human life is to be there, then ordinary necessities are among the elements, the most simple components of human life. It is a further Aristotelian commonplace, that when we want to understand something, we must look first at its simplest parts. To understand the whole, we must understand the elements which comprise it. It follows that if we do not know what the necessities of human life are, we do not know what human life is. The Aristotelian good man of course knows what human life is, and so it follows trivially that he must know what is necessary for that life to be possible and to be maintained in being. It follows from Aristotle's own definitions, that the good man must know what ordinary human needs are.

Must the good man also know how actually to meet ordinary needs? Here again the conceptual structure of Aristotle's view pulls in one direction, while what he says on this topic in the *Politics* pulls in another. What he says, is that the good man does not, and should not think about ordinary needs, because to do so is ignoble and inimical to virtue. But what his view entails, is rather that insofar as the good man is someone able to live an excellent life, he must be able to make the living of an excellent life possible. If you are able to f, you must be able to make f-ing possible: because that is what 'being able to f' means. The good man, then, must be able to meet the needs which are the pre-requisites for the living of an excellent life. He cannot be a good man, if he does not know how to supply the conditions that make his excellent activity possible. So, the good man must indeed know both what ordinary needs are, and know how to meet them. It is worth emphasising that this part of Aristotelian virtue, because it refers to the necessities of human beings as such, rather than those of some particular human being, such as the self, entails that the good man must know and be able to meet the needs of any human being; that is, he must be able to furnish the conditions for excellent human life as such, whoever is to live that life—self or other, individual or community.

Beyond knowing and being able to meet ordinary human needs, must the Aristotelian good man also himself actually meet the ordinary human needs he encounters? Might it not be sufficient for virtue, for him just to know how to ensure that someone else meets the needs he encounters: to know, say, how to get a woman to care for his home, a slave to till his fields, a nurse to tend his bodily needs, a samaritan to deal with the hungry beggar he passes on the roadside? Must the good man be someone who actually meets needs, or can he be someone who snaps his fingers to summon a slave whenever a need arises near him? Here, again, what Aristotle says in the *Politics* is not what his own views imply. He says that the good man should use slaves, women and barbarians to meet the ordinary needs that arise around him, and should concentrate on the higher, leisurely functions of war, politics and religion.

But a more consistent Aristotelian position would say that when an ordinary need arises, in normal cases the good man should actually meet it, rather than summoning someone else to do the 'necessary work'. There are two Aristotelian reasons for this. The first one relates to self-sufficiency. To count as a good person, a person must to the fullest reasonably practicable extent be self-sufficiently good. This means that for all the good man's good functions, he must furnish the necessary conditions for those functions—himself. If I rely on others to make my functionings possible or easy, I am dependent on them, and so less self-sufficiently good and a fortiori less good simpliciter. The second reason relates to the sheer importance of ordinary human life needs. Human life literally cannot go on unless the necessaries are furnished. It is not just that some good will be forfeited or evil suffered, nor that some irrationality or force may have been tolerated or perversely resisted, if such ordinary needs are not met. It is that human life itself, this highest thing which matters to the good man unforsakably and for its own sake, cannot continue unless and until the need is met. This makes it requisite and hence rational for the good man to drop anything of any lesser importance that he might be doing, and meet the need. This requirement will hold for the Aristotelian man pretty much whatever else he is doing—planning his next war, haggling over the right poll tax or over whether someone has coveted his neighbour's wife, or arranging the sacrifice of a goat to appease the gods or keep the slaves happy. The only exception to this would be in a complex case, where the good man is already engaged in a project that is even more necessary for human life.

It might be objected that where others are able to meet the need, allowing the good man to continue his higher activities without interruption, there is nothing in Aristotle's concept of the good man that makes it impermissible for him to delegate the meeting of the need. This is true, but does not establish what Aristotle appears to have wanted: the immunity of the good man to claims of need. That is, it fails to establish that in a case where a need arises which the good man is uniquely (or just best) able to meet, the good man could be immune to the demand. On the contrary, it has been established that the good man must know the need, know how to meet it, and meet it himself.[6]

The conclusion that needs-meeting is the first part of Aristotelian virtue follows straightforwardly from the primacy of needs in human life: unless needs are met, there can be no excellent human life. So we must know what needs are, know how to meet them, and meet them as a matter of priority. This conclusion follows for human life necessities as such—ordinary necessities are no less demanding to the good man than grand ones. The most excellent Aristotelian people will also be most aware of the priority of necessities, and most adept at responding to them. They might do so

---

[6] Thanks to Christopher Rowe, Sarah Broadie and Thomas Johanssen for pressing the objection that having others meet ordinary needs may be consistent with Aristotelian virtue.

discreetly, and they might establish social institutions which discharge this obligation on their behalf most effectively. But what they cannot do, is make it the case that they, as human beings seeking human excellence, are not required to satisfy the necessary conditions for excellent human life.

4. Objections to Aristotle's View of Needs

a. Can Activity and Life aim at Leisure?

One of the reasons that Aristotle offers for attributing the low status he does to the activity of meeting many human needs, is that such activity 'destroys leisure'. I have argued above that it is far from clear that working to meet ordinary needs does this, or that working to meet grand necessities does not do it. But there is a deeper problem, with the very idea of leisure as part of the human good. Aristotle thinks leisure is the first principle of action, and that just as war aims at peace, action aims at leisure (1334a15). Leisure is the 'highest part' of human life, which most clearly expresses human nature, and the best activity is the most leisurely (see e.g. *NE* 1177b4ff; *Pol* 1337b32ff). A leisurely activity is one done for its own sake—it is not required for anything else, and it is not useful. The most perfect leisurely activity for Aristotle is contemplation, because 'nothing arises from it apart from the contemplating, while from practical activities, we gain more or less apart from the action' (1777b3).

This elevation of leisure may be what leads Aristotle into error on the subject of ordinary needs. He recognises in *Nicomachean Ethics X* that a life of leisurely contemplation is impossible for human beings, who must also live in the world and among people, and must look after their bodies. In the face of this difficulty, instead of seeking an alternative to this unattainable ideal, Aristotle places contemplation as the unreachable but still orienting and attractive peak of a hierarchy of human activities, saying that we should do everything for the sake of this. But it is irrational to recommend as a goal something that is impossible. Aristotle should have rejected the ideal, and looked critically at the conceptions of activity, leisure and life that generated it. Conceiving of human activity as aiming at leisure is a fatal error, and it is compounded by the conflation of 'activity desirable for its own sake' with 'activity which produces nothing beyond itself'.

There are the resources within Aristotle's work to solve this problem. For Aristotle, life consists of activity—of the characteristic movements of a natural being. Life thus understood 'aims', if it aims at anything, at the fullest realisation of life. Life has no ulterior or higher purpose or exterior for the sake of which it exists as an instrument. This is the strength of Aristotle's distinction between natural living beings, and other objects. Natural living beings have internal ends of their own—their own lives. Other objects may be instruments to other ends, or inextricable functional parts of other wholes—but they have no internal ends. Why, then, does Aristotle conceive of some human activities as instruments for the achievement of leisure, rather than conceiving of all human activities as among the characteristic activities that together non-instrumentally comprise the life of that organism?

I suggest that what we see here is an unresolved tension in Aristotle's thought, between his homely naturalistic conception of life as a complex of activities which are all and equally 'just what we do', and a more metaphysically grand conception of human life as a quasi-instrumental part of a world essentially striving for the perfection of the eternal unchanging circular motion of divine thought (described in most detail in *Metaphysics XII*). The idea that activity is a means for the achievement of leisure is part of the latter, metaphysically grand conception of life as a means for achieving perfection. Why Aristotle held onto this conception, in his treatment of human needs, but also in his discussion of the contemplative life, is hard to say. Perhaps the persisting influence of Plato. Perhaps a psychoanalytically motivated yearning for independence and an end to all striving.

It is actually easy to generate a *reductio* of the metaphysically grand conception, I think. If we take the limiting case of the supposedly perfect union of activity and leisure, divine thought, we find that what is here called 'activity' looks nothing like any activity we can even imagine. The difference, phenomenologically as well as metaphysically, between the 'perfect activity' of divine contemplation, and the perfect inactivity of non-existence, seems to vanish. Perfect leisure and perfect activity can only be two different ways of describing the same thing—and they are certainly not ways of describing a form of human life desirable for its own sake. Deprived of the affordances and constraints, the contingencies and dependencies of earthly human life, perfect leisure and activity have no matter on which the form of human

194

action can get to work. The error of conceiving action and life as aiming at leisure is compounded by Aristotle's identification of the 'desirable for its own sake' and the 'desirable for nothing but its own sake'. I can desire to meet needs for its own sake, although this may be unusual, since meeting needs is an instrumental business. For example I might desire to feed my family for its own sake because I love preparing food and see this as an important and meaningful part of my life. I cannot, of course, desire to feed my family for nothing but its own sake—if I did, this would show I hadn't really understood what a need is all about. But it is far from obvious that the aspect of the activity under which it is 'necessary work' should loom especially large for me. Indeed, one might reasonably think it would be a good idea to play that aspect down, since the more I experience an activity as 'necessitated', the more coerced I will feel, and the more unpleasant the activity will probably be for me as a result. Why did Aristotle think that if I desired the activity for the sake of the needing being, this entailed I could not desire it for its own sake as well? And anyway, can any activity truly be desirable for its own sake alone? Aristotle offers us contemplation of truth—but even that is desirable for the sake of truth, which is something apart from the contemplation. Aristotle seems to be aware of this, when he says every activity 'gains more or less apart from the action', but he fails to draw the conclusion: the metaphysically grand picture of action and life aiming at leisure and perfection must be sacrificed in favour of the homely empirical picture of life as the set of things that we do, desirable both in themselves and for what they make possible.

b. *Aristotelian Self-Sufficiency Put Right*

Aristotle's concept of self-sufficiency bears some responsibility for his denigration of the work of meeting ordinary needs. For Aristotle self-sufficiency is a very good thing— God is self-sufficient; the perfect state is one that it is independent or self-sufficient; the best activities are those that are 'complete in themselves and lacking in nothing'. But only God and eternal cyclical motion are truly self-sufficient; everything else rests on a bed of necessary conditions which might have been otherwise, and might become otherwise. The most self-sufficiency can be for contingently existing beings like us, is an ideal around which we can organise our lives (as when we emulate God, forget our bodies and lose ourselves in thought—for a time), or as a more or less enabling illusion (as when we forget, or bracket, or put out of our thoughts all the contingent conditions that have to be met for this or that to be possible). Whilst to an extent this forgetting of necessities is itself necessary, it carries risks, and I think Aristotle succumbed to them in his thinking about the place of ordinary necessities in human life.

When we think of a concept or a thing, we can't keep the necessities of that thing before our minds. We can't keep the necessities of a measuring rod before our minds, as we measure with it, and we can't keep the individual trees in mind when we think of the forest. But the difficulty of simultaneously seeing what supports something, and taking for granted that it is so supported, does not license us ever to imagine that the supports are absent or unnecessary. The moment we speak of a contingent thing's being 'self-sufficient', we risk forgetting this. The closest to self-sufficiency a contingent being can come, is to have all its needs met. This is what happens when philosophers talk as if a free rational adult man with resources and skills at his disposal is self-sufficient. The man appears to be self-sufficient, because all his needs are met. But cut off his air or water or food supply, deprive him of a limb or a spouse, vision or language or survival skills, and consider just how 'self-sufficient' he will look then. A contingent being can also be relatively self-sufficient when compared to something else. This is what we might mean when we say a plant is self-sufficient: it has fewer or simpler or more easily met needs compared to, say, a human being. Or a contingent thing could be self-sufficient only figuratively, or under a particular aspect, as a human contemplator of truth may be 'self-sufficient' and 'God-like'. But so long as a being is contingent, it is dependent on its needs—ordinary or grand—being met.

But for Aristotle dependency is an inferior state. Dependent things are like children, helpless and needy. Better to be independent and self-sufficient. But as I argued above, no contingent thing can really be self-sufficient. What Aristotle should have commended to us as the best state for human beings, then, was neither the needless self-sufficiency of God of *Nicomachean Ethics X*, nor yet the state of the 'free' citizen at leisure whose needs are all met by others of *Politics VII*, but rather the state of a person who self-sufficiently has all their needs met. But notice what this would mean: ordinary needs would not be eliminated, transcended, denigrated or delegated; they would be met—and met by the good person himself, in large part. There is a sense in which to have your needs met is to be self-sufficient, namely, that once your needs are met, the capabilities intrinsic to your nature are available to be actualised. Once, and only once, your needs are met, you can be and act as the thing you are, without any further help—so, 'independently'. But it should be obvious that this sense of 'self-sufficient' is nothing like the self-sufficiency of eternal cyclical motion, or God, which so impresses Aristotle.

Because he thinks self-sufficiency is good and dependency is bad, Aristotle argues that the person who delegates needs-meeting to 'necessary people' can be self-sufficient—but he is mistaken. To be 'self-sufficient', human beings have to be able and ready to meet human needs. An individual or community who cannot meet their needs for food, arts, crafts trade and work without depending on slaves, women and barbarians, is a dependent, vulnerable individual or community, not a self-sufficient one. If they lose control of their 'necessary people'—say the slaves revolt—they will be helpless as children, unable to care or fend for themselves. This is not to say the self-sufficient person cannot choose to arrange society in such a way that others normally do a large portion of the 'necessary work'. It is only to say that to be self-sufficient, they must be ready and able to do it themselves.

Aristotle's picture of the self-sufficient citizen, and the self-sufficient state, then, is confused. He slides from seeing self-sufficiency as a matter of having met, but bracketed, needs, to seeing it as a matter of having no needs, and so recommending the less need of some life of contemplation as a human ideal in the *Ethics*.

And he slides from seeing self-sufficiency as being able to meet your own needs, to seeing it as being powerful enough to get others to meet them, in the *Politics*. We can accept his analysis of human necessities, without following him into confusion about self-sufficiency.

c.   *Natural Slaves and Excellent People:*
       The Implications for Needs

Aristotle thought some people are 'natural slaves' while others, because they possess the capacity for rational excellence and leisure, are natural citizens and leaders (1254–60). We modern thinkers find this line of thought alien and repellent. But perhaps Aristotle had a point. Some people by nature do lack a deliberative faculty, and consequently need their lives to be organised by others, and it is perhaps almost forgivable that Aristotle called those people 'slaves' where we would want a much less offensive term to refer to them, like 'those who give us the opportunity to help them'. Whatever we call them, the fact is that many people are not independently capable of autonomous rational agency. Because of accidents of birth or upbringing, and historical contingencies of the established political order, such people cannot engage effectively in politics, they cannot determine their own activities and relationships, they cannot manage to accumulate the goods they need for an excellent human life. They need help; they need the guidance and support of more capable others.

Aristotle may have made the point in the distasteful idiom of 'inferiority' which requires 'superiors' to take charge—but he was right to recognise the reality, and we

199

moderns are wrong not to do so.[7] People who are not self-sufficient need to be helped by others. Our distaste for dependency notwithstanding, it is no crime, nor a mark of inferiority, to be needy in this way. But Aristotle was wrong about the implications for needs-meeting of the natural hierarchy of rational abilities across human beings. He claimed that natural slaves are better suited to meeting needs than others. He thought that people who lack the capacity for rational excellence will do best if they are commanded by others who do have rational excellence, and the best thing for these inferiors to do will be to meet the needs of their superiors, so that the superiors will be in a better position to take responsibility for the lives of their slaves.

To a modern liberal, in theory at least, these ideas are abhorrent. We now think that people who lack the capacity for rational excellence should be helped to acquire as much of it as they can, and should be supported in living lives of their own, rather than used as human equipment to

[7] Our own society, which subscribes to the myth of free rational equal agency, imposes an illusory equality on everyone, and then holds everyone up to the standards of a social game—capitalism—that only highly rational and capable individuals can actually hope to play and win. Adam Smith noted that capitalism depends on some self-deception about just how self-sufficient and independent we can be (see John O'Neill's contribution to this volume). But Smith did not comment on the concomitant deception necessarily perpetrated by the capitalist state on its less able citizens when it embraces 'free trade'. For trade to be 'free', everyone must be equally self-sufficient, have equal access to the market and equal skill in playing it. The capitalist state flatters its less able citizens as it opens the way for the more able to fleece them, and calls this fair play.

enhance the lives of more fortunate others. We think there should be a balance between ordinary needs-meeting, and disputatious, creative, social, political and religious activities in every human life, and we think that a balance between the different areas is desirable and is what good parents, a good education and the good state should foster.

Aristotle's assignment of needs-meeting activities to less rationally capable persons also depends for its plausibility on the underestimation of the importance of ordinary needs that I have described above. Only if you think meeting food needs, or trading, or maintaining a household, say, is actually easy, will you be able to imagine that it is a sensible social arrangement to have less able people do it. We now recognise the complexity and need for skill in previously denigrated ordinary needs-meeting activities, for example those traditionally undertaken by women, like the care of children. We also recognise the complexity and skill involved in making art, in farming, in trading, and the many forms of human labour, including even waste disposal. Whole academic disciplines are dedicated to reinforcing the practical skills and supplying the theory thought necessary to support these supposedly negligible human activities. So Aristotle was wrong, on both moral and rational grounds, to allocate the meeting of ordinary needs to natural slaves. Morally, he was wrong to recommend that less rationally able people should be used as instruments to liberate more fortunate others from ordinary necessities. Rationally speaking, he was wrong to think that the work involved in meeting ordinary needs was either unimportant enough, or easy enough, to make it appropriate work for natural slaves.

5. Conclusion

Aristotle uses an everyday concept of necessity, and describes the things in the world that fall under the concept. Apart from the absolute necessities of eternal circular movement and God, he sees all contingent things as having hypothetical necessities, which fall short of causing the things for which they are necessary, but are their matter, and may or may not be their proper parts. Human needs are the things that must be if human life is to be—they provide the matter of human life. Aristotle thinks that some of these needs are proper parts of human life—warcraft, political judgement and priesthood—but he denies that needs for food, arts and crafts, trade and work are proper parts of human life, on the grounds that they are ignoble and inimical to virtue, not desirable in themselves, and a human life in which they did not arise would be better than the one in which they do.

Arguing against Aristotle on his own terms, I suggested he had identified the wrong set of human needs as 'proper parts' of human life. The ordinary necessities of nourishing, crafting, trading and working can all be proper parts of the best human life; the grand necessities of warcraft, politics and religion can all fail to be. I suggested that meeting ordinary human needs could be desirable in itself, and rejected Aristotle's suggestion that this could not be so for things that are essentially necessities for ends beyond themselves. I argued that the Aristotelian good man will necessarily be a good needs-meeter. Then, challenging Aristotle's terms, I argued that there are mistakes and biases in his conception of good human life. Leisure cannot be the aim of activity, nor can it be the highest or best state for a human being. Further, self-sufficiency for contingent beings like ourselves cannot consist in having fewer needs, nor in getting others to meet our needs, but can only consist in being ready and able to meet our own needs. Finally, I argued that Aristotle was wrong to think less rationally able people should meet ordinary human needs, both because they should really be helped to achieve good lives of their own, and because meeting ordinary needs is difficult, and not particularly well-suited to the limited skills of less able human beings.

6   Need, Care and Obligation

SARAH CLARK MILLER

All humans experience needs.[1] At times needs cut deep, inhibiting persons' abilities to act as agents in the world, to live in distinctly human ways, or to achieve life goals of significance to them. In considering such potentialities, several questions arise: Are any needs morally important, meaning that they operate as morally relevant details of a situation? What is the correct moral stance to take with regard to situations of need? Are moral agents ever required to tend to others' well-being by meeting their needs? What justification or foundation, if any, can be given for requiring moral agents to respond to others' needs?[2]

---

[1] I would like to thank Soran Reader for her very helpful comments on this article.

[2] As a variety of philosophers have it, the scope or extent of our obligation to help others runs the gamut between two extreme positions: the minimal libertarian position that we must only respect the rights of others, leaving charity as optional, not mandatory, and a maximal position like that of Peter Singer's, through which we are required to give to the needy until we are diminished to their level of need. Thomas Hill identifies these two extreme positions in 'Meeting Needs and Doing Favors'. See T. Hill, Jr., *Human Welfare and Moral Worth: Kantian Perspectives* (Oxford: Clarendon, 2002), 201–243. The Singer position (a consequentialist one) can be famously found in his earlier piece, 'Famine, Affluence, and Morality', *Philosophy and Public*

In answering these questions, my argument will take place in several parts. I begin explanatorily, describing care ethics for those unfamiliar with this particular ethical approach. This discussion reveals that care ethicists assert the moral importance of needs. Their position, however, does not offer comment on whether or not we are required to respond to the needs of others. I propose that our human interdependence and finitude give rise to an obligation to care for a certain subset of needs, namely, the constitutive needs of others. Through analysis of both the *Groundwork* and the *Metaphysics of Morals*, I present an interpretation of Kant's duty of beneficence that lays the foundation for the duty to care. After acknowledging the strengths of the Kantian approach, I cite one of its most significant short-comings: although helpful in clarifying the foundation and scope of the duty to care, Kantian ethics requires supplementation with regard to content. Insights from feminist care ethicists provide indispensable enhancement, promoting a robust sense of the content of the duty to care, as represented by two elements: (1) the importance of moral perception and moral judgment in establishing how best to care for others and (2) dignifying care, a notion demonstrating that it is not enough *that* we meet the needs of others, as *how* we do so seriously affects both the agency and dignity of those in need.

Affairs 1, No. 1 (Spring 1972), 229–43. Singer has somewhat modified his position in more recent work. See P. Singer, *One World* (New Haven: Yale University Press, 2002).

1.   Care Ethics: Methods and Themes

The appearance of Carol Gilligan's *In a Different Voice*[3] and, soon after, Nel Noddings' *Caring*[4] marked the emergence of a new moral theory called care ethics. In different ways, both Gilligan and Noddings aimed to uncover the moral methodology and themes inherent in the experiences of women, emphasizing the unique contribution that a 'feminine' approach to ethics can provide.[5] Feminist elaborations of Gilligan's work in particular presented care ethics as an alternative to the so called 'justice perspective', characterised by notions of rationality, autonomy, equality and independence. Such themes, some feminist philosophers have charged, establish a 'masculine' mode of ethics prevalent in the moral theories of many canonical thinkers. Commenting on the origin of this mode of philosophizing, Margaret Urban Walker observes that 'philosophical ethics, as a

---

[3] C. Gilligan, *In a Different Voice: Psychological Theory and Women's Development* (Cambridge, Mass.: Harvard University Press, 1982). See also C. Gilligan, 'Moral Orientation and Moral Development' in *Women and Moral Theory*, ed. E. F. Kittay and D. T. Meyers (Totowa, NJ: Rowman and Littlefield, 1987), 19–33. To understand the theoretical framework that Gilligan was arguing against, see L. Kohlberg, *The Philosophy of Moral Development: Moral Stages and the Idea of Justice* (San Francisco: Harper and Row, 1981).

[4] N. Noddings, *Caring: A Feminine Approach to Ethics and Moral Education* (Berkeley: University of California Press, 1984).

[5] Cf. S. Ruddick, *Maternal Thinking: Toward a Politics of Peace* (New York: Ballantine Books, 1989). In this work, Ruddick draws upon women's maternal experience to articulate new ethical and political insights about peace.

cultural product, has been until recently almost entirely a product of some men's thinking'.[6] Care ethics explicitly challenges this status quo by questioning assumptions concerning, for example, what constitutes moral reasoning, what counts as an ethical issue, and what makes for good moral practice.

In addition to its critical enterprise, care ethics also offers a series of innovative philosophical insights, four of which I treat here.[7] These insights concern the themes of particularity, dependence, interdependence and need. Discussion of these four themes lays the groundwork for a comprehensive definition of care and for an understanding of the relationship between need and care, both of which I provide at the end of this section.

Care ethicists name **particularity** as one feature of their unique moral approach. Caring for others means tending to them in their particularity, responding to them not as abstract 'moral patients' or 'subjects', but rather as unique individuals with distinctive life stories and circumstances. At the core of such an approach one finds significant attention to and respect for forms of difference—expressed through a person's race, class, gender, sexual orientation, religious affiliation, age, physical and mental

---

[6] M. U. Walker, 'Moral Understandings: Alternative "Epistemology" for a Feminist Ethics' in *Justice and Care: Essential Readings in Feminist Ethics*, ed. V. Held (Boulder: Westview, 1995), 139.

[7] Analysis of the role of the emotions and reconceptualization of the public/private split serve as two further examples of significant themes in care ethics.

ability, etc.—that permeate and mould the realities of persons requiring care. The contrast Seyla Benhabib draws between the generalised and the concrete other highlights the particularity inherent within care ethics, while also revealing its dissimilarity from the generalised approach inherited from the early modern era. Benhabib portrays two understandings of self-other relations. As she explains, 'the standpoint of the generalised other requires us to view each and every individual as a rational being entitled to the same rights and duties we would want to ascribe to ourselves. In assuming this standpoint, we abstract from the individuality and concrete identity of the other ... Our relation to the other is governed by norms of *formal equality* and *reciprocity*'.[8] The focus of this perspective draws from the commonality we share with others, which serves as the grounds upon which we can claim equal rights and respect. In contrast, 'the standpoint of the concrete other ... requires us to view each and every rational being as an individual with a concrete history, identity, and affective-emotional constitution ... Our relation to the other is governed by the norms of *equity* and *complementary reciprocity*'.[9] With this second standpoint—one care ethicists readily embrace— moral agents hold the responsibility to respond to others while maintaining a keen awareness of those others' concrete

[8] S. Benhabib, 'The Generalized and The Concrete Other: The Kohlberg-Gilligan Controversy and Moral Theory' in *Women and Moral Theory*, ed. E. F. Kittay and D. T. Meyers (Totowa, N.J.: Rowman & Littlefield, 1987), 163. Emphasis in the original.

[9] Ibid., 164.

specificity: how they understand themselves, what motivates them, and what they want.

A second feature emphasised in care ethics is **dependency**, understood as situations of significant reliance on others that all persons undergo during the course of their lives. Human finitude necessarily gives rise to myriad circumstances of dependency; illness and injury serve as just two cases in point. In addition, dependencies often function as bookends bracing either side of a life: infants are born into radical dependency, while the elderly often encounter it in their waning days. As such, the human experience of dependency is unavoidable. Such a series of observations stands at significant odds with a more traditional picture of the moral agent as autonomous and independent. Although many humans exhibit the capacity of rationality and the accompanying possibility of autonomy, *all* human beings will undoubtedly experience dependency, a fact with noteworthy ethical ramifications. The foundational assumption of the rationality and autonomy of human beings motivates one story about moral agency, one in which often the trick is to adjudicate conflicting moral claims of independent agents. The certitude of dependency, however, tells another story, one in which how we do or do not care for one another in our shared moments of dependence marks a matter of great moral importance.

Care ethics, in underscoring not only the inevitability but also the moral significance of human dependence, calls for an analysis of human **interdependence**. According to the care perspective, persons are not fundamentally independent. Rather, they are *mutually* dependent. Our unavoidable dependency means that if we are to survive, let alone thrive in leading lives that are recognizably human, others must respond to our dependent selves by meeting our needs through their caring actions. During certain life moments, failure on the part of others to so respond could amount to our demise. But I am not solely a dependent being who needs others to bolster my well-being; others, in their inevitable dependence, also need my assistance, hence solidifying the mutuality of the relation. For some care ethicists, our interdependence connects closely with the emotional capacities of empathy and sympathy, moral skills that aid in establishing identification with the plight of others. By conceptualizing ourselves as fundamentally independent of others, we risk stunting cultivation of these, and related, moral emotions. Moral emotions of this nature are clearly a boon in ethical situations hinging on response to needs. But does it make philosophical sense to say that one is required either (a) to feel an emotion like empathy or sympathy or (b) to cultivate within themselves the tendency to feel such emotions? Care ethics, in taking human interdependence as a theme, stirs up these and related engaging questions.

The fourth thematic focus of care ethics is **need**. As the discussion above suggests, talk of need features prominently in the care ethics discourse. More so than other philosophical perspectives, care ethics investigates the subject matter of need in conjunction with both nurturing responsiveness to and responsibility for needs.[10] Although

---

[10] Alison Jaggar, drawing on a comment from Sara Ruddick, comments that beyond responding to needs, 'participants in caring relations also

individual occurrences of need may vary widely (and, indeed, being sensitive to this variance constitutes good care), all humans experience needs. In some sense, care ethics begins from the realization of the role of needs and their significance for our intersubjectively constituted, inter-dependent selves, then moving forward to consider how others' needs can best be met. Thus, care ethics brings about the recognition of needs as morally important.

Although deeply indebted to need discussions in the care ethics literature, this essay also draws upon a second philosophical perspective provided by Immanuel Kant. While not frequently celebrated for its treatment of human need, Kant's practical philosophy incorporates insightful discus-sions of need and obligation, primarily in conjunction with the duty of beneficence. Within the series of needs that a human being can possibly experience, I share Kant's focus on what some have called 'true needs' (Kant's *wahre Bedürfnisse*) and what I refer to as *constitutive needs*.[11] What are consti-tutive needs? Constitutive needs arise in the context of agency-threatening events or circumstances to which another person must respond in order to cultivate, sustain, or restore

strive to delight and empower each other'. A. Jaggar, 'Caring as a Feminist Practice of Moral Reason' in *Justice and Care: Essential Readings in Feminist Ethics*, ed. Virginia Held (Boulder: Westview, 1995), 180.

[11] I employ this term rather than 'true needs' (1) to avoid confusion, as 'true needs' are multiply defined in the literature and (2) because 'constitutive' better captures the dual sense I am trying to convey of a certain set of needs that have the power to establish agency as well as being essential for agency.

the agency of the one in need, as well as to help the individual in need to avoid (further) harm. Such needs can be said to be constitutive in two ways: (1) it is in meeting them that the agency of the one in need is established or re-established, as the case may be, and (2) the needs experienced are generally essential or fundamental to the person in need. I understand constitutive needs to be needs that a person cannot satisfy without the help of others, which is to say that constitutive needs make those in need necessarily dependent upon others to meet their needs. In addition, not responding to such needs often results in serious harm for the individual in need. Constitutive needs can be thought of as ends that agents cannot forgo. They are ends that individuals must attain if they are to exist as agents. In this sense, they function as one of the keys to human agency. Given that humans are finite, experiencing constitutive needs during the course of a lifetime is inevitable and therefore, constitutive needs are inescapable. In order for humans to continue setting subjective ends for themselves—understood to be a characteristically human capability—constitutive needs must be cared for. Other forms of need, such as instrumental needs,[12] do not necessarily require a moral response. Constitutive needs do.

By explaining how need and care relate to one another, the exact nature of **care** becomes clear. Simply put, to have a need is to require care.[13] 'Care' constitutes a

[12] Instrumental needs are required for ends other than (1) avoiding harm or (2) cultivating, maintaining or restoring agency.

[13] J. Tronto, *Moral Boundaries: A Political Argument for an Ethic of Care* (New York: Routledge, 1993), 120.

morally appropriate reaction to another's needs. When a moral agent identifies and responds to a needy individual, the series of actions that moral agent performs to establish or sustain the needy other's agency are caring actions. In this regard, Diemut Bubeck's definition of 'caring for' is quite instructive. Bubeck writes, 'caring for is the meeting of the needs of one person by another person where . . . interaction between carer and cared for is a crucial element of the overall activity and where the need is of such a nature that it cannot possibly be met by the person in need herself.'[14] Elaboration on several aspects of Bubeck's definition provides further clarification of the term. First, the process of caring involves two positions, namely, that of the one who has a need (the 'cared for' or 'care receiver') and that of the one who meets the need of the other (the 'carer', 'caregiver' or 'care taker'). Second, the process is inherently interactive. Although Bubeck initially stipulates that the interaction between caregiver and care receiver must be 'face-to-face', she later qualifies this position to include other forms of interaction and communication.[15] Third, 'self-care' is not possible under Bubeck's rubric. Care must necessarily be other-directed. Fourth, Bubeck distinguishes between caring activities and other activities of love and friendship. Care need not involve the affection present between friends or

[14] D. E. Bubeck, *Care, Gender and Justice* (Oxford: Clarendon, 1995), 129. For a broader definition of care, see Ibid., 102–105.

[15] Bubeck notes that 'the important point is that certain kinds of communication in themselves constitute care . . . whether such communication is immediate or mediate' (Ibid., 129).

213

lovers, although it might. Feelings of affection may or may not be present in the caregiver when meeting the care receiver's needs. Fifth, though other care ethicists have provided much broader definitions of care, Bubeck restricts her consideration of care to humans.[16]

In discussing care, it is important to register two immediate concerns. First, not every act performed in response to need qualifies as care. An individual's reaction to another's need may be brutal, insufficient, or just plain insensitive. Much effort must take place in the instance between the identification of another's need and the performance of a fitting response thereto. Joan Tronto observes that 'what is definitive about care ... seems to be a perspective of taking the other's needs as the starting point for what must be done.'[17] The caring act originates with an accurate perception of and understanding of the needs of the other. This understanding should be gained as much as possible from the needy other's description of his or her own needs. Caring responses, therefore, do not share territory with paternalism. In order to respond in ways emblematic of caring, on my definition, moral agents must advance the *self-determined* ends of those in need to the fullest extent possible.

Second, numerous feminist philosophers have questioned the political implications of care ethics, wondering

---

[16] For a perspective on caring for non-human entities, see M. A. Warren, *Moral Status: Obligations to Persons and Other Living Things* (Oxford: Oxford University Press, 1997).

[17] Op. cit. note 13, 105.

'whether maternal paradigms, nurturant responsiveness, and a bent toward responsibility for others' needs aren't [women's] oppressive history, not [their] liberating future, and whether "women's morality" isn't a familiar ghetto rather than a liberated space'.[18] In essence, some feminists worry that care ethics may further subjugate rather than empower women. Inasmuch as care ethics valorises the 'feminine virtue of care', and inasmuch as the activities and responsibilities historically linked with care have been closely tied to women's oppression, the charge that care ethics draws upon the feminine in a way that renders it unfeminist appears to some extent justified.

As demonstrated above, within the care ethics framework, needs clearly register as morally important. By design, caring actions and attitudes address the needs that others experience. Needs often serve as the catalyst for care. Caring can begin from the other's needs when determining which actions to pursue. Surely, then, needs carry moral weight in an ethic of care. But identifying their moral importance does not necessarily mean that responding to needs must be a matter of obligation. That is, the existence of an individual's morally significant need cannot be said to automatically entail an obligation on the part of others to meet this need. Further argumentation would be required to establish such an obligation. Thus, a critical question remains. Are moral agents required to care for the needs

---

[18] Op. cit. note 6, 140.

of others? And if so, for exactly which needs of which others and when?

It is in conjunction with feminist concerns that an impulse to attach obligation to care—by establishing that there is a duty to care for the needs of others—can initially seem unwise. If care ethics carries with it the danger of further oppressing women by reinforcing the societal expectation that they exhibit the 'virtue' of care,[19] making it a matter of obligation may stir worries that women will become locked in by and loaded down with a *moral requirement* to care for others, hence reifying societal expectations into inescapable demands of moral law. Although these reservations certainly deserve careful consideration, they are ultimately unwarranted. Contrary to some expectations, establishing the duty to care serves feminist goals by making caring a matter of obligation by which all humans, not just female ones, are bound. Such a requirement has potentially liberatory effects, as in conjunction with the duty to care the burdens of care would be more equally distributed, therefore lessening the weight on women's currently overloaded shoulders.

How might the duty to care be established? Given that a number of care ethicists understand care and obligation to be fundamentally at odds with one another, an ethic of care does not provide resources adequate for the task. According to some, the emotions necessary for and central

[19] For an interesting discussion of care and oppression, see C. Card, 'Gender and Moral Luck' in *Justice and Care: Essential Readings in Feminist Ethics*, ed. Virginia Held (Boulder: Westview, 1995), 79–98.

to the act of caring cannot coexist with a sense of caring out of duty.[20] From this perspective, making meeting needs a matter of obligation would destroy the aim of care ethics. Given such objections to connecting obligation with care, alternative philosophical assistance is required.

2. Kantian Beneficence

In searching for help with the present task, it is Immanuel Kant who answers the call. Through the duty of beneficence, Kant demonstrates that there is an obligation to respond to the needs of others, hence replying affirmatively to the question of central importance: Must moral agents care for others by meeting their needs? In short, Kant's account lays the groundwork for and explains why there is a duty to care. In so doing, Kantian moral theory reinforces normative justification for further investigation into moral claims of and responses to human need.[21]

---

[20] This line of critique is captured in a general objection against Kantian ethics that charges it does not allow adequate room for the moral significance of the emotions. For a general description of a feminist take on this issue, see V. Held, 'Introduction' in *Justice and Care: Essential Readings in Feminist Ethics*, ed. V. Held (Boulder: Westview, 1995), 1–3 and V. Held, 'Feminist Ethical Theory' in *Conduct and Character*, ed. M. Timmons. 4th ed. (Belmont, CA: Wadsworth, 2002), 237–243.

[21] Inherent in the turn to Kant is the recognition that feminist ethicists have been hasty in their condemnation of Kant. Despite feminist ethicists' caricature of Kantian moral philosophy as a rule-bound, overly-individualistic, unreasonably autonomous perspective of empty formalism with no bearing on actual moral situations in the real world,

In the *Doctrine of Virtue*[22] Kant poses the question of present interest: 'but beyond *benevolence* in our wishes for others (which costs us nothing) how can it be required as a duty that this should be practical, that is, that everyone who has the means to do so should be *beneficent* to those in need?'[23] (*MS* 6: 452; 201) This question evokes several central features of the Kantian duty of beneficence, features to bear in mind when delineating the Kantian take on need and response thereto.

First, duties of love, of which the duty of beneficence is one, are wide duties. Wide duties carry with them an imperfect obligation to act. (The wider the duty, in fact,

a rigorous approach behooves one to return to the source where answers may be found. (In conjunction with this charge, it is notable that the common feminist interpretation of Kantian autonomy has remarkably little to do with what Kant actually wrote on the subject, inasmuch as it borrows rather heavily from a developmental psychological perspective. This is not to say that such an approach is uninteresting, but only to point out that it promulgates a common misreading of Kant.) In this case, the return is to Kant's duty of beneficence, to see, in conjunction with a detailed and thorough reading, what answers lie therein.

[22] This question is found in a section entitled, 'On the Duty of Love to Other Human Beings.'

[23] I. Kant, *Die Metaphysik der Sitten (1797), Kants gesammelte Schriften, herausgegeben von der Deutschen Akademie der Wissenschaften* (formerly Königlichen Preussischen Akademie der Wissenschaften) vol. 6. Berlin: Walter de Gruyter. Translated as *The Metaphysics of Morals*. M. J. Gregor (trans.) (Cambridge: Cambridge University Press, 1991). *Die Metaphysik der Sitten* will be cited as *MS*, with the volume and page number from the Prussian Academy edition followed by the page number from the English translation.

the more imperfect the obligation to act, as Kant notes (*MS* 6: 390; 153.)) Second, with ethical duties (the duty of beneficence included), the moral law provides agents only with a maxim of actions, thus not detailing exactly which actions one should carry out in order to fulfil the duty.[24] Agents must judge which actions are in accordance with the maxim of actions prescribed by the moral law (*MS* 6: 390; 153). Third, in discussing the duty of beneficence, Kant employs the term 'love' in a special and technical way, one purposely positioned at a distance from individuals' affective involvement with one another. In employing the word *love*, Kant intends what he terms a love of human beings (*Menschenliebe*), or practical love, rather than love as taking pleasure or delight in others (*MS* 6: 450; 199).[25] Thus, for Kant, moral agents cannot be obligated to feel a certain way toward the needy others they encounter. Simply put, the emotion of love is not a matter of obligation. One cannot be morally expected to experience certain emotions toward another human being. '*Love*', Kant writes, 'is a matter of *emotion*, not of willing and I cannot love because I *will* to, still less because I *ought* to (be constrained to love); therefore

---

[24] Kant cautions that a wide duty should not be understood as allowance to make exceptions to the maxim of actions, but rather only to limit one maxim of a duty by another.

[25] On the topic of *Menschenliebe*, Kant writes, 'die Menschenliebe (Philanthropie) muë, weil sie hier als praktisch, mithin nicht als Liebe des Wohlgefallens an Menschen gedacht wird, im tätigen Wohlwollen gesetzt werden und betrifft also die Maxime der Handlungen.' Kant here notes that love of others that is practical is active benevolence, or beneficence, and has to do with the maxim of actions.

a *duty to love* is an absurdity' (*MS* 6: 401; 161). Fourth and finally, there is an important difference that holds between the duty of benevolence and its close compatriot and subject of the current inquiry, namely, beneficence. Kant distinguishes one from the other in a section of the *Doctrine of Virtue* entitled, 'On Duties of Virtues to Others'. One can capture the difference between benevolence and beneficence by examining what each requires of agents in terms of practical action. Whereas the duty of benevolence, which commands the abstract wishing for the well-being of all humans, 'costs us nothing', beneficence requires that individuals with the means to do so take action by responding to true needs present in others (*MS* 6: 452; 201). In responding to another's needs, moral agents are to do so such that they make the well-being and happiness of needy others their end (*MS* 6: 452; 201). In responding to another's constitutive needs, moral agents' actions are such that they take up and promote another's ends as their own.

3. The Kantian Answer

How can it be required as a duty that everyone who has the means to do so should be beneficent to those in need? Explanation of this element in the Kantian moral system provides the much-needed foundation for any moral approach wishing to take seriously a duty to care in the face of need. Kant writes, 'the reason that it is a duty to be beneficent is this: since our self-love cannot be separated from our need to be loved (helped in the case of need) by others as well, we therefore make ourselves an end for others; and the only way this maxim can be binding is through its qualification as a universal law; hence through our will to make others our ends as well. The happiness of others is therefore an end that is also a duty' (*MS* 6: 393; 156). Finite rational beings, in light of their finitude, will require the help of others when they experience need. When I require help, I make myself an end for others inasmuch as they, in helping me, take on my ends as their own. For Kant, my need to be helped by others relates to my need to help others. In addition, the maxim associated with beneficence can only be binding when qualifying as a universal law. This means that when I encounter others experiencing need, in helping them I take on their ends as my own.

But why must this maxim qualify as universal law? Kant claims that our self-love cannot be separated from our need to be helped in the case of need. Finite rational beings have an interest in their own continued existence. In order to go on exercising one's agency as a rational being, certain needs, namely constitutive needs, must be met. They must be met so that finite rational beings can sustain themselves as such and can continue to set ends for themselves. Finite rational beings will sometimes require the help of others, because of the existence of constitutive needs that they cannot themselves fulfil and of certain ends that they cannot achieve without assistance. Some needs will be agency-threatening. In order to ensure humans' continued existence, the possibility that others will respond to them beneficently must exist.[26]

---

[26] At the core of this explanation is the notion that within the spectrum of kinds of agency considered by Kant, not only rational beings, but

Humans are finite in terms of their rationality. But they are also finite in other ways. As embodied and existing in the world, they will be both vulnerable and needy in a variety of ways over the span of a lifetime.

It is in light of this finitude and because rational beings, as rational, will their own continued existence, that finite rational beings must help one another in cases of need as they practice the duty to care. Unlike deception, a principle of nonbeneficence or mutual indifference—that one never helps another in need and therefore never receives the help of others when in need—could, without inconsistency, serve as a universal law (as Kant notes in the *Groundwork*, to be treated shortly) (*G* 4: 423; 32).[27] Finite rational beings, however, could not will that this be so, as doing this would destroy the conditions of their willing their own continued existence. As finite, they will necessarily experience needs that they cannot themselves meet and will then require the help of others. Under a universal principle

also finite rational beings exist. Indeed, Kant's practical philosophy pertains not simply to humans, but to 'finite rational beings as such', though human beings are one kind of finite rational beings to which Kant frequently refers.

[27] I. Kant, *Grundlegung zur Metaphysik der Sitten* (1785), *Kants gesammelte Schriften, herausgegeben von der Deutschen Akademie der Wissenschaften* (formerly Königlichen Preussischen Akademie der Wissenschaften), vol. 8 (Berlin: Walter de Gruyter). Translated as *Grounding for the Metaphysics of Morals* J. W. Ellington (trans.) (Cambridge: Hackett, 1981). *Grundlegung zur Metaphysik der Sitten* will be cited as *G*, with volume and page number from the Prussian Academy edition followed by the page number from the English translation.

of nonbeneficence, such help would not be available to them, thus bringing about their own possible destruction. As universal, the principle of mutual indifference cannot serve all finite rational beings as a principle of action.[28]

A specific example may help to illustrate why finite rational beings are obligated to respond to each others' constitutive needs, that is, why they have a duty to care. In

---

[28] One objection that might be raised at this point concerns the charge that featuring the finitude of finite rational beings treads on the territory of anthropology, which, in the midst of a metaphysics of morals, is not advisable. As Kant notes in the Introduction to the *Metaphysics of Morals*, 'a metaphysics of morals cannot be based upon anthropology but can still be applied to it' (*MS* 6: 217; 10). A metaphysics of morals cannot look to empirical conditions and details of human life in establishing itself; it cannot be derived from anthropology. Onora O'Neill, however, explains that 'although moral philosophy can abstract from anthropology, it cannot abstract from finitude. For the concept of duty is central to morality, and is defined in terms of [what Kant calls] "a good will exposed, however, to certain subjective limitations and obstacles" (*G*, IV, 397)'. O. O'Neill, *Constructions of Reason: Explorations of Kant's Practical Philosophy* (Cambridge: Cambridge University Press, 1989), 71. These subjective limitations and obstacles are part and parcel of finitude. Indeed, the duty of beneficence must not (and perhaps cannot) be established for non-finite rational beings, as without needs produced by finitude, they would not have occasion to care for one another and therefore there would be no reason for an obligation establishing such care. Human beings, however, are not only rational beings, but also finite beings. As such, the situation of their dependence and need means that obligations are necessary for them. Obligations arise in the face of human imperfection. Whereas non-finite rational beings could will that nonbeneficence be made a universal law, finite rational beings, because of the subjective limits of their willing, cannot do the same.

the *Groundwork*, Kant provides an account of non-universalizable non-beneficence or mutual indifference involving the formulation of the Categorical Imperative commonly referred to as the formula of the law of nature. One can read it as revealing and illustrating Kant's position on dependency and response to human need. Kant depicts a man who 'finds things going well for himself but sees others (whom he could help) struggling with great hardships ...' (*G* 4: 423; 32). As Kant tells it, the man responds to need present in other individuals by saying, 'what does it matter to me? Let everybody be as happy as Heaven wills or as he can make himself; I shall take nothing from him nor even envy him; but I also have no desire to contribute anything to his well-being or to his assistance when in need' (*G* 4: 423; 32). The man of mutual indifference takes the stance that individuals can have as much happiness as heaven bestows upon them or as they can generate themselves. He will neither obstruct their given happiness in any way, nor begrudge them it. To underscore a feature of the example important for the present discussion, recall that the man of mutual indifference stipulates, 'I shall take nothing from them', indicating that he will not call upon others to meet his needs. But in addition, he will not respond to needs present in others.

To Kant's mind, a universal law of nature generated from such a maxim 'could subsist in accordance with that maxim', (*G* 4: 423; 32) (that is, it passes the contradiction in conception test), but could not actually function as a law of nature (it fails the contradiction in volition test). Why does Kant hold this position? In willing that this maxim become a universal law of nature, the will of such a man would contradict itself because situations will inevitably arise in which the man of mutual indifference must call for others' help to meet his own needs. He is inevitably dependent upon others. The vulnerability of this finite rational being ensures that at some point (indeed, at numerous points) he will require others in order to meet his constitutive needs. Alan Wood illuminates the premise behind the *Groundwork* indifference example, namely, 'that we humans are highly dependent and interdependent beings, whose ends, projects, and general well-being are vulnerable not only to the violation of our rights by others but to many other misfortunes, and they include many ends that we can achieve only through a voluntary participation of others in our ends that goes beyond what we can demand of them by right.'[29] It is not enough that individuals not interfere in one another's lives. Well-being for finite rational beings can only come about in a world involving beneficence. Perhaps most poignantly, the man of mutual indifference cannot will that he never help another because willing thusly amounts to willing his own possible downfall and destruction. He cannot be assured that in future scenarios he will not require the help of others in meeting his constitutive needs. Given the limitations of his natural powers, to will so as to foreclose this probability amounts to potentially removing the very conditions of possibility of his own willing. The contradiction is generated in conjunction with the limitations characteristic

[29] A. Wood, *Kant's Ethical Thought* (New York: Cambridge University Press, 1999), 95.

of finite, rational beings. It is in light of their finitude, vulnerability, and interdependence that human beings have a duty to care for one another.

4. Strengths of the Duty of Beneficence and the Duty to Care

As I have demonstrated, the Kantian duty of beneficence explains how it is that we are obligated to respond to the constitutive needs of others through the duty to care. Kant's account offers numerous strong points, demonstrating how his practical philosophy provides useful treatments of the concept of need. My comments concerning these strengths are divided into five points.

First, the duty of beneficence, because it is a wide duty, involves an imperfect duty to act. As an imperfect duty, it offers only a maxim of actions,[30] not specifying exactly which actions agents must perform to fulfil the duty and leaving agents with the job of judging whether or not the particular actions they contemplate performing are in accordance with the maxim the moral law prescribes. This is important because when moral agents exercise imperfect duties in particular situations, they are able to exhibit sensitivity as they reflect upon whether or not a specific action fits

---

[30] A maxim of actions, can here be understood in conjunction with O'Neill's depiction of maxims as that which 'can … be interpreted as the *fundamental* principles which guide actions, policies and practices' O. O'Neill, *Faces of Hunger: An Essay on Poverty, Development and Justice* (London: George Allen and Unwin, 1986), 132.

under the maxim associated with beneficence. The duty to care, therefore, allows for a wide variety of possible caring responses to need and can promote forms of caring that respond to agents as differently situated.

Second, although the obligation associated with beneficence is universal in the sense of binding all finite rational agents, it does not require that agents meet every need present in the world (an obvious impossibility), that is, it is not owed to every needy person. This is because the scope of imperfect duties is not clearly defined. As such, it avoids an overload of obligations problem.

Relatedly and thirdly, although 'it is impossible to assign determinate limits to the extent of this sacrifice', (*MS* 6: 393; 156) as Kant acknowledges, he also makes it clear that in being beneficent, an agent should not fully sacrifice his or her own welfare. The duty to care incorporates a fair degree of self-regard and a measured consideration of the extent to which self-sacrifice is possible while still maintaining one's effectiveness as a moral agent. Later in the *Metaphysics of Morals*, Kant queries, 'how far should one expend one's resources in practicing beneficence? Surely not to the extent that he himself would finally come to need the beneficence of others' (*MS* 6: 454; 202). Agents are obliged to respond to the constitutive needs of others. But doing so to the extent that in promoting others' self-determined ends and happiness an agent utterly sacrifices his or her own ends and happiness (and therefore welfare) should not occur, as when elevated to a universal law, such a course of action is not tenable. Thus, Kant does not urge a full sacrifice of the caregiver's needs and life projects to the needs of the recipient of care.

Fourth, in treating the duty of beneficence, one can see a unique form of reciprocity at the heart of the duty to care. Importantly, this version of reciprocity moves beyond an exchange model where one person helps another, thereby placing the first person in her debt to return the favour at some immediate or later point in time. Instead, under the rubric of the duty to care, a more flexible model of help in the face of dependence is present. Obligations exist between those in need and those able to give care such that those who can give care should and those who require care will receive it. Given the realities of human finitude, those providing care one moment may be the very individuals to require care in the next.[31]

Fifthly, beneficence as an imperfect duty is action-oriented, providing an objective for the moral agent of securing (or restoring or maintaining, as the case may be) the agency of the one in need. In general, obligations call for actions and, as such, can be associated with what Onora O'Neill calls 'action-centered reasoning'.[32] The point of the duty of beneficence in particular is to help needy others whose capacities have been lessened or harmed to maintain or regain their ability to act as agents and to advance their own self-determined ends. In the process of doing so, agents exercising the duty of beneficence take up the

---

[31] Cf. J. Ebbinghaus, 'Interpretation and Misinterpretation of the Categorical Imperative', *Philosophical Quarterly* **4** (1954): 97–108 and E. F. Kittay, *Love's Labor: Essays on Women, Equality, and Dependency* (New York: Routledge, 1999).

[32] O. O'Neill, 'Rights, Obligations and Needs', *Logos* **6** (1985), 39.

self-determined ends of the one in need as their own. The duty of beneficence commands that I promote others' happiness in accordance with their self-determined, self-defined ends (hence avoiding paternalistic practices).[33] As Kant notes, 'I cannot do good to anyone in accordance with *my* concepts of happiness ... thinking to benefit him by forcing a gift upon him; rather, I can benefit him only in accordance with *his* concepts of happiness' (*MS* 6: 454; 203). Moral agents are to aid others in need in their attempts to promote ends that those needy individuals understand as a condition of their own happiness. In practising the duty to care, caregivers must endeavour to advance the self-determined ends of the one in need; caregivers are to promote the happiness of the care receiver not in accordance with what the caregiver thinks is best, but rather in accordance with the care receiver's own conception of what constitutes his or her own happiness.[34]

5.   The Content of the Duty to Care

The foregoing account presents Kant's role in establishing the foundation and scope of the duty to care. Although a Kantian approach proves helpful in these two respects, it

---

[33] It is important to note, however, that I cannot promote *any* end that another selects for him or herself. I can only promote another's lawful end. It is not morally permissible for individuals to encourage others in ends that are destructive to them.

[34] In caregiving scenarios, situations of incapacitation do arise in which the one in need is not capable of determining what his or her ends and happiness should be. Such cases, however, are not my current focus.

also carries with it significant limitations. While Kant offers useful insights regarding both foundation and scope, he falls short when addressing the concrete content of the duty to care. Through the principle of beneficence, Kant provides the grounds upon which to establish *that* one must respond to the needs of others, but he has unfortunately little to say about exactly *how* one is to respond. Consequently, a complete account of the duty to care requires supplementation. This moment makes clear care ethics' indispensable role in crafting the duty to care. At this juncture, care ethics steps forward, offering rich resources for fashioning the content of the duty to care. As the literature demonstrates, care ethicists such as Groenhout,[35] Kittay,[36] and Tronto[37] have excelled in analyzing relationships of dependency, articulating what count as good forms of care, while also examining elements of oppression and abuse that can arise in caring relationships. This essential knowledge constitutes the substance of promoting another's well-being in responding to their needs.

Thus, care ethics and Kantian ethics, rather than being understood as standing in opposition to one another, relate symbiotically. Care ethics provides the initial

---

[35] R. E. Groenhout, *Connected Lives: Human Nature and an Ethics of Care* (New York: Rowman & Littlefield, 2004).

[36] Op. cit. note 31.

[37] J. Tronto, 'Women and Caring: What Can Feminists Learn About Morality from Caring?' in *Gender/Body/Knowledge*, ed. A. M. Jaggar and S. R. Bordo (New Brunswick: Rutgers University Press, 1989), 172–187.

necessary awareness of the moral importance of needs, hence flagging the area of concern. Next Kantian ethics offers a way to ground the duty to care, while also delimiting the scope of this duty. Care ethics then takes the lead, providing the substantive details of what moral agents are to do in fulfilling their duty to care. But as we will see below, Kantian ethics does offer a few limited suggestions concerning content. Thus, the two approaches complement one another, and when combined, overcome limits found in each other. Ultimately, the relationship between the two can be characterised as one of mutual benefit.

6. Moral Judgment and Moral Perception

In what follows, I treat two content-oriented suggestions that an ethic of care, and to a lesser extent Kantian ethics, have to offer. I first address the skills of moral perception and moral judgment, then turning to dignifying care, a concept I develop to capture the moral significance of the manner in which we meet others' needs.

Joan Tronto has raised the question of whether or not moral agents are able to properly recognise forms of need when they encounter them. It is competence in moral perception that enables them to do so.[38] Tronto notes that perceptions of need can simply be wrong. What is the moral import of such a failing of moral perception? Are moral agents blameworthy when they do not properly identify

---

[38] Op. cit. note 13, 106–8 and 137–41.

forms of need? Are they, moreover, culpable for responding unsympathetically when faced with others' needs? Difficulties in the midst of the needs meeting process can arise even for individuals with fine skills of moral perception. A person may succeed in perceiving many different forms of need and may be sympathetically disposed toward the individual in need, but may not have the ability to analyze the needs recognised so as to enact effective responses that suit the one in need. Tronto presents one safeguard against such difficulties in her four stages of caring by incorporating a stage with a specific focus on the care-receiver. This stage determines whether or not needs are met from the perspective of the one receiving care. Such a move cautions caregivers against privileging their definitions of need, which may or may not map onto care receivers' understanding and experience of their own needs.

Regarding Kant in particular, his discussions of beneficence offer rather limited guidance concerning quandaries of assessing and responding adequately to needs. As moral principles alone cannot do the job, it is moral judgment that serves as the key component in orchestrating practical efforts of moral perception and proper contextual response to need situations. Although it would be incorrect to say that Kant allows no role for moral judgment rendered through awareness of context (analysis of the *Metaphysics of Morals* demonstrates that moral judgment as practiced by individuals does involve contextual awareness[39]), searching

---

[39] See B. Herman, 'The Practice of Moral Judgment' in *The Practice of Moral Judgment* (Cambridge: Harvard University Press, 1993), 73–93.

for additional philosophical help on the matter proves prudent. Care ethics has done much to draw attention to and fill the gap between moral principles and moral practices, in part because of its innovative treatment of moral perception and moral judgment.

Discussions of moral perception and moral judgment are particularly relevant to the duty to care, especially when keeping its relationship with the duty of beneficence in mind. As an imperfect duty, the duty of beneficence does not tell an agent exactly what she or he must do in order to fulfil the duty (as I noted above). Instead, the duty dictates that moral agents must adopt a general end or maxim. In the case of beneficence, the maxim is one of mutual aid and the ends are the happiness and well-being of the one in need. Given that Kant provides little guidance concerning both how moral agents are to identify situations in which the principle applies and exactly how one is to carry it out once the necessity of moral action is determined, turning to discussions of moral perception and moral judgment is helpful.

Moral judgment and moral perception are distinct, yet closely related, moral operations, both of which aid in elucidating core features of sympathetic response to need.[40] According to Lawrence Blum, moral judgment can be captured via two different characteristics: (1) 'to know what a

---

[40] My discussion here is indebted to Lawrence Blum's work. See L. Blum, 'Gilligan and Kohlberg: Implications for Moral Theory', *Ethics* **98**, No. 3 (April, 1988), 472–91 and L. Blum, 'Moral Perception and Particularity', *Ethics* **101**, no. 4 (July 1991), 701–25.

given rule calls upon one to do in a given situation'[41] and (2) 'the recognition of features of a situation as having moral significance and thus as being features which must be taken into account in constructing a principle fully adequate to handle the situation'.[42] Supplementing (1) and (2), moral perception also involves (3) 'the perceptual individuating of the 'situation' as a morally significant one in the first place.[43] All three features have ramifications for the duty to care.

Starting with feature (2), in order to meet the needs of another person, one must first identify that the other is experiencing a constitutive need. If and how one achieves this moment depends upon one's perception of a particular situation. Care ethics generally advocates a heightened degree of attentiveness to those present in our moral lives. Such attentiveness, and the training to become so,[44] appears to be required by the duty to care, inasmuch as one must first be able to identify another's need in order to respond to it. Beyond care ethics, Barbara Herman offers an additional resource of a Kantian kind that concerns the identification of morally significant features of situations. Herman's 'rules of moral salience' detail how moral agents come to understand which features of a situation are morally relevant, and,

---

[41] Ibid., Blum 1991, 709.   [42] Ibid., 710–11.   [43] Ibid., 714.
[44] Nel Noddings discusses attention to the other and generally how one learns to care. See op. cit. note 4 and N. Noddings, *Starting at Home: Caring and Social Policy* (Berkeley: University of California Press, 2002). In addition, see Ruddick op. cit. note 5 for discussions of attentiveness.

as such, should be contained in maxims of action to be tested by the Categorical Imperative.[45]

Regarding feature (1), a moral agent may acknowledge that a person is in need, and may understand that given that this need is present, she is to respond. Even though this much moral work has gone off without a hitch, the agent may be flummoxed when it comes to figuring out how to apply the principle in the sense of discovering the best action to perform to meet the other's need.[46] But knowing how to meet the needs of others is a skill that can be cultivated. Moreover, it is a skill central to good forms of care, and therefore should be incorporated into one's manner of meeting needs. Practices involving sympathy and empathy—understood as moral emotions that bring needs to our attention and guide us in determining how best to respond—can aid significantly in our endeavours to support and promote another's well-being. Finally, feature (3) denotes a general sensitivity agents can develop that enables them to recognize in the first place that a particular situation has moral import. In the context of the duty to care, this feature amounts to awareness of the interconnected and interdependent nature of the human condition, through which moral agents can become attuned to the

---

[45] Op. cit. note 39. Further exploration of Herman's formulation in conjunction with the duty to care would be an interesting project to pursue.

[46] Tronto comments, 'Even if the perception of a need is correct, how the care-givers choose to meet the need can cause new problems' (op. cit. note 13, 108).

moral salience of constitutive needs as seen in the compromised agency of people in need.

7.   Dignifying Care

The notion of dignifying care serves as the second content-
oriented suggestion engendered by a care ethics orientation.
One of the more interesting features of good care is how it
calls forth the dignity of others, acknowledging and preserving their sense of their own value in the process. It is not the
case that caring actions toward others create dignity in them.
Dignity as inherent worth and value resides in each and every
human being independent of the kind of care bestowed upon
them. Dignity can be conceptualized as a potential implicitly
present in individuals; as such it reaches various levels of
expression in persons depending on their life circumstances.
Good care can bring forth the dignity of individuals, making
explicit and actual what was implicit and potential. In short,
good care can be dignifying. Certain forms of care acknowledge the inherent dignity of human beings, sustaining such
dignity as the agency of those in need flourishes in the
presence of another's caring actions. Through our capacity
to care, we acknowledge the dignity of others. What is more,
good care can empower the one in need to experience and
express her own dignity fully. Thus, although care does not
originate dignity in needy individuals, it magnifies, nurtures,
and promotes the inherent dignity of those in need. It is in
this sense that good care can be referred to as *dignifying care.*

Certainly not all care can be considered to
be dignifying.

Caretaking activities, when performed negligently or malevolently, demonstrate the power of care to be anything but dignifying. The *how* of needs response, that is, the manner in which one meets another's needs, is no less than crucial to the dignity of the agent. If needs are met in a way that demeans the one in need, then that individual can suffer additional damage, further compromising her already attenuated agency. In this scenario, her dignity and worth will in no sense be protected, let alone further fostered. Agents can be harmed by the incivility and humiliation of insulting care. Michael Ignatieff exposes the sense of the harm that a derogating and abasing manner of meeting needs produces:

> Giving the aged poor their pension and providing them with medical care may be a necessary condition for their self-respect and their dignity, but it is not a sufficient condition. It is the manner of the giving that counts and the moral basis on which it is given: whether strangers at my door get their stories listened to by the social worker, whether the ambulance man takes care not to jostle them when they are taken down the steep stairs of their apartment building, whether a nurse sits with them in the hospital when they are frightened and alone. Respect and dignity are conferred by gestures such as these.[47]

Ignatieff reminds us that after recognizing that others require our aid to meet their constitutive needs, we can either respond minimally, providing for their needs in order

[47] M. Ignatieff, *The Needs of Strangers* (London: Chatto & Windus, 1984), 16.

to merely secure their survival, or we can respond robustly, caring for them so as to meet their constitutive needs and therewith preserve or foster their agency. In delineating the content of the duty to care, dignifying care recommends the latter course of action.

A final note on dignifying care: as Julius Ebbinghaus acknowledged, in discussing the duty of beneficence, Kant lays out the terms of what it is to give and to receive help, terms that are enhanced through my account of the duty to care.[48] The picture that emerges is not one in which there are two distinct groups—those who can care and those who cannot—forever etched in stone. In exploring the value of caring and the dignifying effect of care, one sees that the lines are not so clearly drawn. Those of us who lend our dignifying care to others in this particular moment may be the very ones to require the bolstering effect of dignifying care in the next. The value of caring and dignifying care form the warp and woof of interdependently interwoven lives and personalities, from which emerge moments when some are called upon to care, while others receive this care. Bound by the duty to care, we give as we can. Finite and inevitably dependent, we receive when in need.

8.   Conclusion

This paper has featured the duty to care, an obligation that requires moral agents to respond to the constitutive needs of

[48] Op. cit. note 31.

others. This duty combines useful elements of Kantian and care ethics, and reveals their possible symbiosis. Kantian beneficence offers a solid foundation for a universal obligation to respond to the constitutive needs of others. As such, Kant's theory builds upon care ethicists' claim that needs are morally important by establishing that moral agents are obligated to meet others' needs. But this move, absent further consideration of what comprises the content of the duty to care, is lacking. With the addition of care theorists' views on moral perception, moral judgment and dignifying care, the duty to care moves from principle to practice, taking form as a robust moral component delineated in terms of foundation, scope and content.

7   Needs, Facts, Goodness, and Truth

JONATHAN LOWE

In this paper I want to explore certain parallels between the logic of action and the logic of belief or, as it might otherwise be put, between practical and theoretical reasoning and rationality. The parallels will be seen to involve an ontological dimension as well as psychological and linguistic dimensions. It may help to begin by mentioning how I was drawn into an examination of these parallels. This was through becoming convinced of the correctness of an *externalist* account of reasons for action, having been persuaded of this by, amongst other things, arguments found in Jonathan Dancy's recent book on the subject, *Practical Reality*.[1] Externalism about reasons for action appeared to me to be, on reflection, the only view that one could plausibly adopt in conjunction with a libertarian account of free will—the latter being a position which I am now convinced is not only coherent but entirely defensible and indeed correct. Oddly enough, however, recent debates concerning internalist versus externalist accounts of reasons for action tend to have been dominated by moral philosophers, whereas those concerning compatibilist versus libertarian accounts of free will tend to

---

[1] See Jonathan Dancy, *Practical Reality* (Oxford: Oxford University Press, 2000).

have been dominated by philosophers of action. As a consequence of this, the two debates have been carried on relatively independently of each other—in my view, to the detriment of both. The present paper is part of a larger exercise of trying to bring them together.

1.

Very roughly, what I want to say about a voluntary action, freely undertaken after deliberation, is this. The agent makes a choice in the light of reasons disclosed by the deliberative process. This choice is a mental event—what early modern philosophers like Locke would have called a volition or exercise of the will. But it is an event which does not have a sufficient cause in the form of antecedent events of either a mental or a physical nature. This does not mean, however, that it is a mere 'chance' event, like the spontaneous decay of a radium atom. For choice is normally made in the light of reason. Reasons for action are considerations which speak in favour of or against one's acting in a certain way. When one acts freely in the light of such reasons, by choosing to act in one way rather than another, one is not *caused* so to choose by certain of those reasons, for then one's action would not be free. The famous arguments of Donald Davidson notwithstanding, reasons are not causes.[2]

On the Davidsonian account, reasons for action are beliefs and desires, and the reasons for which an agent acted

[2] See Donald Davidson, 'Actions, Reasons, and Causes', in his *Essays on Actions and Events* (Oxford: Clarendon Press, 1980).

on a given occasion are beliefs and desires which caused him so to act, while also 'rationalizing' the action by representing it, under an appropriate description, as something which would serve to satisfy those desires given the truth of those beliefs. However, to be *caused* to act in a certain way by certain of one's beliefs and desires is not consistent with one's acting rationally. It may be that by so acting one is doing something *reasonable*, but because one is not freely choosing to do it in the light of objective considerations favouring that choice, one is not acting rationally. The basic point here is that causes bring about their effects with complete indifference to the question of whether or not there are objective considerations in favour of those effects being brought about. But free and rational agents cannot act freely and rationally with indifference to such considerations and so cannot, in acting freely and rationally, be caused to act by their beliefs and desires.

This is not to deny that we are sometimes caused to act as we do by our beliefs and desires, only to deny that on those occasions we are acting rationally. Nor is it to deny that when we act rationally we possess beliefs and desires whose contents are relevant to the way in which we act. For it is the *contents* of such beliefs and desires that constitute our reasons for acting as we do, though not the beliefs and desires themselves, as an internalist account of reasons for action would maintain. (I shall modify this claim later in the paper, but not in a way that undercuts my opposition to an internalist account of reasons for action.) A simple example may help to illustrate what is at issue here. Suppose that I am standing under the eaves of a dilapidated house and that a loose slate is sliding down the roof in such a way that it is likely to land on my head. This conjunction of circumstances gives me a reason to jump away from the spot on which I am standing. But, obviously, I cannot act on that reason unless I am aware of the circumstances. I must, for instance, believe, or at least suspect, that a slate is sliding towards me and that if it hits me I shall be seriously injured. Now, it may be that my acquisition of this belief, together with other factors, causes me to jump out of the way without any process of deliberation and choice taking place. In that case, my action is instinctive and automatic. It is certainly a reasonable way to act in the circumstances, but it is not a rational action because it is not freely chosen in the light of the reason for so acting which my belief discloses to me.

Saying that the action is in this case not rational is by no means intended as a criticism of it or of myself as its agent. On the contrary, we would surely not survive in a hazardous world if all of our actions had to be freely chosen in the light of reasons disclosed to us. At the same time, it is important to recognize that what makes us different from other animals is that we are at least sometimes able to act rationally. If we adapt the example of the falling slate, allowing me plenty of time to be aware of its trajectory and the danger that its fall presents to me, we can envisage my subsequent act of jumping to be a genuinely rational one. It will be so, if I jump as a result of choosing to jump, in the light of the reason for jumping that is disclosed to me by my awareness of the falling slate and the danger that it presents. But, whether I jump rationally or merely instinctively, in the latter case being caused to jump by my belief that the slate is falling and presents a danger, my reason for jumping is not that *belief*—a psychological state of mind—but its *content*. Or, more precisely, it is *the state of affairs* represented as obtaining by the propositional content of that belief, namely, the fact that the slate is falling and presents a danger to me. It is an insistence upon this point that distinguishes the externalist from the internalist view of reasons for action.

Davidson famously argued that the only way of identifying the reason *for* which an agent acted on a given occasion—as opposed to reasons which the agent may have possessed for so acting but did not in fact act upon—is to pick it out as the one that caused the action. He, of course, was assuming the truth of internalism and took the reason in question to be a *belief* of the agent, not the content of any such belief. (More precisely, he took it to be a conjunction of certain beliefs and desires of the agent.) But it may seem that internalism is supported by the fact that Davidson has this way of answering the question as to which reason was, as things turned out, the agent's actual reason for acting as he did. Not so.

First of all, Davidson's account famously falls foul of the problem of wayward or deviant causal chains, which has never been convincingly solved. The problem involves cases, like Davidson's own well-known example of the nervous climber, in which belief and desire both cause and 'rationalize' an action which is, nonetheless, unintentional on the part of the agent.[3] Secondly, and more importantly in the

---

[3] See Donald Davidson, 'Freedom to Act', in his *Essays on Actions and Events*.

present context, the libertarian account of freedom that I am endorsing has a satisfactory answer to Davidson's question on its own terms. When an agent acts freely and rationally, the reason *for* which he acts is simply the reason on which he *chose* to act. The agent himself determines, by exercising his power of choice, which of various reasons for or against acting in a certain way he acts upon in any given case—selecting, of course, only from those reasons of which he is aware as a result of his deliberations, for one evidently cannot choose to act in the light of a reason of which one is not aware.

2.

So far I have been trying to sketch and defend a picture of rational action which is at once libertarian and externalist, in strong contrast with the dominant contemporary model, which is compatibilist and internalist.[4] Now, however, I have to explain what all of this has to do with the subject of *needs*. For all that I have said so far, it might appear that reasons for action, construed in the externalist fashion that I have recommended, are *facts* or *states of affairs*, disclosed to the agent as the contents of certain of his or her propositional attitudes, most obviously his or her beliefs. This seems to fit the case of the falling slate well enough, at first sight. My reason for jumping out of the way, it may be said,

---

[4] For a fuller account, see my 'Personal Agency', in Anthony O'Hear (ed.), *Minds and Persons* (Cambridge: Cambridge University Press, 2003).

is the fact that the slate is falling towards me and thus presents a danger to me. This fact is something of which I may become aware through perception, thereby becoming the content of a belief of mine, and in the light of that belief I may choose to jump out of the way—assuming that I have time to choose, and do not simply act instinctively on account of that belief.

But now it may be complained, invoking the venerable authority of Hume, that I cannot be expected to jump out of the way in virtue of holding that belief unless I also possess an appropriate desire, in this case the desire not to be injured by the slate. Belief alone, it is said, is insufficient to move any agent to action. My first response to this is to say that this may perhaps be so where non-rational actions are concerned. In the case in which I instinctively jump out of the way of the slate, without exercising a free choice, perhaps it must indeed be the case that I am caused so to move at least in part by a desire not to be injured, not just by the belief that the slate is likely to injure me. However, whether or not this is so seems to me to be an empirical psychological question, which cannot be settled by a priori philosophical reflection on the nature of such actions. Be that as it may, I am not primarily concerned, in any case, with non-rational actions in which I am caused to act as I do by my antecedent psychological states, whether these be beliefs or desires or combinations of them both. I am primarily concerned with rational actions, taking these to be understood along the lines sketched previously. So the issue for me now is whether any comparable complaint can be raised against this view of rational action on account of its taking reasons for action to be constituted solely by *facts* or *states of affairs* disclosed to the agent through his or her beliefs.

It would seem that an analogous complaint can indeed be raised. This is that facts can only constitute reasons for *belief*, not reasons for *action*. If it sometimes seems as though we can present reasons for action as being facts of a certain kind, this is really only a subterfuge, or so it may be said. For example, the fact that the slate is falling and about to hit me certainly constitutes a reason for me to believe that I am likely to be injured unless I take avoiding action by jumping out of its way. But it doesn't seem that this fact, or this fact alone, suffices to constitute a reason for me to jump in these circumstances. Something is still missing from our account. It might be suggested that what is missing is the fact, or supposed fact, that being injured in this way is *not in my interests*. After all, it may be said, we can surely envisage cases in which it *would* be in an agent's interests to be injured by a falling slate—for example, so that he or she could collect a large amount of money from an insurance company. We were just taking it for granted in the present case that it was not in my interests to be injured, so this presumed fact must be added to give a proper and full account of what constituted a reason for me to jump on this occasion.

But what kind of *fact* is it that something or other is 'not in my interests', or that something else *is* 'in my interests'? This sort of locution is hardly perspicuous, even if it is commonplace. The danger at this point is that we shall fall back into the clutches of internalism and be persuaded to say that what something's being 'in my interests' ultimately amounts to—all that it *can* ultimately amount to—is the fact that I desire it. The very word 'interest' encourages this identification with something of a psychological character, and desire naturally presents itself as the appropriate psychological category to invoke in order to classify it. The only way to avoid this sort of psychologism about reasons for action and to represent reasons for action as something objective and external, while at the same time locating them within the realm of facts or states of affairs, is to invoke some sort of distinction between those facts or states of affairs which are apt only to constitute reasons for belief and those that are apt instead to constitute reasons for action. The former may perhaps be distinguished as being purely 'descriptive' facts, the latter as being 'normative' facts—in a broad sense of 'normative', no doubt, which is suited to embrace both properly 'moral' facts and also merely 'prudential' facts.

However, if we proceed down this route we shall obviously find ourselves enmired in the seemingly endless disputes about the so-called fact/value distinction. Many philosophers find the notion of a 'normative fact' virtually a contradiction in terms. Facts as such, they say, are value-free. Values are projected by us and perhaps by other intelligent beings upon a world that is essentially or intrinsically valueless. The idea that there might be moral or even prudential facts is dismissed as 'queer' and incompatible with a naturalistic view of the world as disclosed to us by science.[5] Such facts, it seems, would not be empirically detectable in

[5] I have in mind here J. L. Mackie's famous 'argument from queerness': see his *Ethics: Inventing Right and Wrong* (Harmondsworth: Penguin Books, 1977), 38–42.

248

the way that scientific facts supposedly always are, unless we impute to ourselves a special faculty of moral sense which is apparently inconsistent with a naturalistic account of the physical and psychological make-up of human beings and other animals.

In the light of such seeming metaphysical difficulties, the advocate of normative facts may be pressured into according them a subordinate status, constructing them as 'social' facts founded on culturally accepted conventions or as 'subjective' facts resulting from the 'projection' of our desires and emotions upon aspects of our social and physical environments. Such subterfuges should be resolutely resisted by advocates of the objectivity of reasons for action. A wrong turning was taken in trying to force reasons for action into the mould of reasons for belief, for this is almost bound to result in the former being construed as facts or states of affairs of a peculiar and ill-defined kind. A better strategy by far for the objectivist is to find an altogether different ontological category to house reasons for action. And, indeed, the very language of action and practical reasoning suggests that precisely this is the right strategy to adopt.

3.

Belief is rightly classified as a propositional attitude whose aim is truth—and truth consists in correspondence to fact. I take this to be a truism, rather than a rash commitment to a specific theory of truth. That is to say, I am not suggesting that the concept of truth may be defined in terms of independently intelligible concepts of 'correspondence' and 'fact', though nor do I wish to rule out the possibility of such a definition. My point at present is just that the verb 'believe' may be complemented by a 'that'-clause and that when it is the case that S *believes truly* that *p*, it follows that it is a *fact* that *p*, or that what S believes is a fact. This is a purely semantic point which can hardly be denied by any theory of truth that aspires to respect the meanings of the words 'believe', 'true', and 'fact' that belong to the English language and have their equivalents in all other human languages known to us. Because it is the case that *what* we believe, when we believe truly, is a fact, it is also the case that *facts* are those items that are apt to constitute reasons for belief. A fact can be a reason for belief, because it can entail or confirm—more generally, it can *support*—the truth of a belief. For example, the belief that the earth is round is supported by the fact, amongst others, that ships disappear over the horizon as they get more distant from the observer.

In order to see what sort of item can constitute a reason for action, it will help to consider how the language of action both resembles and differs from the language of belief. Beliefs, we have noted, are propositional attitudes: they are psychological states whose 'contents' are propositions. We may say this much uncontentiously, without delving into the metaphysics of propositions. For present purposes, we need not concern ourselves overmuch with what propositions themselves are. Now, actions are certainly not propositional attitudes. For one thing, they are events rather than states. Still, an action has an agent, just as a belief has a subject. And in both cases this is a person, or at least an animal of some kind. Indeed, it would seem to be the case that those things that are subjects of belief are necessarily also agents of actions, and vice versa: only a believer can be an agent, and only an agent can be a believer.

However, while subjects 'hold' beliefs, they 'perform' actions. We can regiment belief-statements in the general form 'S believes that p'. Here the subject of the belief is S, the belief held by the subject is the belief that p, and the content of the subject's belief is the proposition p. How can we analogously regiment action-statements? In the following way, which brings out both the similarities and the differences between belief and action. The general form of an action-statement, we may say, is 'A does x'. Here A is the agent of the action, the action performed by the agent is the action of doing x, and finally, we might say, the content of the agent's action is the act x. An example will help. Suppose that A raises his arm. We may regiment this in the form—which admittedly sounds either slightly strained or somewhat archaic—'A does raise his arm'. The point to get across, however, is that *what* the agent does—raise his arm—is distinguishable from his *action* of raising his arm in a manner that is analogous to the distinction between a belief and its propositional content. I propose to reserve the term 'act' for the 'content' of an action, and refer to this kind of content as 'actual content', in deliberate contrast with the 'propositional content' of beliefs and other so-called propositional attitudes.

The virtue of this kind of analysis lies not only in the comparisons it sustains between belief and action but also in the means it provides to distinguish perspicuously between *actions*, conceived as particular events, and the abstract items that form the 'contents' not only of actions themselves but also of those psychological states of an agent that are specifically 'directed' upon action—states such as intending and trying, which we could collectively call 'conative' states and which constitute the present-day equivalents of the volitions or acts of will favoured by early modern philosophers of mind and action like Hobbes and Locke. *What* we intend or try is to do *such-and-such*, where 'such-and-such' is a place-holder for what I am calling an 'act'. (Of course, it is also sometimes what we *desire*, for we must distinguish between desiring *that* and desiring *to*.) I intend or try, for instance, to *raise my arm*. If I am successful, I perform an action which consists in my doing just what I intended or tried to do, namely, *raise my arm*. It is important here to appreciate that what I intend or try to do is not *the action* which, if I am successful, I will go on to perform. That action is a particular event, which has not yet occurred when I begin my attempt to act. To be successful in my attempt, I do not have to intend to bring about the very event which, as it turns out, will constitute my successful action. That would make intentional action virtually impossible for beings with our cognitive limitations. For my attempt to be successful, it suffices that *some* action of mine should ensue which satisfies the content of my prior intention, which was to *raise my arm*. Any one of many—perhaps even infinitely many—numerically distinct possible actions could meet this requirement. This sort of consideration, then, appears to justify the kind of articulation of action-statements that I am proposing, with its distinctions between agent, action, and act. Acts, thus conceived, are abstract items in the same way—whatever exactly that is—that propositions are and must be distinguished clearly from the concrete events that are particular actions, just as propositions must be distinguished from the concrete states that are particular beliefs.

However, there the similarity between acts and propositions ends. Propositions are expressed by that-clauses, or by whole sentences, whereas acts are expressed by infinitival verb-phrases, such as '[to] raise my arm'. This verb-phrase is apt, as we have seen, to express both what I may intend or try to do on a given occasion, and what it is that I succeed in doing when such an intention or attempt is successful. In both cases, it expresses a certain *act*. Because acts are not propositions, they cannot, of course, have truth-values. Propositions are true or false, and beliefs are correspondingly true or false in virtue of the truth or falsehood of their propositional contents. Because acts cannot have truth-values, however, *reasons* for action, unlike reasons for belief, cannot be facts. They must be items belonging to some other and suitable ontological category. What could that category be? The items in question must be ones which in some appropriate sense *support* actions, in a manner analogous to that in which facts support beliefs.

We do not have to look far for a suitable category of items. The category in question is surely the category of *needs*. These items have, as it were, precisely the right sort of 'logical shape' to constitute reasons for action. Again, a simple example will help. Just as the fact that distant ships disappear over the horizon supports the belief that the earth is round so, it might well be said, the need to eat supports the action of sowing corn. Or again, to return to our example of the falling

253

slate, the need to avoid life-threatening injury supports the action of jumping out of the way of a falling slate. But what exactly *is* a need, then? This is a bit like asking: what exactly *is* a fact? By pointing this out, I don't mean to suggest that the question is an illegitimate one, only that it is no less difficult than the corresponding question concerning facts and also that this difficulty should no more deter us from referring to needs and citing them as reasons than we should be deterred from doing the same in the case of facts. I hope it will not seem disappointing if I say that I shall not attempt to answer this difficult question in the present paper. For my present purposes it suffices to identify needs as items belonging to a distinct ontological category and as having a 'logical shape' which suits them, unlike facts, to constitute reasons for action of an objective kind.

Some may press me at this point concerning my assumption that needs may be 'objective'—by which I mean 'mind-independent', in the sense that a need is an item that can exist whether or not anyone is aware of its existence and so does not exist simply because one or more people believe that it exists. However, there are philosophers who would equally want to press my assumption that *facts* are 'objective' in this sense—anti-realists of various stripes. This is much too big an issue to take on here. And the same applies with regard to the corresponding question concerning needs. The important strategic advantage of identifying reasons for actions as needs rather than as a putative special class of 'normative' facts is that it puts needs and facts on the same footing with regard to such big questions of realism versus anti-realism.

4.

There is an obvious question which arises at this point, given that the parallels between reasons for action and reasons for belief so far advanced are accepted. What is it that stands to needs as truth stands to facts? We have noted that acts—the contents of actions—cannot have truth-values in the way that the contents of beliefs—propositions—do. Correspondingly, actions cannot be true or false in virtue of their contents, in the way that beliefs can. The obvious, and I think correct, thing to say is that the equivalent of truth in the domain of action is *goodness*, understood in a suitably broad sense which is not exclusively moral in import, but which includes moral goodness as a special case. Just as a true belief is one which corresponds to fact, so a good action is one which corresponds to need. In another idiom, just as facts are the truth-makers of true beliefs, so needs are the goodness-makers of good actions.

We can extend the parallel between goodness and truth to capture what is similar and what is different between practical and theoretical reasoning, or the logic of action and the logic of belief. A valid argument in the logic of belief is one that is *truth-preserving*, while an inductively strong argument is one which preserves probability of truth. Analogously, then, we may say that a valid argument in the logic of action is one that is *goodness-preserving*, while an inductively strong argument is one which preserves probability of goodness. A simple example will serve to illustrate the notion of goodness-preservation. Given that it is good to do both x and y, it follows that it is good to do x. For instance, given that it is good for me to both eat and drink, it follows that it is good for me to eat. However, we should not expect the logic of action to resemble in every respect the logic of belief, simply because goodness-makers are very different from truth-makers. Needs are very different from facts. One very important difference is that facts cannot conflict with one another, but needs can—both the needs of different people and different needs of the same person. Because facts cannot conflict with one another, truth is unitary and indivisible. But goodness, it seems, is not like that.

Suppose, for example, that I am lost in the desert with a very small supply of water in my water-bottle. I need to drink, but I also need to conserve water. These needs conflict, however. The action of drinking would be good, as would be the action of conserving water, but I cannot perform both actions—at least, I cannot both drink all of the water in the bottle now and also conserve some of it for later use, or both conserve all of it for later use and drink some of it now. The good thing to do is to compromise, by drinking some of the water now and conserving the rest for later use. By contrast, compromise is never required in the domain of facts, because facts cannot conflict. Formally, this difference is reflected in the contrast between the following two inference-patterns, the first of which is valid and the second of which is not: 'It is true that p and it is true that q, therefore it is true that p and q', as opposed to 'It is good to x and it is good to y, therefore it is good to x and y'. We have already seen one putative counter-example to the validity of the second inference-pattern. Here is another. Suppose it is agreed that it is good to be self-sufficient and that it is also good to give all of one's possessions to the poor. It can hardly be concluded that it is good to both be self-sufficient and give all of one's possessions to the poor, because it is impossible to do both. We have to choose between two incompatible courses of action, each of them good in its own way—or else we have to compromise. While we likewise have to choose between incompatible beliefs, however, we cannot regard each such belief as being true in its own way, nor can we compromise about truth. There is only one way in which beliefs can be true. Truth is single and indivisible, but goodness is not.

What I have said about this matter is extremely sketchy and may fail to convince for that reason. In a fuller account, I would need to be much more specific about the individuation of acts, actions, and needs. I have spoken, for instance, of a need to eat, an action which satisfies that need—someone's eating something—and the act that is the 'content' of such an action, the act of eating something. But, of course, we could and perhaps should be much more specific about all items of these kinds. In like manner, we may loosely speak of the belief that it is raining, appreciating that we should more precisely talk about a particular person's belief on a particular occasion that it is raining in a specified place at a specified time. Similar precisifications no doubt can and in principle should be included in our talk about acts, actions, and needs. We could talk, thus, of a particular person's action on a particular occasion of eating some specific object in a specified place at a specified time. However, I see no reason to suppose that the main thrust of what I have said so far about the logic of action and the relationship between goodness and needs would be at all affected by such precisification. Sometimes being precise is not a virtue in philosophy, because it hinders our ability to see the main features of a position clearly.

Another issue that I have skirted around is the following apparent difference between goodness and truth: goodness seems to be a matter of degree, while truth does not. Relatedly, it may be said that the goodness of some actions outweighs that of others, but that all truths have the same weight. However, these apparent differences between goodness and truth are not incontestable. Some logicians maintain that there are degrees of truth and try to explain various semantic phenomena of vagueness in these terms. Again, it is often urged by philosophers of pragmatist leanings that some truths are more important than others. In view of such disagreements, I think it better to leave these questions aside for present purposes, important though they are.

5.

What I have been proposing in this paper is that we should take needs seriously, from an ontological point of view. Only then, I have suggested, shall we be able to understand clearly how the logic of action both resembles and differs from the logic of belief and how practical rationality both resembles and differs from theoretical rationality. Needs constitute objective reasons for actions. They are what make actions good, analogously to the way in which facts make beliefs true. Very arguably, just as we do not need to invoke false-makers to account for false beliefs, neither do we need to invoke badness-makers to account for bad actions. Plausibly, just as a false belief is one that fails to correspond to any fact, so a bad action is one that fails to correspond to any need. Be that as it may, the important point, ontologically speaking, is that needs exist and are items which belong to a distinctive ontological category, different from that of facts. To articulate clearly the nature of needs, we would need to provide a full account of the existence- and identity-conditions of needs, and that is not something that I have attempted to do here. It is a very big task which goes far beyond the limited ambitions of the present paper. The central lesson, however, of the present paper is that the world is not just a world of states of affairs—to echo the title of a well-known and excellent book by David Armstrong.[6] To put it another way, the world is not just, in the famous words of Wittgenstein, 'everything that is the case'.[7] Rather, it is a world that is also permeated by needs—to the extent, at least, that it is a world inhabited by agents who possess reasons for action. Whether those needs can be accounted for in wholly 'naturalistic' terms—whatever precisely that is taken to mean—is another question that is too big for me to address on this occasion. I would only emphasize that if, by a 'naturalistic' account of needs, is meant one which somehow reduces the existence of needs to the existence of certain scientifically describable facts, then I hold out no hope for such an account.

[6] See D. M. Armstrong, *A World of States of Affairs* (Cambridge: Cambridge University Press, 1997).

[7] See Ludwig Wittgenstein, *Tractatus Logico-Philosophicus*, trans. C. K. Ogden (London: Routledge and Kegan Paul, 1922), 1.

8   Fundamental Needs

GARRETT THOMSON

The concept of need is promising and alluring because of three factors:

1. Needs are objective because it is a discoverable matter of fact what needs a person has and yet this fact has a bearing on what one ought to do. The concept is both factual and evaluative.
2. Needs are matters of priority; what we need usually overrides other reasons for action.
3. Needs are unimpeachable values. We cannot say truly that a person ought to have different needs and, in this sense, they are fundamental.

In this paper, I shall be concerned primarily with explaining the third of these features. I am interested in fundamental needs, but not necessarily basic or minimal needs, such as those pertaining to survival. Furthermore, I shall not be concerned directly in the strength of claims to need on other people, but rather on oneself. I shall use 'need' in such a way that the term indicates a disposition and does not imply a lack. I need food even when I am eating.

A definition of 'need' requires a distinction between 'need' and 'desire' and, perhaps more problematically and centrally, between fundamental and instrumental needs. An instrumental need is a necessary condition for the obtaining of a goal or for the satisfaction of a desire. To claim that X is needed instrumentally is simply to assert that X is a necessary condition for the obtaining of the contextually relevant goal, whatever that happens to be. It does not imply that the goal or desire in question is in any special way important or even good for the life of the subject.

In contrast, to claim that X is a fundamental need for person A is to assert that X is a non-derivative, non-circumstantially specific and an inescapable necessary condition in order for the person A not to undergo serious harm. There is nothing that the person can do to change this fact. In this manner, one of the main features of the concept of a fundamental need is that it makes a virtue of natural necessity by cutting down options and, thereby, simplifying choice. One has no choice except having X or undergoing serious harm.[1]

I will assume that there is a distinction to be drawn between instrumental and fundamental needs, and I shall examine the implications of this for the concept of serious harm. How can we explicate the nature of 'serious harm' in such a way that allows us to maintain this distinction?

1.   Inescapability

Let us examine the ways in which the concept of need exploits and is shaped by natural necessity, or the different

---

[1] D. Wiggins, *Needs, Values, Truth: Essays in the Philosophy of Value*, (Oxford: Blackwell, 1987), and G. Thomson, *Needs* (London: Routledge, 1987), Chapter 1.

respects in which fundamental needs are inescapable. This feature of 'need' is important because one way of challenging a claim to X, which is different from showing that it is overridden as a reason, is to undermine it. One undermines a claim to X by revealing that it is dependent on conditions that ought not to obtain. For instance, a claim to X that is derivative on desires can be undermined by showing that the person would be better off not having, or ought not have, the desires in question.

In contrast, in the case of inescapable needs, such an undermining is by definition impossible. If a need is inescapable then it is redundant to ask whether we ought to have it. 'Ought' implies 'can' and, therefore, 'cannot' implies 'not ought.' There can be no question of whether one ought or ought not to have the inescapable needs one has. Consequently, we are justified in treating inescapable needs as given in practical reasoning in the sense that such 'need'-claims cannot be undermined by showing that they depend on conditions that ought not to obtain. We have to accept the fact that we have the fundamental needs that we do have. In this manner, such needs are different from addictions, which one might be better off not having; and, in this sense, I cannot reduce my needs.

Fundamental needs are inescapable in two related ways.

1. A fundamental need for X is itself inescapable in the sense that the fact that X is causally necessary for not suffering serious harm cannot be altered. The causal link is inescapable.

2. The harm itself must be inescapable. The fundamental sense of 'need' determines that the antecedent of a 'need'-statement must be A's life or the quality of his or her life, or more specifically, the avoidance of an especially serious type of harm. The concept of need, in this rich sense, also determines that what counts as relevant harm to A must be inescapable. One cannot escape a fundamental need by altering what substantially counts as harm. In this way, the concept of harm as employed by 'fundamental need' requires a certain lack of plasticity.

I would like to end this section with two observations regarding the inescapability of fundamental needs.

First, the term 'need' in its fundamental use has a connotation of practical necessity. What one needs, one cannot forgo. Objects of fundamental need are practically necessary in part because needs are naturally necessary. In using the term 'need,' we exploit the notion of natural necessity so as to force our hand practically.

Second, the notion of inescapability can help explain why or in what sense fundamental needs may form part of the essential nature of a person. 'Need' contains the idea that A needs X to be A or to function as A, and this implies that the end-state for which X is needed by A is defined by A's essential nature. In order to avoid some of the metaphysical complications that arise from such a claim, I suggest that we should understand it in terms of three points, namely that:

a) A's need is non-derivative; if A needs X fundamentally then A needs X not in virtue of needing something else.

b) A's need is non-circumstantial; it does not depend on specific circumstances but rather is a need that the person carries from one situation to another.

c) A's need is inescapable.

The third of these implications has the most obvious significance for practical reasoning.

2. Harm

A person is harmed when he or she is deprived of engaging in non-instrumentally valuable experiences and activities, as well as the possibility of appreciating them. By 'experiences,' I mean something we undergo or live through. An important task in explicating 'harm' is to explain what constitutes the value of these activities and experiences.

A desire theory of harm would explain such values in terms of the activities being desired by the subject. However, if there is a distinction between fundamental and instrumental needs, then harm cannot be constituted by the non-satisfaction of desires or preferences. If it were so constituted, then all so-called fundamental needs would be a species of instrumental needs. The distinction requires that harm should not be explicated in terms of desire-satisfaction.

The desire account tries to define the value of activities in terms of their being the objects of desire or of informed preferences.[2] In so doing, it urges us to accept our desires at face value, as a given. To understand

---

[2] J. Griffin, *Well-Being* (Oxford: Clarendon Press, 1986).

well-being and harm, one does not have to look beyond them and ask why we desire what we do. In this way, it urges an uncritical attitude to our wants and preferences. In opposition to this, I would suggest that desires act as a guide to the relevant kind of non-instrumental value and that, as a guide, they can mislead us. If they are merely guides then desires do not constitute the relevant kind of non-instrumental values. This suggestion indicates the need for a critical attitude towards one's desires. Such an attitude does not imply mistrust, but it does necessitate trying to identify the interests that motivate our desires, as we shall see.

It is time to sketch briefly the beginnings of an alternative theory. Activities and experiences are worthwhile because they have desirability-characteristics. When we explain what makes an activity worthwhile, we usually cite general desirability features of the activity. For example, an activity is exciting, soothing, engaging, and so on. Such characterizations show what makes the activity valuable.

What is the relation between these characteristics and our desires? There are two extreme positions. On the one hand, there is the desire theory, which we have already rejected, which claims that desirability features are entirely derivative on our wants. On the other hand, some thinkers advocate that desirability characterizations do not depend at all on our wants, but rather explain them. We want things that we perceive to have such characterizations.[3]

[3] See M. Platts, *Ways of Meaning*, (London: Routledge, 1979) and 'Morality and the End of Desire', in M. Platts (ed.) *Reference, Truth and Reality* (London: Routledge, 1980).

I shall advocate a view that combines these two positions. It rejects the idea that desirability is entirely independent of desire on the grounds that what is desirable for one person might not be for another. (This is not the claim that what a person thinks is desirable for himself might be different from what another thinks is desirable for herself; it is the assertion that what actually is desirable for one person might not be for another.) In other words, some of the psychological differences between people will amount to the fact that, for one person, X is desirable and for others not. On the other hand, the position we are advocating rejects the identification of the desirability of X for A with A desiring X. Part of the problem is that object-individuated desire is too specific. Although these characterizations depend on general features of our desires, they do not depend on specific conscious wants.

Our motivational make-up cannot be entirely irrelevant to our well-being. The fact that we are broadly socially motivated creatures is surely relevant to what constitutes a good life and harm, even if that cannot be spelled out directly and specifically in terms of what a person wants (or would want under certain conditions).

Freud realized that even our deepest desires have a motivational source behind them, of which we are not usually aware.[4] Unfortunately, he tended to think of this as yet another desire, albeit unconscious. Freud's insight does

[4] S. Freud, 'Instincts and their Vicissitudes,' *Standard Edition of the Psychological Works of S.Freud*, Vol. 14, 111 (International University Press, 1964).

not have to be couched in Freudian terms of repressed unconscious sexual desires. Freed from the particularities of the Freudian message, the important insight is that desires for very different things can have a similar motivational source. Wants are structured by this source.

This insight is important, and should be developed, because it allows us to recognize that our motivational nature as individuals, as members of a culture and of a species, is relevant in determining what counts as well-being and harm. It permits us to recognize this, without trapping us in the idea that obtaining what one wants is all there is to value. It allows us to distinguish between the feeling 'I have to get what I want' and the idea that one's life has to fit one's nature as a person. It requires us to separate the specific thing that a desire is directed towards (the object of desire) and the general source or motivational nature of the desire. This permits a mature attitude towards wanting than that which exclusively focuses on getting exactly what one desires.

To develop this idea, we require a theory of the interpretation of desire, which allows us to distinguish interests and desires in a way that is relevant to well-being. First, in our everyday life, we need to understand our motivational natures in a way that transcends knowing our existing preferences identified in terms of their specific objects. We need such comprehension in order to be able to predict what people would want and like in hypothetical situations, and to anticipate how our desires alter in changing circumstances. For example, when one cannot obtain exactly what one wants, one's desire switches to something relevantly similar. The standard desire or preference account cannot explain adequately what counts as 'relevantly similar' insofar as it simply lists preferences and thereby ignores their structure or the patterns of our desires.

Furthermore, the desire theory implies that value must be defined in terms of getting exactly what one wants. It disallows the idea that it can be defined more broadly using the concept of something relevantly similar to an existing desire. For these reasons, to understand harm, we require an account of desire that does not take wants at their face value and which attempts to interpret them. Implicitly, this critical attitude implies that there is more to the concept of 'better' than simply the satisfaction of preference.

Second, our capacity to live well and fully is not restricted to satisfying our existing desires, which are limited by our beliefs and character traits. We can reach beyond them to something better. In other words, new situations can bring new desires or preferences that the individual might never have imagined and which can constitute an improvement over the actual. Once again, this implies that there is more to the concept of 'better' than simply the satisfaction of preferences.

Third, in effect, the standard economic theory of utility ignores the intentionality of desire. Desires are intentional, and this means that an object of desire is always wanted under a certain description and not under others, and that we are not necessarily aware of every aspect of our desire. Because of this intentionality, the process of understanding desire should be thought of hermeneutically. It is a question of interpreting or reading desire and not just identifying the object that is wanted.

3. The Hermeneutics of Desire

In our everyday practice, we interpret people's desires without necessarily taking at face value their word concerning how this should be done. We read between the lines of verbalized conscious desires to find broader patterns but without impugning unconscious drives to the individual. Hermeneutics constitutes an approach to understanding desire that is significantly different from both the economic model and psychoanalytic theory, which postulates unconscious drives. In our everyday interpretations of people's wants, we usually employ a method that is hermeneutical. It is holistic and self-critical.

At the same time, this interpretation often involves characterizing desires in terms of their motivating interests. Here I am employing the word 'interest' in a special and unusual way, which needs explanation. Desires can be instrumental or non-instrumental; instrumental desires are directed to things wanted as means to something else. Things wanted non-instrumentally are desired for their own sake. The term 'interest' refers to the motivational sources or nature of non-instrumental desires. In this sense, interests indicate from a psychological viewpoint the desirable aspects of what we desire. Interests are not *things* separate from our normal desires, but rather they are facets of our wants. An alternative term might be 'core motivations.' They constitute a way of characterizing desire that is distinct from specifying the object of desire. They indicate *why* we want and not *what* we want.

The notion of interest allows us to see what apparently disparate desires have in common. For example, the interest people have in belonging may express itself in many different ways. It may be manifest as a general desire for certain kinds of friendship or to live in a community. Alternatively, it may express itself as a desire to conform or to outshine others in competition. It is also an important factor in the way people decorate their houses and tend their gardens. In each case, these general wants will generate more specific desires in particular circumstances. These very different object-individuated desires can have a unifying aspect, namely shared motivating interests. In this way, the notion of an interest enables us to understand how wants for disparate things are nevertheless similar.

Additionally, 'interest' is often necessary to interpret how desires change. For example, it allows us to comprehend how a desire for material success might be replaced later by a desire to conform. As a person acquires new beliefs and his or her character traits change, his or her desires alter. However, such change need not amount to transformation insofar as the motivating sources of the desires remain constant. If our motivational nature is structured like a web, the outer part consists in specific desires individuated by their objects, which change with belief. In contrast, the central core remains relatively stable and permanent, constituted by general motivating interests, which are belief-independent. Changes in the central core constitute a transformation in character and nature. As the outer ring of the web alters, sense and order can be made of this flux by concentrating upon the relatively stable motivating interests. In summary, without the notion of an interest, one cannot see the patterns in the ways that desires change, nor structure in the varieties of our wants.

Interests explain desires by structuring them into choice-independent groupings.

I need to clarify why interests are not simply general desires. In fact, the two are significantly different. First, object-individuated desires are often belief-dependent, and interests are not. For instance, a person's desire to buy a specific painting depends on the individual's judgments about its desirability and cost. On the other hand, if a person has aesthetic interests then he or she has aesthetically motivated desires, and this is not dependent on beliefs regarding the desirability or cost of beautiful things. Indeed, the person may not even realize that he or she has aesthetic interests. Second, desires act as potential causes of actions in conjunction with suitable beliefs. For example, I want to eat ice cream and believe that the ice cream is in the refrigerator; jointly, these explain my action of walking towards the fridge. They constitute my reason for action. In contrast, interests act as potential explanations of desires without the need of a relevant belief. Such explanations indicate the reason for a desire by revealing its motivational nature, but they do not give the person's own reasons. The individual may not acknowledge these reasons, and so such acknowledgment cannot be essential to their existence, nor to the fashion in which they explain the desires in question. In summary, a description that characterizes a person's interests indicates the motivational nature of the individual's desires; they inform us of the non-instrumental reasons *why* a person desires, but without necessarily specifying *what* he or she desires.[5]

---

[5] Thomson, op cit., Chapter IV.

Finally, I should explain why this distinction is important. First, we have seen why the desire-based theory of value is unsatisfactory. We have now offered the preliminaries of an alternative account based on interests, which avoids the problems of the desire theory. In particular, it allows the idea that value does not have to be tied to the specific things wanted, and yet does depend on the patterns of our motivations. One of the interesting points apparently in favor of the misguided attempt to explain value in terms of desire is that it permits individual variations in what counts as value. However, an interest-based account has the same advantage but without the problematic aspects of the desire theory.

Second, interests provide a basis for the critical evaluation of desires. For instance, social forces can lead to a situation where the object of a person's desire clashes with the interests that motivate the want. For example, many people aspire for status and this aspiration generates many more specific wants, which can demand tremendous effort. However, suppose that the desire for status is largely an expression of an interest in belonging. If this is true, then it is worrying because trying to attain status is a muddled way to belong. Indeed, the search for status, which will make a person ambitious, may actually thwart the possibilities to belong, for example, by making a person work too hard, thereby ignoring his or her friends and family. In which case, what the person actually desires (status) is incongruent with the interest that motivates the want (belonging). The satisfaction of the desire and the effort that this entails frustrate the interest that motivates the want.

Third, we interpret desires in part because often we cannot obtain exactly what we want. This interpretation consists in characterizing the interests that motivate the desires, and it shows what is valuable about the desire without indicating its specific object. For example, when your child wants a popsicle and the shop is shut, you might cool a banana on a stick. Now, imagine that there is no banana and no fridge. What should you do? It depends on the nature of your child's desire. Is she thirsty? Does she have a bad taste in her mouth? Does she just want a treat? Is she hot? Or, is it more than she wants loving attention? If it is the latter, then a walk in the park might be better than a popsicle. This ability to predict what people will want in new circumstances is crucial to the understanding of well-being.

In conclusion, let us summarize these points.

1) First, non-instrumental desires have a motivational source, which we may call an interest and which is not another more general desire. Our belief-dependent desires and preferences are expressions of such interests. Because such interests are not based on choices and beliefs, they constitute a feature of desire distinct from what is wanted. However, although interests are different from object-individuated desires, they are not some *entity* completely distinct or separate. They are facets of our wants.

2) Second, these interests define the temporal patterns and non-temporal structures of our desires. They permit us to see that desires for very disparate things may have common motivational sources. In this way, they make interpretation of desire possible.

3) Third, what is important in desire satisfaction is not the obtaining exactly of what one wants, but rather that the interests behind the desire are satisfied. If I need more beauty in my life, then it is not so important that I obtain exactly the specific beautiful things that I want, but rather that there is more beauty of a certain kind in my life. Indeed, I may not be aware that my desires are aesthetically motivated.

4) The fourth point is that the objects of desire do not necessarily express well the interest behind the desire. For example, I may have an interest in belonging, and this may express itself as a range of desires pertaining to status, which drive me to work so hard that I end up feeling alienated. In this sense, interests provide a way to evaluate desires.

The truth in the desire model is that our motivational patterns can define what has non-instrumental value for us. In this sense, our desires are relevant in defining what constitutes harm, without it being the case that harm consists in the satisfaction of desire or informed preferences. Desires bid us to do, but what they urge is not automatically good for us. The promptings of desires can be fickle voices and, when they are clear, they are sometimes a stubborn and persistent nagging that leads us away from what is good. Yet, at the same time, desires have motivational sources that reveal our deeper interests, which do define, in part, what has non-instrumental value for us. Being deprived of activities and experiences that answer such interests is part of what counts as harm.

4. Conclusion: Back to Needs

Let us now return to the concept of need and the two aspects with which we started. First, if we are to maintain a distinction between instrumental and fundamental needs, this requires that the antecedent of a fundamental 'need' claim (i.e. not undergoing serious harm) should not be explicated in terms of desire-satisfaction. Second, the concept of a fundamental need is characterized in part by the way it employs the notion of natural necessity and, more specifically, inescapability to limit choices. For a fundamental need to be inescapable, the nature of the harm caused by the lack of the object of need must itself be inescapable. The interest/desire distinction allows us to maintain with some plausibility the claim that certain features of harm are inescapable. Desires individuated and identified by their objects usually are alterable; perhaps none of our desires are inescapable. But, although we can exercise control over what we desire, we can exercise much less over the motivational nature and the structure of our desires. Therefore, the distinction between interests and desires is required for the claim that some primary values are relatively inescapable because they are subject to the constraints of natural necessity. If certain general types of activity are inescapably valuable, then this is because the interests that define them are themselves inescapable.

The concept of an interest must form an integral part of the concept of a fundamental need because our interests determine in general terms what types of activities and experiences we are deprived of when we are harmed. We require the notion of an interest to explain what harm is, and we require the notion of harm to explain what a fundamental need is. The concept of an interest demonstrates in what sense our well-being consists of living in accordance with our nature, rather than consisting of getting what we desire. The significance of inescapable interests is that these define in what way we must treat this nature as given. They provide a certain starting-point for deliberation and a certain fixedness in what is to count as good or bad for a person.

Prudence can require us to change ourselves, and thereby what has primary value for us. The significance of inescapable interests is that they set limits to how radically and deeply we can change ourselves, and that they determine ends that must be taken as given in prudential deliberation. It is in relation to this given multiplicity of goods that we can assess whether we ought to change the more optional sides of our nature. In this way, it is possible to include the more optional and plastic aspects of our nature, as well as the inescapable, in our conception of the range of goods relevant to well-being and harm. In other words, our conception of primary goods does not have to be restricted to our inescapable interests. It can include more optional interests, so long as prudence does not require us to change these. Thus, starting from inescapable interests, we can build a more full-bodied picture of the types of primary goods relevant to harm and well-being.

9 Needs, Rights, and Collective Obligations

BILL WRINGE

1.

Normative political discussion can be conducted in a variety of different vocabularies. One such is the vocabulary of rights; another is that of needs. Others, with which I shall be less immediately concerned, are the vocabularies of common good and perhaps—although one might regard it as such a general term as to be common to almost all the terms in which one might conduct normative discourse— that of moral obligation.[1]

It is often pointed out that the use of particular normative vocabularies can have significant effects on political practice. So for example, it can be said that the vocabulary of needs carries with it implications of urgency which talk of preferences—which in this context almost always seem to attract the epithet 'mere'—cannot.[2] To those who

---

[1] This is not intended to be an exhaustive list. One vocabulary which I have not mentioned here, but which is closely related to those which I shall be discussing, is that of capabilities—see M. Nussbaum, *Women and Human Development: The Capabilities Approach* (Cambridge: Cambridge University Press 2000) for further details.

[2] See D. Wiggins 'Claims of Need' in his *Needs, Values, Truth: Essays in Philosophy* (Oxford: Blackwell 1987), 1–57 esp. 6; G. Thomson, *Needs*

think that the notion of need can play a valuable role in political discourse, this can be supposed to be one of its virtues. To those who are suspicious of it, it may, equally seem like further grounds for suspicion.[3]

Similarly, use of the vocabulary of rights is often thought to encourage those designated as right-holders to take an active role in securing the new or continued performance of such obligations as they take to be owed to them.[4] By contrast, use of the vocabulary of obligation may encourage them to take up a more passive or less strident attitude to the same matters. Depending on one's point of view, this may seem like either a good thing or a bad one.

Different sorts of normative discourse can come into conflict with one another. Part of the job of the philosopher is to uncover and articulate relationships between concepts we should expect that when conflict occurs, we will

---

(London: Routledge and Kegan Paul 1987); H. Frankfurt 'Necessity and Desire' *Philosophy and Phenomenological Research* **45** (1984), 1–14. I should perhaps emphasise that none of these writers thinks the difference between preferences merely and desires can be accounted for just in terms of their urgency—and nor do I.

[3] For further discussion of these points see the exchange between Frankfurt op. cit. note 2 above and R. Goodin, 'The Priority of Needs' *Philosophy and Phenomenological Research* **45** (1985) pp 615–626. Interesting further discussion of these issues can be found in G. Brock 'Morally Important Needs', *Philosophia* **26** (1998), 165–178.

[4] O. O'Neill, 'Hunger, Needs and Rights' in *Problems of International Ethics*, S. Luper-Foy (ed.) (London: Westview, 1986) reprinted as 'Rights Obligations and Needs' in *Necessary Goods: Our Responsibilities to Meet Others' Needs* G. Brock (ed.) (Lanham: Rowman and Littlefield 1998) 86–106 (page references to this reprint).

need to engage in philosophical investigation.[5] One part of the point of this investigation will be to discover whether the conflict is deep or contingent: whether it stems from features of the concepts which are expressed in those vocabularies or only from the personal preferences or the particular allegiances of those who find themselves articulating their views in terms of one or other of them, or on accidents of political and intellectual history.

Onora O'Neill has claimed that there is a tension between the normative uses of the vocabulary of needs and the vocabulary of rights which results from conceptual rather than contingent features of the two discourses involved.[6] The aim of this paper is to show that O'Neill's contention is overstated, and that the tension can be resolved.

The alleged tension, which I shall describe in more detail below, arises when we try to articulate a set of rights whose consistent observance will ensure that every person's

---

[5] Why does the fact that two forms of normative discourse come into conflict (if they do) matter? Part of the reason will have to do with the practical consequences of adopting one form of discourse or another. But if the conflict is deep (in the sense I have suggested, and in the sense which O'Neill's arguments seem to suggest) then it may be impossible to use both vocabularies without falling into incoherence. This strikes me as particularly significant for someone who wants to give the vocabulary of needs an important role in normative political discourse, since the vocabulary of rights is so deeply embedded in that discourse as to be for all practical purposes inextricable. (I am indebted to Sandrine Berges for pressing me on this point.)

[6] O'Neill op. cit. note 4.

basic needs are met. It arises because—she claims—rights can only generate two kinds of obligations, special obligations, which specific individuals owe to particular others because of historical circumstances, and general obligations, which everyone owes to everyone else. However, the obligations which would be generated by subsistence rights cannot fall into either category.[7]

I shall argue that O'Neill does not succeed in showing that the vocabularies of rights and needs are in conflict in the way in which she suggests. She fails to do this, I shall claim, because she takes an overly restrictive view of the sorts of general obligation which rights can generate. I shall try to show that rights can also generate a kind of collective obligation which is distinct both from our special obligations and from the sorts of general obligation she recognises. Obligations of this sort fill a gap, which is left by the other two sorts of obligations—a gap to which O'Neill rightly draws our attention.

The main philosophical work to be done here will be in explaining what I take collective obligations to be, defending the claim that they exist and arguing that they do indeed fill the gap which O'Neill points out. Along the way, I shall also try to make clear how my response to her views differs from that put forward by other critics.

---

[7] In what follows I concentrate on what O'Neill (op. cit. note 4) has to say about general obligations—what she says about special obligations strikes me as mostly correct.

2.

Before going any further, I need to say something more about the terms of the debate. I shall start by making some fairly basic remarks about needs.

It is often observed that there are important differences between a statement such as 'I need five pounds in order to be able to enter the office sweepstake' and 'human beings (like me) need to eat.' Two such differences are that in the first case, but not in the second, what is needed is spoken of as being needed for some further purpose—namely, entering the office sweepstake; and in the second, but not the first, the question of whether the need gets satisfied seems to have some moral significance.[8,9]

If I am unable to eat, through no fault of my own, then it is possible that someone might be obliged to help me. If I am unable to enter the office sweepstake, the same is less likely to be true—and if it is true, then unlike the case in

---

[8] Wiggins op. cit. note 2, 7–10.

[9] For some skepticism about the significance of the distinction, see B. Barry, *Political Argument: A Reissue with a New Introduction* (Berkeley and Los Angeles: University of California Press, 1990.) In my view Barry's critique of Wiggins relies on attaching too much importance to the claim that 'needs' has two distinct senses, and not enough to the idea that different kinds of need claim can have different sorts of significance. As far as the first claim is concerned, I am not sure that questions about how many senses a word has always admit of determinate, context independent, answers. But in any case there seems no clear inference from the claim that 'need' is univocal to the claim (which Barry goes on to make) that claims about certain kinds of need are not morally distinctive.

which I am unable to eat, it will only be true because of a set of very particular circumstances. Unless these circumstances are described in detail, the claim that the first sentence has some moral significance will just seem bizarre.

It is very tempting to think that the two distinctions here are connected. In other words, it is because the alleged need for five pounds is only a need relative to some apparently morally insignificant further goal that it lacks any moral significance. However, it is important to notice that what makes the need morally insignificant is not that it only exists relative to some further goal, but that that goal is morally insignificant. We would not be similarly dismissive of the moral significance of the need claim if someone said 'I need five pounds in order to be able to eat'. Any skepticism that one felt here would be directed to the truth of the claim, and not to its significance if true.

A more plausible suggestion is that when needs claims have moral force they have it in virtue of the inescapability of the ends to which they are relative. As David Wiggins has pointed out 'I need five pounds to enter the office sweepstake' can be met by the retort 'But you don't *really* need to enter the office sweepstake'.[10] By contrast the retort 'But you don't *really* need to eat' would be argumentatively inept, as well as grossly insensitive.[11,12]

---

[10] I have altered Wiggins' example for purely rhetorical purposes.

[11] Cf Wiggins op. cit. note 2, 7–8.

[12] At least, in a situation where the person addressed was unable to eat. In other circumstances it might be merely inane.

Philosophical controversy lurks in the wings, however. It is not obviously true that every kind of inescapable need has moral significance. For example, a heroin addict's need for his daily fix may be just as inescapable as his need for food but, arguably, does not make the same moral call for satisfaction.[13] Considerations of how needs are acquired seem to play at least as much of a role in judging their moral significance as considerations about how easily we might divest ourselves of them. Furthermore the observation that certain needs do seem to have moral significance does not tell us anything about why they have this significance—or, in particular, whether they have this significance just in virtue of being needs of a particular kind.

What does not seem especially controversial, though, is that there is a class of needs whose satisfaction is necessary not just for the satisfaction of particular goals, but as a precondition for pursuing any goals at all. The most obvious such needs are human needs for food and shelter. However, if we look not just at what is required for pursuing goals, but at the conditions for forming goals, and for forming them autonomously, in the manner characteristic of mature human beings, we may arrive at a more expansive list, which includes needs for a relatively stable upbringing, education, and access to information about the opportunities available in one's society.

---

[13] G. Brock, 'Justice and Needs' *Dialogue* 35 (1996), 81–6.

If there are any needs which have moral significance it will be these.[14]

3.

To identify a set of needs which have moral significance, if any do, is one thing; to give a convincing account of the *sort* of moral significance they have, and a defence of the claim that they do indeed have this significance is another. A natural strategy to adopt is to argue that the central significance of these needs means that human beings have rights to their satisfaction. I shall call such rights 'subsistence rights', following a long tradition, although the characterisation I have given of them here makes them extend beyond what is required for bare subsistence.[15]

There are a number of strategies which one might adopt in order to defend this claim. One would be to argue, along lines pioneered by Alan Gewirth, that the fact that these needs are among the preconditions of any form of rational agency gives rise to a right to their satisfaction.[16] An

[14] L. Doyal, 'Basic Needs' in *Necessary Goods: Our Responsibilities to Meet Others' Needs* G. Brock (ed.), Lanham: Rowman and Littlefield (1998), 66–86.

[15] Someone who has argued recently for this view is Charles Jones: C. Jones, *Global Justice—Defending Cosmopolitanism* (Oxford: Oxford University Press, 1999). Although I am in agreement with many of the points he makes, my own strategy for responding to O'Neill's objection is rather different.

[16] A. Gewirth, *Reason and Morality* (Chicago: Chicago University Press, 1978).

alternative, more *ad hominem* approach would be to start with examples of rights which almost anyone would acknowledge, and then to claim that any plausible account of the considerations that lead us to recognise rights of this kind would, if applied consistently, also lead us to recognise subsistence rights.[17] A third strategy would be to argue that given the overwhelming role that the needs I have identified play in the well-being of those that have those needs, the recognition of subsistence rights is the best way of protecting human welfare.[18,19] I shall not examine any of these strategies in detail, since my concern here is with an argument that purports to show that none of them can succeed.

---

[17] J. Sterba, 'From Liberty to Universal Welfare' in *Necessary Goods: Our Responsibilities to Meet Others' Needs* G. Brock (ed.), (Lanham: Rowman and Littlefield 1998), 185–216.

[18] Jones op. cit. note 15.

[19] Other strategies have also been suggested by David Braybrooke (D. Braybrooke *Meeting Needs* (Princeton: Princeton University Press, 1987)) and David Wiggins (Wiggins op. cit. note 2). For a discussion and criticism of these attempts see Brock op. cit. note 13. I am not sure whether Brock's criticisms of Wiggins are on the mark. In any case, both Wiggins and Braybooke seem to be concerned with our obligation to meet the needs of members of our own political community. But for reasons which I explain below, I am not sure this goes far enough: if I am right obligations to meet needs can extend beyond national boundaries. I express this point with a certain amount of tentativeness, however, since the criticism depends on identifying nations as the most extensive political communities of which we are members. For doubts about this, see T. Pogge *Realizing Rawls* (Ithaca: Cornell University Press, 1989); from a very different perspective S. Berges, 'Loneliness and Belonging: Is Stoic Cosmopolitanism Still Defensible?', *Res Publica* **11** (2005).

4.

O'Neill's objection to the idea of subsistence rights can be summarised fairly quickly. The objection is that, whereas liberty rights, as these have traditionally been conceived, give rise to obligations on the part of every individual, subsistence rights seem to generate unallocated obligations. To assess whether this line of argument is a good one, however, we need to know why subsistence rights generate unallocated obligations, and why this should matter. In order to do this we will need to look more carefully at the differences between liberty rights and subsistence rights which O'Neill takes to be significant in this context.

The significant difference between these two sorts of rights (or, if O'Neill is correct, supposed rights) stems from differences in the sorts of obligation which such rights give rise to, if they really exist. According to O'Neill, we can distinguish between two sorts of obligation to which rights might give rise—special obligations which fall on individuals because of the particular social roles they occupy, and universal obligations, which fall on everybody. For example, an individual's right to free speech might be thought to give rise to a universal obligation not to interfere with his or her expression of her opinions. It might also give rise to certain special obligations as well. For example, if I am an election official, and a candidate complains of being intimidated by members of a rival political party, her right to free speech may also give rise to a special obligation—one which would not exist if I were not an election official—to investigate the complaint and take appropriate action if it turns out to be well-founded.

For reasons which will become apparent, I think there are problems with O'Neill's attempts to classify all obligations as being either universal or special. I shall be arguing, in effect, that this dichotomy leads us to overlook another kind of obligation which is significant in this context. For purposes of exposition I shall ignore this point for the time being, but it will be significant later.

For the purposes of this discussion we can also set aside special obligations: although O'Neill makes some mention of them—presumably for the sake of completeness—their existence does not play an important role in the argument that subsistence rights are incoherent. That argument depends on a problem about the universal obligations to which subsistence rights give rise.

One idea about why the distinction between liberty rights and subsistence rights which might carry some weight arises from considering the following claim:

L: A person's liberty right (for example, their right to free speech) is adequately respected only if everyone avoids interfering with the exercise of certain capacities (for example, the right to formulate and express opinions on matters of judgment).

If this claim is correct, then the sense in which the right in question generates specific obligations is clear: it generates an obligation on everyone to avoid interfering with the exercise of this capacity.

What about subsistence rights? The following claim is formally analogous to L:

s: A person's subsistence right (for example their right to a reasonably nutritious diet) is adequately respected only if everyone avoids interfering with their enjoyment of certain resources.

S is not entirely without teeth. Depending on how one understood the notion of interference it might, for example, justify prohibiting various environmentally disastrous farming practices, or some inequitable trade arrangements. Taken as such it need not be just a notational variant on particular liberty rights such as the right to property.

Indeed, one might go even further than this. If we take 'holding goods which one doesn't need' to constitute a form of interference with others then S could be thought to have very radical implications indeed, as Thomas Pogge has, in effect, argued.[20] Some might protest against this conclusion on the grounds that it is hard to see how merely 'holding' something could count as 'interfering' with anything. But of course this is one case where the linguistic expression of the point is far from being philosophically neutral. Typically those who 'hold' goods which they do not need are far from passive in their attitude to them: they do not only 'hold' them but enforce, or manifest their readiness to enforce, and support institutions that do in fact enforce property rights over such goods. Behaviour of this

---

[20] T. Pogge, *World Poverty and Human Rights: Cosmopolitan Responsibilities and Reforms* (Malden, MA: Polity Press, 2003).

sort can easily be cast as 'interference' without any linguistic or conceptual strain at all.

Assessing the significance of this line of argument about the implications of S is far from straightforward. One thing it will depend upon is the balance between the respective contributions of the roles played by enforcement of property rights on the one hand and other mechanisms for ensuring their observance such as ideological legitimation of the status quo on the other. If, as seems likely, both play a significant role in preserving existing patterns of property holding, then even if everyone abided by the obligations which S imposes on us, the basic needs of many individuals would remain unmet.

Many of those who have wanted to argue for the existence of subsistence rights have thought that such rights have implications beyond their imposing on us the sorts of obligations to which S gives rise.[21] They have wanted to claim that the existence of subsistence rights does not just require individuals to avoid interfering with other people's enjoyment of resources they already possess. It also requires them to make some form of provision for individuals who lack those resources.

How might we formulate this claim in a way which preserves the analogy to L? Here is a first attempt:

S^1: A person's subsistence right is adequately respected if and only if everyone provides them with the goods to which the subsistence right entitles them.

---

[21] Jones op. cit. note 15, H. Shue, *Basic Rights: Subsistence, Affluence and US Foreign Policy* (Princeton, NJ: Princeton University Press, 1980).

But S¹ is absurd, for two reasons. First, the obligations that it generates are unduly demanding. According to S¹ if I am to respect everyone's right to adequate nutrition, then I need to provide every starving person in the world with an adequate diet. But this is not merely something that it is unreasonable to ask of us. It is something which, for most people, is literally impossible. Call this problem with S¹ 'Impossibility'.

A distinct problem with S¹ I shall call 'Overgenerosity'. Suppose we lived in a world with an enormous population in which there were comparatively few deprived individuals, so that it was in fact possible for most people to comply with the obligations generated by S¹. If everybody who could comply with S¹ did so, then the deprived individuals would acquire far more than they needed to satisfy their needs.

How can we avoid these absurdities? We seem forced to say that if subsistence rights generate obligations, they are unlike liberty rights in that they do not generate an obligation on the part of each individual to respect them. But if they do not (as they cannot) generate such obligations, then it is not clear what obligations they do generate, or who they fall on. That is what is meant by calling the obligations generated by subsistence rights unallocated.

However, although the argument above does seem to show that subsistence rights do generate unallocated obligations, it is not immediately obvious why this should be a problem. The answer seems to depend on two further claims. The first is that obligations which are unallocated are unenforceable; the second is that obligations which are unenforceable are rarely taken seriously.[22]

It is not immediately obvious what the force of these points is. However O'Neill can have no principled objection to a moral theory's generating unenforceable obligations since the sort of Kantianism which she prefers to rights theories generates as many, if not more unenforceable obligations as rights theories do.[23] Her view seems to be that rights theories which generate unenforceable obligations are problematic in a way that Kantian views are not. This is because the stress that rights theories place on enforcement means that unenforceable obligations are less likely to be taken seriously within the context of rights theories than within other contexts.

This point needs handling carefully. It is not enough for O'Neill's purposes if the connection between rights and enforceability is just a contingent feature of the way we respond to rights discourse. If this were the case, then O'Neill would not have shown, as she thinks she has, that there was some conceptual tension between the discourse of needs and the discourse of rights. She would only have shown that we need to be more careful about how we think about rights.

Unfortunately for O'Neill, however, it seems that the connection between rights discourse and enforceability must be a merely contingent one. For as Charles Jones has pointed out, it is arguable that all forms of rights, and not just subsistence rights generate unallocated obligations.[24] To see this consider L again. One natural response to L is that because it

---

[22] O'Neill op. cit. note 4, 98–9.   [23] O'Neill op. cit. note 4, 105 ff.
[24] Jones op. cit. note 15 chapters 3–4.

leads us to focus on what we most do in order to comply with liberty rights it leads us to underestimate the obligations which liberty rights generate. As well as generating obligations of non-interference such rights also generate obligations of enforcement. If someone prevents me from exercising my right to free speech, then someone ought to do something about it.

But who? There is no obvious answer to this question—the obligation is unallocated. So if rights which generate unallocated obligations are problematic the problem seems to be one which arises for all kinds of rights.[25]

5.

A natural response to these points is that O' Neill is right to think that there is a problem about the unallocated obligations that subsistence rights seem to generate, but that she has mislocated it. The problem with unallocated obligations is not that they are unenforceable but that the very idea of an

---

[25] This matters because O'Neill thinks that there is no similar problem about liberty rights. One might resist this conclusion by appealing to the Nozick/Locke view of rights in which rights do not generate a obligation to enforce but only rights (on the part of the possessor) to enforce. (R. Nozick, *Anarchy, State and Utopia* (Oxford: Blackwell, 1974); J. Locke, *Two Treatises of Government*, P. Laslett (ed.), (Cambridge: Cambridge University Press, 1968). But even if this can be done, it doesn't really help O'Neill's case, for the upshot is that the success of her argument depends on adopting an account of rights which is (at best) contentious. Nor would it help to conclude that rights discourse as a whole is incoherent—although this might be true, it is sufficiently implausible to motivate us to look for another response to the problem.

unallocated obligation is incoherent. Obligation is a relational term: the idea that there are obligations to do things
which do not fall on anyone makes no more sense than the
idea that there are people who are heavier, without there
being anyone specific who they are heavier than.
Furthermore, one might add, if other forms of rights generate this kind of obligation, so much the worse for the
coherence of rights discourse as a whole.

If this is the correct diagnosis of the problem which
O'Neill has identified, then we can make two points. The
first is that the problem is a fairly significant one for anyone
who wants to rely on rights discourse to do a significant job
in moral philosophy. The second is that there seems to be a
fairly obvious strategy for solving it—namely to find some
agent to whom the unallocated obligations can be allocated.

I think that both of these points are correct.
However, they call for further comment in two respects.
First, it is probably philosophically uncontroversial that
obligation is a relational term, and that one of the relata of
the relation in question is either an action or an action type.
When we come to the question of what sorts of things can be
obligation-bearers, matters are much less straightforward.
However, we cannot simply assume without further argument that only individual human beings can be obligation
bearers. Indeed there is even a *prima facie* case for thinking
that other things can bear obligations.[26] We certainly often

---

[26] I should emphasise that at this point I do not take the case to be
anything more than *prima facie*. Arguments in favour of my
contention are to be found in section 7 below.

talk as though this is so—we talk of corporations, governments and states as having obligations. It is certainly not
obvious (although it may ultimately be true[27]) that this is
just a *façon de parler*.

Secondly, talk of 'allocating' apparently unallocated
obligations might suggest that the philosopher's job in this
area is that of a cosmic bureaucrat making sure that no
moral or metaphysical loose ends were untied. The language
in play here naturally gives rise to this way of thinking.
However, there is one important difference between the
job of the philosopher and that of the bureaucrat. As far as
the bureaucrat is concerned it need not matter, except for
purely local reasons, how responsibilities get allocated, provided that everything that needs to get done gets done.
Matters are different for the philosopher: we need not only
to find some way of allocating these obligations but also to
find some rationale for this allocation. Ideally this will be
one which will justify us in thinking that the obligations
were so allocated all along, if only we could have seen things
sufficiently clearly.[28,29]

---

[27] I make the concession only for rhetorical purposes—see section
7 below.

[28] It might be thought that this claim prejudges the issue between realist
and constructivist metaethical views. However, I think that any viable
version of constructivism needs to respect this intuition—even if it
does so in the sort of weasely way that Wittgensteinian accounts of
mathematics respect the necessity of mathematical judgments.

[29] A third more strategic comment may also be called for here. Earlier,
I argued that both liberty rights and subsistence rights give rise to
apparently unallocated obligations. Although I stand by this claim, in

6.

One possible response to the problem of unallocated obligations would be to argue that these obligations should fall on states.[30] I shall now argue that this response is unsatisfactory. I shall then suggest an alternative response and argue that it is more satisfactory.

We need to distinguish between two significantly different strategies that one might adopt in arguing that states can act as the bearers of the unallocated obligations that O'Neill is worried about. One would be to argue that each state has obligations generated by the subsistence rights of its own citizens. The second is to suggest that individuals' subsistence rights generate obligations which fall on all states. On the first strategy we are saying that the obligations are, in O'Neill's terminology, 'special' obligations; on the second that they are general obligations.

At first sight it is the first strategy which seems more promising. One might think that on many accounts of the state, states have obligations to their citizens which might extend to seeing that their subsistence rights are respected. For example, one might hold that the purpose of the state is to pool the cost of reducing vulnerability to risk, and that

what remains of this paper I shall only be attempting to solve the problem as it arises for subsistence rights. Whether my solution can be used to cope with the unallocated obligations to which liberty rights give rise, and how it might be adapted, are matters which I shall leave for a future occasion.

[30] Cf Jones op. cit. note 14; R. Goodin, 'What is So Special About Our Fellow Countrymen?' *Ethics* **98** (1986) 663–686.

one significant risk to which citizens might collectively wish to reduce their vulnerability to is the risk of the harm that ensues when their needs are not met.[31]

However, I do not think that this strategy for dealing with O'Neill's worry is likely to succeed. O'Neill's objection to subsistence rights was that they seemed incoherent because of some of the general obligations they generated. It is hard to see how it could help to suggest that they also generate a set of special obligations as well. It seems to me that it could only do so if the special obligations somehow cancelled out the general ones. The only suggestion that seems plausible here is the possibility that the existence of the special ones somehow guaranteed that the general ones never needed to be met. In that case it wouldn't really matter whose obligations they were.

But the sad fact is that this is far from being true. Even if states do have obligations to see that the subsistence rights of their subjects are respected, nothing guarantees that they will be capable of doing so. So we have no reason to think that the problematic general obligations lapse, and we do need to worry about who they can be allocated to.

This might lead us to try the second strategy instead. This would be to argue that general obligations arising out of subsistence rights fall on all states. One reason why it has seemed appealing to respond to the problem of unallocated general obligations by arguing that these obligations fall on states rather than individuals is that it seems clear that states

---

[31] I am grateful to Soran Reader for pressing this suggestion.

can do things which individuals cannot. While it might be impossible for individuals to satisfy all the obligations which subsistence rights generate, it is not so obvious that this is impossible for states—at least not fairly large, affluent states.

Nevertheless, there are some problems with the idea that states should be the bearers of otherwise unallocated obligations. One which should be set aside almost immediately is that states cannot bear obligations either because they are not agents at all, or because they are agents which are constituted in the wrong kind of way—for example because they are constituted in such a way that the only things that can be reasons for them are considerations of power or of the welfare of their citizens. Whatever the merits of these suggestions—and I do not think they are great—they are ones which a defender of O'Neill's position should be wary of appealing to, if for no better reason than the fact that O'Neill herself is committed to the view that states, along with multinational corporations and some supra state entities are both agents and obligation-bearers.[32]

A more serious concern is that there seems to be something arbitrary about the suggestion that states should be the bearers of otherwise unallocated obligations. Even if it is true that states can do things which individuals cannot, they are not the only bodies that can do so. Supra-state organisations such as the United Nations are one example of such bodies. Still it might be argued that supra-state organisations can only have obligations in virtue of the

---

[32] O. O'Neill, 'Agents of Justice', in T. Pogge, *Global Justice* (Oxford: Blackwell, 2001).

obligations which their members have. If so then their existence does not undermine the case for thinking that the unallocated responsibilities which subsistence rights generate should fall on states.

However, there are other bodies that can do things which individuals cannot, such as multi-national corporations. Of course, the idea that multinational corporations have obligations to meet people's subsistence needs is not one which is likely to find much practical or philosophical support. However, this is not the reason for raising the possibility in this context. The reason for doing so is that it shows that the idea that unallocated obligations should fall on nations is, in an important sense, arbitrary. Since there are other bodies which could fulfil these obligations, the claim that states should do so cannot be defended just by appealing to the fact that states can do things which individuals cannot.

It might be possible to rebut this line of argument by showing that there was something about the nature of the state which made it peculiarly suitable to be a bearer of otherwise unallocated general obligations. However it is far from clear what the details of such an argument would be, and it is difficult to see how it could avoid relying on controversial claims about the nature and function of the state.

In any case we need not pursue this argument with excessive vigour. The idea that unallocated general obligations should be allocated to states faces another problem. Consider the role of S in generating the problem of unallocated obligations. Earlier I observed that there was a problem about seeing S as generating obligations for individuals for two reasons which I called 'Impossibility' and 'Overgenerosity'. If S is regarded as generating obligations for states then 'Impossibility' is not a problem. However 'Overgenerosity' remains in place.

7.

In the rest of this paper I want to sketch an alternative response to the problem of unallocated obligations. Stated as briefly as possible, the suggestion that I want to make is that unallocated obligations should be seen as obligations which fall on the world's population collectively. This suggestion has two advantages.

The first advantage is this. An obligation which falls on everyone cannot be regarded as arbitrary: arbitrariness—in so far as it is a problem for the idea that unallocated obligations fall on nations rather than individuals—arises from selectivity, and the suggestion that I have put forward is maximally unselective. The second is that if the obligations which S generates are regarded as one single collective obligation then the problem of Overgenerosity does not apply. That problem was generated by the existence of a set of different obligation bearers all of whom were obligated by S. On my view there is only one obligation bearer—namely, all of us.

Despite its virtues, my solution to the problem of unallocated obligations will be met with a certain degree of skepticism. There are two obvious lines of resistance. The first is to argue that the view I am putting forward is unintelligible. The second is that, although intelligible, it does not solve the problem. I shall start by defending the intelligibility of my claim.

The main reason for finding the view I am putting forward unintelligible is the idea that, properly speaking, we cannot make sense of the idea of collective obligations. Since we often do speak in ways which suggest that there can be collective responsibilities, people who hold this view are likely to hold that there is a sense in which the apparent existence of collective obligations arises out of the actual existence of individual obligations. If a view of this sort is right then collective obligations will not help us to solve the problem of unallocated obligations.

I shall try to undermine this view by describing a situation in which the idea of collective obligations seems to make sense. Consider a situation where two people share an office. Due to bad weather, the roof starts to collapse. In this situation, we might well want to say there is a joint obligation to inform a responsible person about the state of the roof before a passerby is injured.

Why does this seem like the right thing to say? Well, it is more plausible than the claim that we *each* have an obligation to tell someone. What makes that claim implausible is that we both discharge our obligation by seeing to it that one of us tells the responsible person. If we both had an obligation, then only the person who did the telling would succeed in discharging it.

One might think that we could correctly describe the situation by saying that in the imagined circumstance, we each have a *conditional* obligation to inform a responsible individual provided the other person does not. But this does not capture everything we want to say here either. Imagine a situation where, for one reason or another, each of us is individually unable to inform the responsible individual. Since ought implies can, any conditional obligation we might be taken to have lapses. But it may be that we can somehow contrive to do things together that we cannot do individually.

For example—suppose that the person who needs to be informed has to be informed by email. Person A has the technical expertise necessary to describe the damage to the roof in an informative manner but doesn't know how to use email. Person B is a computer wizard who doesn't know the first thing about roofs. Between them they can pass an informative message to the right person, but individually neither of them can. In a case like this, we would not say that the people involved had fulfilled their obligations if having reasoned that their individual conditional obligations lapsed they then went on to do nothing. We can explain why this is so by appealing to the idea that A and B have a collective obligation here which does not lapse under exactly the same circumstances as their individual obligations lapse.

It is true that even here we can find obligations that fall on individuals—namely the obligation to engage in some suitable co-operative scheme. However, this does not show that collective obligations are a myth. This observation suggests that in any case where it is plausible to say that a joint obligation exists, we can find individual obligations, or in other words the existence of collective obligations always entails the existence of some individual obligations. It does not follow from this that claims about collective obligations can always be dispensed with in favour of claims about individual obligations.

This is because it is plausible to think that the existence and structure of the obligations which fall on individuals in these cases can only be explained by reference to the collective obligation. When we look at cases where it is relatively easy for one individual to discharge the collective obligation this fact is masked. We need to focus on cases where discharging the obligation requires co-operative action—and where more than one scheme of co-operation might be possible in order to see that collective obligations are met—to see that collective obligations are not dispensable epiphenomena.

8.

In the previous section I made a case for recognising the existence of collective obligations. I also claimed that once we recognised this fact we could see how to respond to the unallocated obligations. However, one might concede in principle that collective obligations exist, but deny that they could be used as a way of dealing with the problem which O'Neill identifies.

I shall consider two objections along these lines. One focuses on enforceability. A natural worry about collective obligations is that they are unenforceable. If O'Neill was right to think that it was the unenforceability of unallocated obligations that made them problematic, then talk of collective obligations would not help to solve the problem.

But I have already argued that O'Neill's focus on enforce-ability was misguided. If my arguments there were correct, then this objection fails.

A second worry is this. I conceded above that where collective obligations exist, they entail the existence of indi-vidual obligations. It is natural to ask what individual obli-gations might be entailed by the existence of a collective obligation to meet subsistence needs. A further, skeptical question might follow. Can we be sure that these obligations can actually be met? If not, then since ought implies can, and since one person's *modus ponens* is another person's *modus tollens*, then it might be the case that the collective obligation lapsed. This would be true if it was impossible for individ-uals to carry out the obligations on them that the existence of the (supposed) collective obligation entailed.

As far as the first question is concerned, I shall start by entering a plea of ignorance. Knowing what sorts of individual obligations are entailed by our collective obliga-tion to meet individuals needs would require knowing what forms of collective action would be sufficient to solve these problems—and to know this one would need to know a lot more about such things as the economic and practical con-sequences of various schemes of food distribution. However I think there are good reasons for thinking that these are problems which could be solved by collective action of one sort or another.[33] Saying this, though, seems to entail that

[33] Especially if, as Amartya Sen and Jean Dreze have argued, famines, for example, typically arise out of problems with the distribution of entitlements to food rather than simple insufficiency of food. (A. Sen

there is a set of actions by individuals that they could actually carry out that would constitute the taking of such collective action—and this, if true, would be an answer to the objection.[34]

However, moving the focus in this way from the issue of collective obligation to that of collective action does help to shed light on some of the concrete individual obligations that our collective obligations might entail. At least this is so if it is true that the discharge of collective obligations requires collective action, and if it is also true that collective action, properly so called, requires the existence of what Margaret Gilbert calls 'plural subjects'.[35] On Gilbert's account, the existence of such a plural subject requires a form of mutual recognition by the members of a group of people (in this case the population of the world) that they are ready to participate in joint action of the relevant sort.

and J. Dreze, *Poverty and Famines* (Oxford: Oxford University Press, 1984)).

[34] Perhaps it would not fully answer the charge that these obligations might turn out to be unduly burdensome, in the same that way many people have thought that the obligations to which Peter Singer takes us to be subject are too burdensome. (P. Singer, 'Famine, Affluence and Morality', *Philosophy and Public Affairs* 1 1972, 229–243.) But there is no reason to think that my proposal does generate Singer-style obligations on individuals: the stringency of those obligations seems to derive from Singer's focus on what I have called conditional rather than collective obligations. (I am indebted to Sandrine Berges for this point).

[35] M. Gilbert, *On Social Facts* (London: Routledge, 1989); G. Simmel, 'How Is Society Possible' in *Georg Simmel: On Individuality and Social Forms* (Chicago: University of Chicago Press, 1971).

We might think that ideas of this sort would constitute a serious objection to the claims that I have been making about the existence of collective obligations. This would certainly be true if we thought that the existence of collective obligations required the existence of plural subjects as obligation bearers, since the population of the world does not at present constitute such a plural subject. However, I think that a demand of this sort is too strong. This can be seen by reflection on the example of the roof which I used in arguing for the existence of collective obligations. It was no part of the situation as I described it that, in order for the collective obligation to exist the two individuals implicated in this scenario recognise themselves as a plural subject. Still, if Gilbert is right, the discharge of the obligation does require this—at least when collective action is required for its discharge.

This, though, is highly suggestive. A reasonable inference—and one which I am tentatively inclined to draw—is that the existence of collective obligations which require joint action for their discharge entails an obligation on individuals to set about constituting (and doing whatever might be necessary to constitute) the sort of plural subject that can perform such actions. In cases where the constitution of such a subject is a non-trivial task, this will entail non-trivial obligations for individuals. Moving down from the highly abstract level at which I have been discussing, this might have such (relatively) concrete implications as requiring individuals to act in a way that will bring into existence and support institutions and projects which can act in such a way as to fulfil our collective obligations, and to undermine institutions which stand in the way of the realisation of such goals.

9.

The skeptical reader may still have some reservations. One might wonder how much difference there is between the view that I have been advocating and O'Neill's own position. For O'Neill holds that we have an imperfect duty of beneficence towards individuals in need, and she argues that this imperfect duty gives rise to obligations to work towards setting up institutions that can combat severe poverty.[36] These obligations do not seem very different from the obligations which I have been suggesting individuals have in virtue of our collective obligations. So one might think that my view amounts to little more than a 'notational variant' on hers.

I think that this is a mistake. There are clearly substantial philosophical differences between O'Neill's view and my own; and these philosophical differences also give rise to practical differences. The most obvious difference between O'Neill's position and my own is that O'Neill holds that claims about subsistence rights are incoherent, while I think they are coherent. It seems hard to deny that a disagreement about whether a certain way of framing a normative claim is coherent is a substantial *philosophical* difference. Claims about whether concepts are coherent are part of the philosopher's stock-in-trade.

It would be a mistake to characterise my difference with O'Neill as nothing more than a preference for one sort

[36] O'Neill op. cit. note 4.

of rhetoric over another. This characterisation of matters would be appropriate if O'Neill was merely claiming, as she sometimes seems to be, that rights talk was unhelpful. But the points she makes about unallocated obligations seem designed to show that such talk is unhelpful because it is incoherent.

Does the philosophical difference between our views make any practical difference? As I have already observed, some might think that it does not. It certainly seems plausible that, for example, the extent and frequency of an individual's donations to Oxfam or whether they vote for political parties that support inequitable trading regimes does not depend on whether they view these obligations as arising from the facts that rights are being violated. (It may be this that leads people to suspect that differences between the two views are 'merely rhetorical'.)

However, I suspect that even on this level, matters are not as straightforward as they might seem at first sight. After all, someone who thinks that claims about subsistence rights are incoherent is likely to be somewhat dismissive of the attempts of individuals to have those rights enforced, however sympathetic they may be to the plight of the starving individual. And it is not too difficult to see why this should be. Obligations arising out of the violations of rights often strike us as particularly urgent. If we think the rights being claimed do not exist, we are likely to feel piqued by the stridency of demands for their observation.

This will be true, even if we take ourselves, as good Kantians like O'Neill do, to have some duties arising out of imperfect duties of benevolence towards the needy. For on the Kantian picture we have many other imperfect obligations, including self-regarding obligations, such as the duty to develop our talents. On this picture, there doesn't seem to be any reason why I should think that imperfect obligations derived from a duty of benevolence should be given a particularly high priority. On the other hand if I think rights are being violated then matters will seem a little bit more urgent. Although this might not lead to differences at the level of individual actions, it may well affect the shape of the lives that people choose to live. If that is not a practical matter, then it is difficult to see what is.

10 Where Does the Moral Force of the Concept of Needs Reside and When?

DAVID BRAYBROOKE

1. Does Moral Force Reside in a Systematic Schema? Not in Any Simple Way

My point of departure in the book *Meeting Needs* was the conviction that the concept of needs has moral force, but the force has been dissipated and anyway made hard to see by multiple complications including but not confined to multiple abuses.[1] I now think that is only half the problem.

To help restore the moral force to view for systematic application, I worked out a philosophical construction – a schema – designed to give a stable foundation for the concept of needs in the uses in which it carries moral force. It is this schema on which I shall focus in the present paper. If vanity in addition to familiarity plays any part in my decision to do so, the vanity is offset, I hope, by the fact that I shall be carrying out an exercise in self-correction; and by the reasonable expectation that what I say in correcting the view to be taken of my own schema will apply to other attempts to systematize the concept.

---

[1] Princeton: Princeton University Press, 1987.

309

The schema specified a list of matters of need and minimum standards of provision for each need and each person. The matters of need were course-of-life needs, that is to say, needs (like the need for food and for being spared terrorization) that people have throughout their lives, or at least (like the need for sexual activity) in certain stages of their lives. The minimum standards of provision varied with persons (some people really need more to eat than others). They varied with climates (in some climates shelter is needed more to reduce exposure to the sun than to keep warm). They varied with cultures (the forms of food acceptable as provisions differ from culture to culture in respect to the animals that people are ready to eat).

Both the list and the minimum standards were governed by a Criterion. The Criterion certified each matter of need on the list and – person by person – each of the associated minimum standards of provision as something to be met as an indispensable condition of being able to perform four basic social roles: citizen, worker, householder, and parent.

Within this schema, I allowed for discussion and negotiation to fix the content of the list and the level of the minimum standards of provision. Negotiation (which I did not then distinguish, though it was allowed for) differs from discussion in bringing in bargaining. Bargaining in the case of settling upon the features of the schema consists, I suppose, mainly someone's agreeing to a more exacting concept of needs on one point (say, recreation) in return for getting someone else's agreement on a less exacting concept of needs on another (say, shelter).

In the discussion and negotiation, the main issue would be what list and what minimum standards would be generally accepted by people of good will in a certain policy-making population or community as having priority under a Principle of Precedence. The Principle consisted in giving needs precedence over less important matters, both for themselves and for other people in their own community or in one or another population otherwise defined for which they were ready to take some responsibility.

The moral force of the concept of needs would thus be fixed – though subject to further discussion in future rounds of policy-making – by the combination of the other features of the schema with the Principle of Precedence, when agreement was reached on how the schema is to be filled out.

It might seem that the Criterion, resting on empirical evidence, would not leave much room for discussion. And indeed I think there is a tension in the schema between what can be established by common sense or science as a fact about needs and what is accepted as the meaning of needs by people ready to agree to being guided by considerations of needs in making policies. But this tension in the schema reflects a real tension in the world of policy-making. Furthermore, it does leave a good deal of room for discussion: People may disagree, for example, on whether the indispensable conditions related to being barely able to perform the basic social roles or being able to with some room to spare (and hence some energy for trying out new ways of performing the roles). They may disagree about how far the deliverances of science or other bodies of evidence were to be taken as well-established or even relevant. They could disagree about what population or populations they would assume any responsibility for and about modifications to the list or modifications to the minimum standards of provision as one population after another came into view. They may disagree about other things as well, for example, the liberty to review in a later round of discussion and negotiation any agreement that they make about the schema for this round.

I owe to a student in a graduate seminar at The University of Texas, Brandon Butler, or perhaps better, I owe to Brandon Butler's father and grandfather,[2] whose position in these matters was invoked by Brandon in discussion – the stimulus for thinking again about just how the concept of needs has moral force. If it does, does all or any of the force reside in a schema of the sort that I constructed? Is there any force in the schema abstracted from the urgency of specific occasions? How, and in what terms does the urgency manifest itself?

In use, the concept of needs is infected by non-motivating aspects of the concept of neediness. Neediness is a tiresome subject, of which bleeding hearts, among whom I daresay I should count myself, may often make too much. Neediness also raises – directly, perhaps, but certainly in reaction to the bleeding hearts – a question about how the needy got that way. Was it through their own current

[2] Brandon is now inclined to invoke his grandfather (Sam Collins) rather than his father, as having the more explicit and trenchant position, but I'll keep them both in view.

shiftlessness? Or ready to work as they now may be, did they fail in their grasshopper days to acquire marketable skills? Approaching needs in this way, through the concept of neediness, Brandon Butler's father and grandfather might well find, as Brandon reports, nothing particularly moving about the concept of needs.

Their position (as Brandon suggests) may be tied up with notions about desert. Do the needy in this instance deserve to be helped? Short of bringing in an issue about deserts, the position might be, simply, that through their own improvidence the needy in question had created a difficulty about meeting their needs. One might hold that it was now up to them to get out of the difficulty as best they could without going on to blame them for their improvidence or to treat their difficulty as a natural or divine punishment. Even the feeling, 'Serves them right!', might not go that far; it might just mean, 'What did they expect, if they spent all that time dancing about, and neglecting their crops?'

But I expect that for many people, without their necessarily subscribing to a Calvinist-like religion, in which divine punishment is a prominent feature, the improvident deserve blame and punishment. Brandon Butler's father and grandfather may look upon withholding help from the undeserving as punishment, though they do not need to do this to feel justified in the withholding.

Up to a point, I sympathize. I want to be a grass-hopper, as Isaiah Berlin's Tolstoy wanted to be a hedgehog, but I am an ant at heart, just as Berlin's Tolstoy was a fox. I think that there is a moral and practical issue about whether measures set on foot to meet needs benefit some shiftless people. At any rate, there is a moral and practical issue about whether this possibility is an important obstacle to supporting the measures or something that can be tolerated, like having an occasional man live with a welfare mother. It is an obstacle really present; and an obstacle difficult, perhaps counterproductive, to root out.

It is, I suspect, frequently untimely to appeal to anything like a schema for needs. For, logically, as I point out, all the needs may currently be met, and so why ask for contributions? Let people go on taking care of themselves. If they do not succeed, it may be for reasons that Brandon's father and grandfather would not respect. The schema thus should not be treated as if it continually entered into the policy-making process, even if it helps explain why shortfalls of personal resources in some connections turn out to be urgent issues, and how the episodic use of 'needs,' which calls attention to the shortfalls, comes into play. It is a use with a footing in the schema, though it is not logically present there, just because if all the needs are currently met, though they certainly remain needs, there is no occasion for the episodic use.

Furthermore, I think that the moral force that I assumed is to be attributed to the concept of needs as exhibited in the schema may as well be attributed to specific instances of needs, and perhaps better so attributed, in the view of some people (Brandon Butler's father and grandfather and other people with whom Brandon has affectionate acquaintance in the State of Georgia). I treat needs as surrogates for whatever directly falls under the concept of utility, which I regard as too abstract for practical use – so abstract that it has not yet been firmly associated even in theory with a calculus both wholly intelligible and wholly acceptable. But the concept of needs as systematically presented in the schema may itself be too abstract, too far removed from the actual practices of policymaking to be useful. When needs are appealed to during those practices, does the denomination 'needs' bear the moral force? Or does the denomination as a specific need? Is it denomination as a specific need only in the context of a shortfall in meeting the need? Is denomination as a need then even necessary?

Even more important, some respect should be given to the fact that people may quite reasonably not want to be bound as private persons to meet the needs of other people, especially people outside their family circles. Would any of us be happy writing a blank cheque in this connection? Many of us would not be happy to write a blank cheque within our family circles. I don't think philosophers would want to write blank cheques themselves; so far Brandon's father and grandfather and other philosophers will be allies.

What citizens might bind themselves to is another matter. Then the responsibility, even if it is blanket, is not so overwhelming, since it is shared and can be limited to taxes, which are not usually so burdensome as politicians vie to make out. However, citizens, too, will sooner or later want to know whether there is any limit to the number of needs that they are invited to attend to; and what serious footing the needs all have. Moreover, to say the least, the moral obligations that people have as private persons do not neatly divide from the moral obligations that they have as citizens. We should want to keep up certain parallels between the two sets of obligations. Bodies of citizens can squander resources just as private persons can; and neither bodies of citizens nor private persons should ignore the extent to which on occasion efforts to meet people's needs miscarry.

2. Needs v. Capabilities as Alternatives to Utility

In Britain, there is a sharp increase in mortality among old people during especially cold weeks in the winter. In Chicago and Texas, there is a sharp increase during especially hot weeks in the summer. In the one case, the old people do not have enough heat; in the other, they have too much, because they lack air conditioning. The consequences are morally horrifying. I do not entirely know why the horror seems not to be felt among those economists who incline to dismiss basic needs, when the needs can be agreed upon, as too trivial in their claims on the Gross National Product to be worth talking about.

Economists will not do any better with the concept of utility. The notion of utility, along with the project of getting from this notion exact optimal solutions to problems about the choices of policies affecting human welfare has bewitched even economists who are thoroughly alert to unmet needs and thoroughly committed to getting them met. The bewitchment survives, even in the case of Amartya Sen (at one point at least in his recent writings[3]); and Sen is an economist who could not be more fully aware

---

[3] E.g., Amartya Sen and others, *The Standard of Living* (Cambridge: Cambridge University Press, 1987).

of the theoretical disasters to which attempts to found social choices on utilities and preferences have led in welfare economics and social choice theory.

Sen, in the book that I have in mind, is reluctant (even though tempted) to endorse the concept of needs, in the absence, he intimates, of a demonstration that the concept of needs can meet the test of utility, that is to say, among other things, of the expectations of precision associated with utility.[4] I think that here he has got things just upside down. The concept of utility is nowhere in direct application in practical discussions of policymaking;[5] and though Sen has a lot to say, all of which I applaud, in objection to relying on the concept of utility for the evaluation of policies, its absence from practical policy discussions is not something that he makes any fuss about or even notes.[6] This omission is, I think, a predictable consequence of his approaching practical discussions, much as he is concerned with them, from the viewpoint of an economist. Habituated to discussions with economists and philosophers, in which utility is an ubiquitous concept, Sen has not looked to see whether it is in use in practical discussions, at any rate in use by other people in such discussions. In sharp contrast to the concept of utility, the concept of needs is

---

[4] Op. cit., 25–6, 105.

[5] The qualification 'direct' allows for the application through surrogates that I am about to describe.

[6] This is true not only of his contributions to *The Standard of Living*, but also of his later book, *Development as Freedom* (New York: Knopf, 1999).

in application on every hand (though not always under that name, and in a complex pattern of representation and application that I am about to describe). If utility works out in a way that seems to conflict with the concept of needs, reflective equilibrium is not going to give so much weight to utility as to needs. Indeed, insofar as utility (as advanced by the utilitarians) has had any application in choices of social policies during a history now of two and a half centuries, it is by way of the concept of needs, with provisions for individual needs serving as surrogates for utilities. Utility is too refined a notion, and even so too problematical in application, for economists to deal with when they give advice about policies, and certainly for people generally and politicians.

Moving away from utility notwithstanding any lingering bewitchment, Sen would have us deal with the 'capabilities' (or freedoms) that people enjoy given appropriate resources.[7] These extend far beyond provisions for basic needs to include having the resources to take part in

---

[7] G. A. Cohen has said, 'Sen arrived at what he called "capability" through reflection on the main candidates for assessment of well-being that were in the field [in 1979], to wit, utility, or welfare, and Rawlsian primary goods' (see Cohen's 'Equality of What? On Welfare, Goods, and Capabilities,' in Martha C. Nussbaum and Amartya Sen (eds.), *The Quality of Life* (Oxford: Clarendon Press, 1993), 9–29, at 17. That's not so; it misdescribes Sen's reflection, even if his reflection was limited to 'the main candidates.' Provision for needs (something different from welfare occupied with utility or preferences) was a main candidate, as it had been from time immemorial, though disregarded by most sophisticated thinkers. Moreover, Sen has reflected on needs, and I expect he did so before 1979.

higher cultural activities and in politics, indeed, to all the aspects of living largely and generously, attaining what Thomas Hobbes would call 'commodious living'. (Curiously, the functionings that Sen's capabilities serve are just what would in the eyes of Karl Marx, young and old, be needs in a rich and expanded sense.)[8] In writings later than the book that I have just cited, Sen clearly treats needs as I understand them, to imply conditions indispensable for having important freedoms, among which he includes the freedom to survive.[9] There is no disagreement between us on this point; even if I would use 'freedom' in a more restricted way, I am ready, indeed eager, to go along with him in advocating effective practical attention beyond needs to the whole range of capabilities. I do not hold that everything important in life or social policy is covered by the concept of needs.[10]

---

[8] In an early writing, Marx says, looking forward, 'To take the place of wealth and poverty as political economy knows it, there comes forward the rich man, fitted out with rich human exigencies. The rich man is at the same time the man who, to live, has need of a totality of human manifestations, the man for whom his own realization is an interior necessity, a need'. (*Economic and Philosophical Manuscripts of 1844* (London: Lawrence and Wishart, 1959), 111–12.) The English here is my translation from the French of the *Pleiade* edition. This is the sense in which Marx is to be understood, late in life, putting forward in the *Critique of the Gotha Program* the principle, 'From all according to their ability, to all according to their needs.'

[9] See, for example, *Development as Freedom*, 4, 64, 82, 84.

[10] Thus the concept of needs, in the use that I advocate for it, is not open to the fifth of the five criticisms of the concept that Sabina Alkire (*Valuing Freedoms* (Oxford: Oxford University Press, 2002), 166–170)

We can try to expand the list of basic needs and raise the standards for meeting them, and this is plausible up to a point, but it risks diminishing the force of the appeal to needs. We can leave off expanding when the application of the concept is felt on every hand to have become tenuous; then we can build into our system of evaluation a level above needs to deal with personal values, which are to be taken seriously in the same way as needs, but perhaps in a lexicographically secondary place.

Sen's 'capabilities' may be regarded as doing much the same work as a two-level construction of this kind. His concept of capabilities, I might say, focuses on the Criterion that figures in the sort of construction or schema that I associate with needs. That Criterion already takes some of what Sen calls 'functionings' into account: specifically, functionings in the roles of householder, parent, citizen, and worker. As it stands, moreover, with the role of 'citizen', the Criterion already has implications for political liberty and justice, since no one can play the role of citizen in the absence of these things. But in effect Sen generalizes the Criterion to embrace functioning in all the roles that people might want to have the freedom to play – to do 'one thing today and another tomorrow, to hunt in the morning, fish in the afternoon, rear cattle in the evening, criticize after dinner'.[11] It is having with the appropriate resources the

finds in Sen's writings, the only one to which she thinks final weight should be given.

[11] Karl Marx and Friedrich Engels, *The German Ideology* (Moscow, 1964).

capabilities of functioning in all these ways to which Sen wants to direct comprehensive attention in making social policies.

Sen's approach has the advantage (against the concept of needs, as stabilized in the construction) of giving more weight to agency, an effect of using the term 'capability,' which connects with agency more directly than the term 'needs'. Moreover, Sen, in his discussion of the approach, returning to the subject of agency repeatedly, gives more weight to it, weight that I welcome, than I have done in my discussions of the schema for needs. Yet agency is already allowed for in the expectation that the details of the schema will be fixed by negotiation and discussion among the agents who will act on the schema. Again, agency is already allowed for with the schema, not only in the role of citizen, but also in the other roles that figure in the four-role Criterion, since the roles are to be played by agents. This may be the best place to make the allowance, given that agency and capability do not always operate in receiving and realizing the benefits that Sen wishes to capture.[12] Meeting needs, in another part of the schema, has no implication that they do so operate.

The 'capabilities' approach has the advantage, shared with the concept of needs on the first level of the construction, of not concentrating even on the second level on preferences. When I want to emphasize the distinctive weight to be given to needs, I refer to a second level of

---

[12] A point made in 'Equality of What?', 19–20, by Cohen, detecting an ambiguity in Sen's use of 'capability'.

'matters of preference only', but this makes the second level sound unduly frivolous. No doubt some things there are frivolous; but many of the added functionings are important aspects of good lives, personal fulfillment, and civilized societies. Of course, the added functionings would have a plausible place in a second level of construction only if the roles with which they are associated were roles that people choose to play, in choices expressing their preferences; but the same could be said of the functionings in the basic four-role Criterion. People's preferences operate in their choosing to be citizens and householders. Furthermore, whether the resources supporting the capabilities are used or not depends on people's preferences regarding taking them up; but this is true, too, of the provisions for basic needs – people sometimes refuse to eat, or prefer to sleep 'rough' in the streets. Yet the three-term relation between resources, capabilities, and functionings is an objective one, which does not depend on preferences. One will not have the capability to function as a pianist if one does not have access to a piano.

To all these advantages must be added the overarching one of being comprehensive in a way that it would be unwise (in spite of Karl Marx) to think of needs as being. The approach through 'capabilities' helps make sure that concerns stretching beyond needs will get due consideration; and thus lays to rest the misgivings of some thinkers that a preoccupation with needs will distract people from these other concerns, which include, for example, the concerns at stake with affirmative action. No one, in a cautious use for purposes of social policy of the concept of needs, needs to be a lawyer or a doctor, a university professor or an actress. To give people the capability – the freedom – to pursue such careers (given aptitude) is notwithstanding an important objective of social policy.

However, here we touch upon a limitation of the capabilities approach. It may have the opposite disadvantage from making too much of needs. Great strides in American social policies have been made with affirmative action (a feature of those policies that gives an advantage in present competitions for places to groups that have suffered discrimination in the past); but simultaneously the basic needs of many people in the same country – for not too much heat and not too little; for food; for shelter; for provisions suited to their disabilities (something much in Sen's mind) – go unmet. The capabilities approach may distract policy-makers from giving sufficient weight to needs.

I think Sen does not make as much as can (and should) be made of the concept of needs. The concept of needs, along with the term, is familiar to everyone, and by everyone regarded as relevant, though with some uncertainty how it is to be used if it is left unstabilized. Moreover, even with Brandon Butler's father and grandfather in mind, I expect that not only will it be easier to get people to commit themselves to providing for other people's needs than to get them to commit to heeding other people's preferences; it will also be easier than to get them to commit to enlarging other people's objective capabilities. It may be a fine thing for N to be able to play a musical instrument; but how compelling is the call to help him acquire this capability? The capabilities that do have some moral force get it from an extended

323

argument showing how they figure in human welfare. Needs already have moral force, I want to say *prima facie*, and by the very use of the term. That's one reason why the concept of needs is so much abused; it pulls, or at least tends to pull, on people's heartstrings. Caution about uses comes in, but only in second thoughts.

Part of the trouble with capabilities here is the fact that in their upper range they are very diverse and not capabilities that everyone has to have to lead a good life. Some people will want one; other people, another. People who go in for extreme sports are not likely to be the same people who want to play in string quartets. Needs, by contrast, in the first level of the schema are, some of them, like food and freedom from harassment, universal; and others, like recreation and companionship, at least presumptively so. I do not say that lack of universality puts the higher capabilities out of account morally; but it must complicate the argument for giving them moral force, since this may best go by way of citing universal human properties, shall I say universal needs, like having some at least of one's preferences heeded, or having heeded one's most heart-felt desires, if this is feasible? The complication is so serious that the argument is not likely to get off the ground with Brandon's father and grandfather.

I do not come away from this comparison of the capabilities approach with the needs approach with any sense that either approach has won the victory and displaced the other. On the contrary, I think that the two approaches should be combined. I can only speculate that the strategy of getting basic needs met first, before putting full moral effort into achieving the capabilities in the second level of construction, is more likely to be successful. It may, judiciously used, make some headway on some occasions with Brandon's father and grandfather. Trying out capabilities first may be rejected out of hand, especially when Brandon's father and grandfather learn that affirmative action is one of the connections in which efforts to enlarge capabilities is most active. I suspect that Brandon's father and grandfather do not bring much fervor to affirmative action.

Support for enlarging the higher capabilities may demand altruism of a sort that people cannot reasonably be expected to practice. Altruism is commonly defined as putting other people's preferences or interests (in which preferences are commonly and wrongly accorded a basic part) ahead of one's own. There is vanishingly little appeal in that. On the other hand, suitably presented, an altruism that to some extent puts other people's needs ahead of one's own preferences may well have widespread attraction. Concern with other people's needs, moreover, is something that can be more convincingly advanced by judicious moral education. (In a judicious moral education Economics 101 is postponed until the students' benevolence has been fully established.)

3. Needs as Surrogates and Surrogates for Needs

Needs (provisions for needs) are surrogates for utility. However unrefined may be our practical ideas about utility or even about the less recherche subject of happiness, we may, while we are waiting for the concept of utility to be perfected, assume that to meet the needs that people have for pure water, unpolluted air, heat neither too little nor too much, food, clothing, shelter, education, along with recreation, will favor their happiness. So we act to meet those needs, perhaps by establishing a truly competitive market, perhaps by setting up along with the market arrangements to correct the imperfections of its operations. The schema shows how to keep the uses of the term and concept of needs in these connections under control. (So it is at least a barrier to losing the moral force of the concept by using it too loosely.)

But is it the term 'needs', designating the concept as exhibited in the schema, that we most commonly and effectively invoke? The term in its 'episodic' use, to designate a shortfall in meeting one of the Matters of Need on the List, may be more effective. Is it as effective even so, however, as simply describing as such people who are starving, or dying of exposure? To activate the good will of people like Brandon Butler's father and grandfather, I expect we commonly bypass the term 'needs' even in its episodic use to resort to surrogates for needs, or at least to surrogates for the term, namely, terms that alert people to specific instances where help is urgently called for: thirst, starvation, exposure, illiteracy.[13] We commonly also supply, along with these terms, respectable explanations of why they have come to apply. The wells and creeks have dried up, so people have run out of potable water;

---

[13] These, related to comparisons of policies, are instances of what Sen, in *Development as Freedom*, 82, calls 'distinguished capability comparisons,' in which 'concentrated attention [is] being paid to some particular capability variable, such as employment, or longevity, or literacy, or nutrition'.

their crops have failed because of drought and they are starving; their homes have been demolished by tornadoes; their schools have been closed because rebel forces have trashed them and anyway funds and teachers for them are not available. We do not – and the victims do not – have to use the term 'needs' to call for help; it would be idle or redundant in the immediately practical context to use the term; to insist on it would be puzzling.[14] For that help (from some source) is called for is obvious; it goes without saying.

Brandon Butler's father and grandfather and other people in the State of Georgia may be moved by these terms whether or not they would be moved by our saying that here there is an unmet need and here another one. They may be moved whether or not they would be moved by our presenting to them a list of needs and a schedule of minimum standards of provision and calling upon them to support standby arrangements for meeting them should they ever be in danger of not being met.

[14] A comment at the conference in Durham by Bill Pollard led me to recognize that I have brought forward not just one, but two types of surrogate for the term 'needs' – not just the term or phrase identifying the plight of the people in need, e.g., that they 'have run out of potable water,' but, secondly, this identifying term or phrase combined with a term or phrase that gives 'a respectable explanation' of how their plight came about. The surrogate without the explanation will sometimes suffice, especially in very urgent cases. We would move to extract Mencius's child fallen into the well without asking for an explanation about how she got there; and likewise move without further ado to rescue an old woman from a burning house. At other times, with some people, only the combination including the right sort of explanation will be moving.

Yet once being moved by more immediate terms is something acknowledged to occur we can see more easily how the term 'needs' becomes ready for use for special purposes. The situation may compel us to recognize that any one of these shortfalls is a shortfall in meeting one need among others. We say, 'we have to do more than provide shelter; these people need education, too'. So considered, all of the shortfalls have some moral force, but some may require more urgent attention than others. Disaster comes more speedily with lack of water than with lack of education. We have to balance these matters just because we understand that they are needs. We do not have to balance them against the victims' preferences in the same way (even if, other things being equal, we are ready to arrange for provisions that they prefer instead of provisions that they do not).

Moreover, the force that they have in common can be exhibited in a systematic construction, for example, in a schema of the sort that I constructed. This, when there is occasion to bring it in, explains and justifies the moral force, besides showing how the force can be both limited and (by, among other things, being limited) kept alive.

4. The Practical Timing of Appeals to Needs

What I have just done is lay out the elements of a pattern of presentation for needs. The elements of the pattern are so many vehicles, operating on different occasions, for presenting the concept to attention. More specifically, the vehicles are utterances in which figure:

the immediate descriptions of shortfalls;
or their descriptions by the episodic use of the term 'needs',
or the designations of individual standing (course-of-life)
    needs that lie behind each of the episodic uses;
or references (including references expansible into refer-
    ences of this kind) to the schema in which standing needs
    and the minimum standards of provision for them are
    marshalled under a Principle of Precedence.

All these things can be distinguished by reflecting on the use
of the term 'needs' and testing the reflections in dialectical
intercourse with other theorists. So, concurrently, can some
at least of the typical occasions for relying on one vehicle
rather than another. What cannot be done without empirical
non-philosophical research in social science – systematic
survey research – is confirm the hypotheses embodied in
these distinctions by establishing how far the distinctions are
heeded (and, as well, recognized) by the general public.
Empirical research of a specialized kind is also needed to
establish firmly how often in practical discussions about
public policy one or another of the vehicles distinguished
is used, on what occasions, and in what sequences. Research
of this kind though not yet specifically in application to
needs is notably carried on in the empirical investigations
of practical discussions by my friends at the University of
Amsterdam who are advancing argumentation theory under
the banner of pragma-dialectics.[15] I am not now in a

---

[15] See, for example, F. H. van Eemeren (ed.), *Advances in Pragma-
Dialectics* (Amsterdam: SicSat, 2002); or the special issue of the journal

position to conduct such investigations myself. I can say some things speculatively, which empirical investigations may confirm or disconfirm.

In the book *Meeting Needs*, I allowed for some important complications in applying the schema – the list of needs; the minimum standards of provision; the Criterion; the Principle of Precedence. I distinguished between strict final priority and a looser sort of priority in which the priority given needs varied with different social roles that would figure in policy-making. Strict final priority means giving for a specified population lexicographical priority over mere preferences to the whole list of matters of need together with the whole schedule of settled minimum standards of provision. In a real world policy-making community, perhaps only experts working out ideal plans for public policy would heed strict final priority; people in other roles, as legislators, citizens, and consumers, would invoke needs less systematically and less trenchantly. As consumers, for example, they may go on smoking, while as citizens they support vigorous measures to curtail the sale of cigarettes.

I have allowed, more in the essay that I contributed to Gillian Brock's collection[16] than in my book, for there being rounds of discussion and negotiation in which changes in the schema or in any part of it could be introduced. I had chiefly in mind rounds of discussion within a

Argumentation **17**(4), 2003, of which I am titular editor; in particular the contributions there from Amsterdam.

[16] Gillian Brock (ed.), *Necessary Goods* (Lanham, Maryland: Rowman & Littlefield, 1998).

given policy-making community, preoccupied with the needs of its own members. Furthermore, I made a beginning to allow for the untidiness of the practice of policy-making. The distinction just recalled from the book *Meeting Needs* between the two sorts of priority is already a beginning. In Gillian Brock's collection, I went further, opening the way to allow for discussions that, far from taking a systematic view of the whole range of basic needs, concerned just a few needs, maybe only one, and did not press the discussion even of them to the end, that is to say, to a settled conception of them of the kind called for in the schema. Real-world discussions are continually being interrupted by other considerations; so an issue about a need may be resolved only in part before public attention shifts to something else entirely. Much more has to be said, however, both to be more realistic about contexts of application and to explain where in bearing on any given occasion the moral force of needs resides. It certainly does not reside time after time in the schema alone. I now think that it resides in the schema, so far as guiding choices of actions and policies goes, only on specially suitable occasions for invoking it. The schema belongs, on most occasions when it is in view, to the philosophical theory of needs rather than to applications bearing on choices of actions and policies. On most occasions in real-world policy-making, I expect, nothing like the schema is brought into view at all. It is, furthermore, if it is brought into view, more often brought in only part by part than as a systematic whole.

Let us imagine, however, an occasion on which it might be brought into view during the exploration of certain ramifications of an issue about needs. Civil war breaks out in a poor country, quickly depriving the population of security of life and limb. No one who wishes to help or to appeal for help has to say that their need for security is not being met, though this is as real as a need can be.

It risks redundancy even to say they have an urgent need (the episodic use) for security. Yet suppose someone does say this. An expectable response is that they need food and shelter just about as urgently. The point made by bringing in the term needs is to align the one shortfall with the others in the spectrum of needs – on the list of matters of need. Suppose someone now asserts that the population in view has a need for education that must not be overlooked. Other discussants question whether the shortfall in education is anything that needs immediate attention. 'Perhaps not this week or next,' says the discussant who brought up education, 'but in the long run, even over the next couple of years, if the need for education is not met, the people we are discussing will remain in a desperate condition. They will not be able to understand or apply the agricultural techniques that they must employ to prosper; they will miss opportunities to defend their interests as farmers; they will not do anything to reduce the birthrate'.

Someone may not see the connection with needs, or at least be a little unsure about just what the connection amounts to. Is education more than a means to meeting the needs for security, food, or shelter, and a rather indirect means at that? The response might run on two tracks. On one path, it would be pointed out that even if it is no more than a means, it is a means to meeting a number of needs all of which will have to be dealt with urgently in the case of shortfall. On the second track, it might be argued that the need for education has the same footing as the need for food and shelter. This is just because unless it is met, people will not be able to carry out their roles ('functions', Sen would say) as householders or parents or workers or citizens as fully as can reasonably be demanded. Unless it is met, along with meeting the other needs provisions for which have to be made if the community and its members are to thrive, there will be shortfalls that give rise to urgent needs – needs in the episodic sense. The schema is here being drawn into the discussion, even if it is not laid out in full elaboration.

It may not require to be fully elaborated even if economists, or other people misled by economists to disdain the concept of needs, question whether the concept is not too fluid and too much compromised by expressions of wants – mere preferences – to be useful. For it may suffice to answer this question to show that the one or two needs that may be under discussion do satisfy a criterion that mere preferences do not; and call for arrangements for steady provision if the community or population in view is to thrive or at least survive.

What, however, is the status of the schema? It is a philosophical construction that can be described as useful in answering questions about the footing that course-of-life needs share; and in limiting the recognition of such needs to those that have this footing. Such questions may sometimes, if only rarely, arise in real-world policy-making processes; I have just outlined an illustration in which they do (or at least are on the point of arising). 'Rarely' here is perhaps too lightly conceded, under a presupposition narrow in its view of policy-making processes. On a broader view, books like Sen's *Development as Freedom* are contributions to real-world policy-making processes; that is just what Sen says he intends this book and his other writings on the same and related themes to be;[17] and they are all writings at a level of discourse that invites presentation of a schema of needs, with which Sen's concept of capabilities intersects and has clear affinity.

The particular philosophical construction that I have offered, however, contemplates having its features – the schema with its list of matters of need, its schedules of minimum standards of provision, its Criterion – settled by some sort of agreement among the people who are to apply it in conjunction with the Principle of Precedence. When and where was this agreement ever reached and who took part in reaching it?[18] Has it ever been anything more than a hypothetical topic in philosophical theorizing?

I give a three-part answer: (1) If the agreement has never been more than hypothetical, nevertheless, as a feature of the schema it has a part to play in showing how the

---

[17] See the moving passage in the Preface to *Development as Freedom*, xiii–xiv, which ends, after saying that the book is aimed at 'nonspecialist readers' for 'open deliberation and critical scrutiny' in 'public discussion,' with Sen saying, 'I have, throughout my life, avoided giving advice to the "authorities". Indeed, I have never counseled any government, preferring to place my suggestions and critiques – for what they are worth – in the public domain.'

[18] Is it as elusive in respect to time and place as the historical contract that Locke postulated as the foundation of English government?

concept of needs is to be given a systematic basis; (2) agreement on something like the schema, or at least the beginnings of it, if not often explicit in domestic politics, is present in the lists of basic needs adopted by agencies and advisers active on the business of the United Nations and other international organizations; (3) ad hoc agreements on parts of the schema come about from time to time in real-world policy-making processes. Is it really no more than moonshine to suggest that there is something like this agreement on the standard provisions for housing offered by Habitat International? To be sure, most people leave action on the standards to others; or, making too much, among other things, of the ways in which appeals to the concept of needs may abuse the concept, may not support action on the standards by anybody.

I might say a little more about point (3), about ad hoc agreement on parts of the schema. On occasion, an appeal to a need (say, to recreation, or even to education) is questioned as having to do with something dispensable, or maybe something with no firm basis distinguishing it from things that it would be nice to have, but that answer to nothing more than mere preferences.[19] Suppose the question – either question – is answered by bringing up a criterion (about survival; about thriving) that the needs in question satisfy just as much as the most obvious needs like

---

[19] In *A Strategy of Decision* (New York: The Free Press, 1963), C. E. Lindblom and I quoted Sydney Smith: 'Education has many honest enemies; and many honestly doubt and demur, who do not speak out for fear of being assassinated by Benthamites.'

the need for food or (in some climates) the need for clothing. It is admitted that some discussion about minimum standards of provision has to take place before the answer is entirely satisfactory – otherwise the dimensions of provision that fall outside the criterion, into what in this connection may be tendentiously reckoned the realm of matters of preference only, will be given undue relevance. Suppose as one after another need comes up and on every occasion the same criterion (or at least a criterion belonging to the same family of criteria) comes up and the same discussion of minimum standards of provision takes place, ending in tentative agreement. This is surely a plausible process. Does it not amount to building up step by step a comprehensive agreement of just the sort that the schema calls for? The agreement at each step brings into operation an application of the Principle of Precedence; and every application is formally, even if imperfectly coordinated in a schematic way with every other.

Epilogue

In the body of this paper, I have relied for the most part on an intuitive understanding of moral force, except that at one point, where I identified a pattern of presentation of needs with a number of alternative vehicles for presentation, I said something that foreshadows what I am now about to offer as a sketch of how I think moral force may be explicated. I said there, 'The vehicles [of presentation] are utterances in which figure the immediate descriptions of shortfalls; [or, alternatively] their description by the episodic use of the term "needs", [or, alternatively] the designation of individual standing (course-of-life) needs that lie behind each of the episodic uses; [or, alternatively] references (or references expansible into references of this kind) to the schema in which standing needs and the minimum standards of provision for them are marshalled under a Principle of Precedence.'

I shall treat moral force as relativized to a certain population (which may be as large as all human beings of good will, but which in practice may be much smaller). An utterance has moral force if it is accepted by the population in question in four respects. First, it is accepted as expressing an emotion favoring an action of some sort and capable of inducing a like emotion in other members of the population. Second, it is accepted as expressing in standard cases, where present time actions and policy-making are at issue, an imperative to settle the issue in one specified way, with action in accordance following. Third, the utterance, in both its emotive and its imperative aspects, expectably has the implied perlocutionary effects on other people. Fourth, it is accepted that all of these things can be associated with a convincing moral argument that is itself accepted. The argument may be simple or elaborate: simple, if it involves no more than saying something like, 'We can't let people starve, can we?'; elaborate – the acme of 'elaborate' – if it brings forward a full-blown ethical theory, utilitarianism, contractarianism, or natural law theory.

On various occasions, all of these things will be present for any of the vehicles that I distinguish: for utterances describing shortfalls ('These people are starving'); for utterances describing the shortfalls by the episodic use of the term 'needs' ('These people have urgent need of food'); for utterances designating the individual course-of-life needs lying behind each of the episodic uses ('People cannot survive or thrive unless their need for food is met'[20]); for utterances embodying references (or expansible into references) to the schema ('People not only have a need for food; they have a need for shelter and a need for education, among other things; and they must have a minimum of provisions for these things if they are to thrive, even survive').

The moral force of the vehicles will vary not only with occasions, but also with the population to which the force is relativized. If we start with a diverse population, like the body of citizens in any one of the United States, say, Georgia, only a subset of that population may be moved by a given vehicle on a given occasion. No doubt there will often be efforts by moralists and politicians to enlarge the subset. The general picture, however, is one in which it cannot be safely expected that the whole of the initial population will be moved by any vehicle on every occasion. This does not seem to me to impair the notion of moral force. It is always an empirical question whether the force is felt by a given set of people in a given connection.[21]

---

[20] A point emphasized in just these terms by Sen in *Development as Freedom*, 84.

[21] An earlier version of this paper was read and discussed – much to its advantage – in a colloquium of the Department of Philosophy at Dalhousie University in June 2003. I have also benefitted not only from Brandon Butler's bringing his father and grandfather into the discussion, but also from Brandon's comments on a version of the paper even earlier than the one discussed at Dalhousie. Mats Furberg's reactions helped me understand the paper better as well as to make some corrections.

11   Needs and Capabilities

SABINA ALKIRE

1.   Abstract

How should actions to redress absolute human deprivation be framed?[1] Current international coordinated actions on absolute poverty are framed by human rights or by goals such as the Millennium Development Goals. But appropriate, effective and sustained responses to needs require localized participation in the definition of those rights/goals/needs and in measures taken to redress them. Human rights or the MDGs do not seem necessarily to require such processes. For this reason some argue that no universal framework can describe economic, social, or cultural rights. Yet to address absolute poverty purely from the local perspective still requires the identification and prioritization of capabilities or needs, and often requires actions by greater-than-local institutions, so in practical terms a framework is not rejected without cost. This paper argues that the identification and prioritisation of rights or MDGs can and should be done at an international level, but that they might be framed as capabilities, and that far greater

---

[1]   I am grateful to David Wiggins, Soran Reader, Melissa Lane, Ian Gough, Ingrid Robeyns, and participants at the Needs conference in Durham for their comments. Errors remain my own.

attention need be given to the iterative specification of these rights, and to the ongoing protection of certain agency freedoms. The paper explores how Wiggins' account of need can fruitfully inform the specification of needs claims. It also draws significantly on Sen's work to identify the intrinsic importance of process and opportunity freedoms, and to identify how these can relate to universal priorities.

2.   Introduction

'We will spare no effort to free our fellow men, women, and children from the abject and dehumanizing conditions of extreme poverty, to which more than a billion of them are currently subjected.'[2]

That sentence, taken from the 2000 Millennium Declaration of the United Nations, is an oft-cited introduction to the eight 'Millennium Development Goals' (MDGs) that the United Nations together with 189 countries pledged to achieve by 2015.[3] Rhetorical fashions shift, and words

---

[2] *United Nations Millennium Declaration* (8 September 2000), General Assembly Resolution 55/2.

[3] The goals are to:

   i. eradicate extreme poverty and hunger
   ii. achieve universal primary education
   iii. promote gender equality and empower women
   iv. reduce child mortality
   v. improve maternal health
   vi. combat HIV/AIDS, malaria and other diseases
   vii. ensure environmental sustainability
   viii. develop a global partnership for development

such as 'need' or 'right' do not appear in the favourite caption of this initiative. Unsurprisingly, though, the word 'need' threads through the Millennium Declaration and subsequent documents. For example the UN Secretary General Kofi Annan reported in 2002 that more progress was required. 'Otherwise the ringing words of the Declaration will serve only as grim reminders of the human needs neglected and promises unmet'.[4]

However, the MDGs and related accounts of human needs such as the second generation human rights (economic, social, and cultural rights), have been criticised by those who firmly support the commitments the MDGs seek to embody and advance. One salient criticism is that the MDGs are not conceptually framed so as to ensure that the *process* by which the MDGs are met is empowering, and that the MDGs are appropriately adapted in different settings. For example David Wiggins writes that proposals such as the MDGs are 'insufficiently rich or robust to withstand commercial or political exploitation and abuse and insufficiently informed by the local realities of a myriad [of] very diverse supposed beneficiaries – an understanding insufficiently rich or robust, certainly, to sustain argument worthy

---

[4] Kofi Annan, 'Implementation of the United Nations Millennium Declaration' A/57/270 (31 July, 2002). David Wiggins, 'Claims of Need' in *Needs, Values, Truth* (Oxford: Clarendon Press, 1998) 1–57. Martha C. Nussbaum, *Women and Human Development: The Capabilities Approach* (Cambridge: Cambridge University Press, 2000).

of the high aspirations that underlay the [Millennium] Declaration itself'.[5]

But could there be an adequate way of framing goals for concerted action to redress absolute human deprivation? This paper will argue that such goals can and, for pragmatic reasons, should be framed universally, but as capabilities or freedoms. It will further argue that to identify and locally adapt a set of freedoms of vital importance requires an iterative approach that does indeed address the 'process' considerations mentioned above.

The paper will engage the writings of David Wiggins and Amartya Sen, both of whom work, in different ways, towards rights conceived as 'ethical affirmations' – Wiggins using vital needs, and Sen using freedoms.[6] The identification of particularly crucial needs, or especially important capabilities is a central component of rights, particularly when these rights are normative for individuals and groups (whether or not they are also to some extent legally protected).[7] What I propose is that we might interrupt the full determination of needs in Wiggins' account in two ways. First, we might frame goals at a sufficiently general level to

---

[5] Hart Lecture (17th June 2004), 32, fn 23. Len Doyal and Ian Gough, *A Theory of Human Need* (Basingstoke: Macmillan, 1991). Ross Fitzgerald (ed.), *Human Needs and Politics* (Sydney: Pergamon, 1977). Patricia Springborg, *The Problem of Human Needs and the Critique of Civilisation* (London: George Allen & Unwin, 1981).

[6] Sen Forthcoming Mimeo p. 6.

[7] Wiggins and Sen both follow H.L.A. Hart in viewing a purely legal account of human rights as too narrow. This paper will not, however, explore further the similarities and dissimilarities in their accounts.

guide international action by focusing on capabilities rather than needs or their satisfiers. Second, we might frame vital needs not necessarily as needs for commodities (to have or use *x*), but in ways that can create ongoing space for individual and group agency, choice, and other processes of the kind that Sen and, it would seem, Wiggins, envisions contributing to a fully specified determination of vital needs. Finally, I propose an iterative sequence so that any account of needs can be revisited and revised.

This is a narrow and limited treatment, which compares needs and capabilities as the central space in which to articulate international goals. The paper will not enumerate needs thresholds, discuss institutional obligations, or scientific reasoning, or consider in anything more than a passing glance the normative 'frames' such as human rights. A further narrowing: the paper restricts its consideration of needs to Wiggins' account in 'Claims of Need' and its consideration of capabilities to Amartya Sen's writings.[8] Of particular note in Wiggins' account of needs are various conditions for the identification of certain needs as 'vital,' and the relativities that shape how an essentially contestable need can nonetheless be specified. Sen's writings identify

---

[8] Wiggins op. cit., paragraphs 1–11, and postscript 2, 319–328. It would perhaps be a more obvious comparison to use Nussbaum's account of the capabilities approach as she also argues that the state should support a 'threshold' of central human capabilities (Nussbaum 2000). But as this paper turns on the role of freedom and agency, I use Sen's writings as they consider the role of freedom rather carefully.

indelible roles for human freedom in the identification and pursuit of needs.

3. Need Claims: Inherently Particular

Wiggins argues that while it is valid to proscribe universal evils such as torture, genocide, or slavery, one cannot validly propagate universal goals to meet human needs.[9] He argues this while holding that needs should command political and ethical attention. Indeed Wiggins argues (in ways this paper will not explore) that appropriately defined vital needs should in principle have priority over other desires, and over non-vital needs. He speculates that '*it is pro tanto unjust* if, among vital interests actually affected by such interventions, the greater strictly vital need of anyone is sacrificed in the name of the lesser needs of however many others'.[10] This section traces Wiggins' account of needs claims.

To begin with a common observation, consider how the phrase 'this group is deprived of basic capabilities' strikes the ear versus the phrase, 'this group has unmet basic needs'. The word 'capability' or 'freedom' or even 'basic capability' does not *prima facie* carry a comparable normative force. Wiggins argues that the difference between the impact of stark claims of 'need' on the listener, and the impact of claims of 'want' or 'desire' or 'preference', [or, we might add, capability / freedom] explains the 'constant recourse

---

[9] Hart Lecture (17th June 2004), 32, fn 23. [10] Wiggins op. cit.: 45.

to the idea of need' in western political discourse.[11] He makes the case that although the concept and conceptualization of need is difficult, it is nonetheless crucial: 'given the special force carried by "need", we ought to try to grasp some special content that the word possesses in virtue of which that force accrues to it. It would be a sort of word-magic if so striking a difference as that between "want" and "need" could arise except from a difference of substance'.[12] But a great deal of confusion is evident in how to define needs in a sufficiently flexible manner as to avoid producing an imposition, and a sufficiently robust manner as to command political attention.

Need turns on the observation that some things are required *despite* what one chooses, and however hard one struggles against the need. Marta keenly desired to subsist on the oranges she was picking and send her entire earnings home, but she began to fall ill. The other pickers told her to buy protein-rich food from the canteen with some of her wages or she would become too weak to work at all. She *needed* other food besides oranges (and her need, as we shall see, was basic). Thus Wiggins describes needs as '*states of dependency (in respect of not being harmed)*, which have as their proper objects things needed (or, more strictly, *having* or *using ... x*)'.[13] In contrast to needs, 'capability' – in seeming contradiction – represents precisely a potential for [often intentional] choice and action.

---

[11] Op. cit., 4. This argument is common in basic needs literature: see also Doyal and Gough, op. cit., Fitzgerald, op. cit., and Springborg, op. cit.
[12] Op. cit., 6.   [13] Op. cit., 16.

Wiggins works towards defining the most fundamental or 'vital' needs by first defining *absolute* needs and
then identifying five other possible qualities of needs –
which are 'overlapping but independent categorizations' –
all of which vital needs satisfy.[14]

Absolute, or categorical needs refer to needs which,
if unmet during a relevant time period, *blight one's life* or
cause serious harm. Consider x to be something that is
needed – something that one cannot get on without – such
as food or emergency health care when one has been in a
serious accident. Wiggins defines absolute needs in the
following way:

(i) I need [absolutely] to have x if and only if
(ii) I need [instrumentally] to have x if I am to avoid being
     harmed if and only if
(iii) It is necessary, things being what they actually are, that
     if I avoid being harmed then I have x.[15]

So a person needs x *absolutely* 'if and only if, whatever
morally and socially acceptable variation it is (economically,
technologically, politically, historically ... etc.) possible to
envisage occurring within the relevant time-span, she will be
harmed if she goes without'.[16] Consider the example of a
person needing one pound to buy a kilo of rice. To test this
claim one would first need to ascertain that one pound is the
price of a kilo of rice (it could not be bought more cheaply or
borrowed); second, one would need to ascertain whether the

[14] Op. cit., 16   [15] Op. cit., 10.   [16] Op. cit., 14.

person would be harmed if she did not have a rice by time t (say, Sunday at five). The first set of investigations consider the scientific connection between the satisfier and the need, as well as the feasibility of meeting *that* need with *that* satisfier (in this case, the fact that one pound will indeed buy a kilo of rice). The second set of investigations examine harm, which plays a pivotal role in the determination of need (a fuller account of harm is required for basic needs as we shall see).

Another feature of needs that Wiggins identifies is that they are expressed in a general way.[17] This is because 'we must start to see any statement of the form "y needs x [absolutely]" as tantamount to a challenge to imagine an alternative future in which y escapes harm or damage without having x ...'.[18] As Wiggins put it, often we might recognize that we can slightly weaken the statement because 'he will get by if he has x or y or z. Overspecificity in a "needs statement" makes it false'.[19]

Wiggins then canvases additional distinguishing characteristics of needs. (1) *badness or gravity* refers to 'how much harm or suffering would be occasioned by going without'. (2) *urgency* refers to 'how soon must this thing be supplied?'[20] (3) *substitutable* needs are those which could be met by a different satisfier if the standard of harm is slightly lowered (hence the value of generality mentioned above).

---

[17] Wiggins follows Hare's distinction between universality and generality – see R. Hare, *Freedom and Reason* (Oxford: Oxford University Press, 1963), 38–50.
[18] Op. cit., 22.   [19] Op. cit., 23.   [20] Op. cit., 14 both quotes.

(4) *entrenched* needs are those which cannot be changed, even if gradually or over time.

If a need is *entrenched*, other routes of action would not avert the harm. If Murial is lacking an *entrenched* need, say food, then no matter whether the political leaders assume that Murial's only possibility is to beg, or whether they assume that in fact there are many alternatives Murial could take to avoid being hungry (she could migrate and work, or live with relatives, or frequent charity kitchens in another area), they will have to recognize that within the next five days (for example – any time period could be specified) *in all cases Murial will be harmed* if she does not get food. Wiggins writes, '*y*'s need for *x* is *entrenched* if the question of whether *y* can remain unharmed without having *x* is rather insensitive to the placing of the . . . threshold of realistic envisage-ability-cum-political and moral acceptability of alternative futures'.[21] This would not be the case, for example, if Murial had a need to work in McDonald's because she was a teenager and found meaningful employment by the image of, and income from, McDonald's. Because if Murial matured, changed professions and found an alternative future in which she was fulfilled by managing a furniture workshop, the need to work at McDonald's could disappear (note that the need might still be absolute in the short term).

(5) *Basic* needs are a subset of entrenched needs. An entrenched need is further defined as *basic* 'if what excludes futures in which *y* [the person, i.e. Murial] remains

---

[21] Op. cit., 15.

unharmed despite her not having x [the basic need-satisfier, i.e. food] are *laws of nature*, unalterable and invariable *environmental facts*, or facts about *human constitution*'.[22] If Murial's need were basic it could not 'disappear' by a change in her job preferences. Basic needs are rather unavoidable, as Marta the orange-picker learned.

Thus in these stages Wiggins identifies **vital needs** as those basic (hence entrenched and absolute) needs which are grave and scarcely substitutable. Vital needs thus lie at the intersection of the different considerations.

Vital needs may have a claim to political attention because even if a person twists and turns to avoid them, the person cannot disrupt laws of nature, unalterable and invariable environmental facts, or facts about the human constitution. This might *seem* to explain part of the appeal of the Millennium Development Goals. Three of the MDGs clearly aim to reduce mortality. If claims of need, as Wiggins has them, 'may be pressed from a simple passion to subsist'[23] then

[22] Op. cit., 15; A. K. Sen, 'Capability and Well-Being', *The Quality of Life*, A. Sen and M. Nussbaum (eds.) (Oxford: Clarendon Press, 1993), 30–53.

[23] Op. cit., 29. Amartya K. Sen, 'Equality of What?' *Tanner Lectures on Human Values*, S. McMurrin (ed.) (Cambridge: Cambridge University Press, 1980a). Amartya K. Sen, 'Plural Utility,' *Proceedings of the Aristotelian Society* **81** (1980/81), 193–215. Amartya K. Sen, 'Well-Being Agency and Freedom: The Dewey Lectures 1984', *Journal of Philosophy* **82**, 4 (1985a), 169–221. Amartya K. Sen, *Commodities and Capabilities* (Amsterdam: Elsevier, 1985b). Amartya K. Sen, 'The Standard of Living', *The Standard of Living: The Tanner Lectures on Human Values*, A. Sen, J. Muellbauer, R. Kanbur, K. Hart, and B. Williams (eds.) (Cambridge: Cambridge University Press, 1987).

premature preventable death seems to constitute a grave blight
(related to a fact about human constitution). Chronic hunger
and undernourishment – the halving of which is contained in
the first goal – are also usually recognised as harmful: persistent
child malnutrition stunts physical growth and development
thus affecting the child for life. The widespread support for
MDGs may suggest the plausibility of these interpretations of
blight although they were 'arrived at without consultation of
the opinions of [all] other[s]'.[24]

Amartya K. Sen, 'The Concept of Development', *The Handbook of
Development Economics*, Volume I, H. Chenery and T.N. Srinivasen
(eds.) (Amsterdam: Elsevier Publishers, 1988a). Amartya K. Sen,
'Development as Capability Expansion', *Human Development and the
International Development Strategy for the 1990s*, K. Griffin and J.
Knight (eds.) (London: MacMillan, 1990). Amartya K. Sen, *Inequality
Reexamined* (Cambridge, MA: Harvard University Press, 1992).
Amartya K. Sen, 'Capability and Well-Being', *The Quality of Life*,
Amartya Sen and Martha Nussbaum (eds.) (Oxford: Clarendon Press,
1993), 30–53. Amartya K. Sen, 'Well-Being, Capability and Public
Policy', *Giornale degli economisti et Annali di economia* **53** (1994),
334–347. Amartya K. Sen, 'On the Foundations of Welfare Economics:
Utility, Capability and Practical Reason', *Ethics, Rationality and
Economic Behaviour*, F. Farina, F. Hahn and S. Vannucci (eds.)
(Oxford: Clarendon Press, 1996a), 50–65. Amartya K. Sen, 'Freedom,
Capabilities and Public Action: A Response', *Politeia* 12, 43/44
(1996b), 107–125. Amartya K. Sen, On Economic Inequality: *with a
substantial annexe 'after a Quarter Century'* by J. Foster and A. Sen
(Oxford: Clarendon Press, 2nd Edition, 1997a). Amartya K. Sen,
Development As Freedom (New York: Knopf Press, 1999).
[24] Op. cit., 60 where Wiggins discusses the epistemological role
consensus can play.

Yet, in contradistinction to the MDGs and any other needs of ostensibly universal applicability, Wiggins identifies three ways in which needs are also relative. They are:

1. *Relative to an account of well-being*: as the words 'harm' and 'blighted' suggest, the particularization of what needs actually are, is not 'innocent of the metaphysics of personhood'[25] but requires some account(s) of human well-being or flourishing.
2. *Relative to culture and individual understanding*: Harm (or suffering, or wretchedness) 'is an essentially contestable matter, and is to some extent relative to a culture,

---

[25] Op. cit., 11. Martha C. Nussbaum, 'Nature, Function and Capability: Aristotle on Political Distribution', *Oxford Studies in Ancient Philosophy* 6, Supplementary Volume (Oxford: Clarendon Press, 1988), 145–184. Martha C. Nussbaum, 'Aristotelian Social Democracy', *Liberalism and the Good*, Bruce Douglass, Gerald Mara and Henry Richard (eds.) (London: Routledge, 1990), 203–252. Martha C. Nussbaum, 'Human Functioning and Social Justice: In Defense of Aristotelian Essentialism', *Political Theory* 20, 2 (1992), 202–246. Martha C. Nussbaum, 'Non-Relative Virtues: An Aristotelian Approach', *The Quality of Life*, Amartya Sen and Martha Nussbaum (eds.) (Oxford: Clarendon Press, 1993), 242–269. Martha C. Nussbaum, 'Aristotle on Human Nature and the Foundations of Ethics', *World Mind and Ethics: Essays on the Ethical Philosophy of Bernard Williams*, J. Altham and R. Harrison (eds.) (Cambridge: Cambridge University Press, 1995), 86–131. David A. Crocker, 'Functioning and Capability: The Foundations of Sen's and Nussbaum's Development Ethic, Part 2', *Women, Culture and Development: A Study of Human Capabilities*, Martha Nussbaum and Jonathan Glover (eds.) (Oxford: Clarendon Press, 1995), 153–199.

even to some extent relative to people's conceptions of suffering, wretchedness and harm'.[26]

3. *Relative to feasible possibilities at the time:* Needs are necessarily temporally indexed – need at time *t*. This limits consideration of alternatives to futures 'that (i) are economically or technologically realistically conceivable, given the actual state of things at *t*, [presumably in a particular place] and (ii) do not involve us in morally (or otherwise) unacceptable acts or interventions in the arrangements of particular human lives or society or whatever, and (iii) can be envisaged without our envisaging ourselves tolerating what we do not have to tolerate'.[27]

This relativity means that although overspecificity is to be avoided, Wiggins' needs can only be specified locally, with reference to a particular time, and with a deep understanding of, or in partnership with, the concerned individual(s) or group(s). Wiggins thus objects to the MDGs and, similarly, to second generation rights such as the right to development, or to education, or to food, because they cannot incorporate these relativities, thus are liable to be (and have a history of being) interpreted and implemented in inappropriate ways.

[26] Op. cit., 11.

[27] Op. cit. 1998, 12. Amartya K. Sen, 'Rights and Agency', *Philosophy and Public Affairs*, **11**, 1 (1982a), 5–29; Sen, 'Liberty as Control: An Appraisal', *Midwest Studies in Philosophy*, 7 (1982b), 207–221; Sen, 'Freedom of Choice', *European Economic Review* **32** (1988b), 269–294.

4.   Practicality, Process, and Open-endedness

Wiggins' sophisticated account of needs introduces a number of careful distinctions, some of which were set out above, and articulates the kinds of sensitivities, flexibilities, and considerations that would characterize a full determination of important needs. It also lays a possible foundation for a needs-based approach to rights. But the distance between Wiggins' account of needs and a universal or global description of deprivation-related goals or rights that could guide public action is considerable. I will briefly mention a set of practical difficulties, and certain conceptual concerns.

Clearly the need for local specification of needs is durable and inescapable. But if we can only specify needs locally, then would the staff of every institution that is designed to meet terrible human deprivation at the national or international level have to hold their breath in suspense until the mystery of what vital needs are in a particular situation at a particular time was revealed? Or might these needs – in a sufficiently general way – be predicted and anticipated? Another problem is data collection and analysis. If we have no hypothesis regarding what needs might be, then we would not gather data on them (on nutritional status, on causes of mortality and morbidity, on ability to drink clean water, etc) nor compare how they are fulfilled in different situations. Yet perhaps some of our understanding of human need is further deepened by such information and analysis (which could be used for descriptive purposes to inform, rather than dictate, responses). Further, if not all needs can be met locally nor by the relevant state but require global or non-state interventions, then how do we craft more efficient processes by which those with unmet vital needs, and those potentially responsive to them, can interact? These clearly practical problems would be encountered if responses to need were confined to deeply sensitive local accounts.

Certain conceptual issues may bear consideration. Does Wiggins' own account adequately address the problems that many have detected in the MDGs – namely, (first) their lack of mechanisms by which to tailor the goals to local values and circumstances, and (second) their inability to distinguish whether or not the *process* by which the goals were realized was itself humane at the very least? Third, how does this account address ongoing human diversity among those with unmet vital needs?

As regards the first issue, Wiggins clearly identifies the considerations that should guide the local specification of needs (urgency, gravity, substitutability, etc). He also clarifies that the identification of needs is time-sensitive. This account is, indeed, strong and flexible, and although he does not specify who is to undertake these considerations, or how value conflicts are to be managed, these questions are often enough addressed, and vary by context anyway. Because for Wiggins needs are *only* identifiable locally, he does not spell out how to take a general need (for nourishment), and further specify it. Yet a clear strength of this account is that it identifies the concerns that would arise in such a specification.

While recognizing that unmet needs may cause multiple harms, Wiggins defines needs with reference to

the objects of need '*x*'.[28] The second key question is how *x*
can be interpreted.

Wiggins describes needs as '*states of dependency (in
respect of not being harmed),* which have as their proper
objects things needed (or, more strictly, *having* or *using*
things)'.[29] He gives no examples of his own; as examples of
what people have claimed to be needs (whether or not they
are) Wiggins cites 'more roads, more fast reactors, more
animal experiments'.[30] This goes back to Wiggins' definition

[28] 'Needs are *states of dependency* (*in respect of not being harmed*), which
have as their proper objects things needed (or, more strictly, *having* or
using . . .x)'. Op. cit., 16.

[29] Op. cit., 16.

[30] Op. cit., 9. Ruut Veenhoven, Carla DenBuitlaar and Henk de Heer,
World Database of Happiness: Correlates of Happiness (Rotterdam,
Netherlands: RISBO, 1994). Peter B. Smith and Michael Harriss Bond,
Social Psychology Across Cultures: Analysis and Perspectives (Hemel
Hempstead: Harvester Wheatsheaf, 1993). G. Hofstede, *Culture's
Consequences: International Differences in Work-Related Values*
(Beverly Hills, CA: Sage Press, 1980). Ronald Inglehart, *Modernization
and Postmoderization: Cultural, Economic, and Political Change in 43
Societies* (Princeton, NJ: Princeton University Press, 1997). Ronald
Inglehart and Wayne Baker, 'Modernization, Cultural Change, and the
Persistence of Traditional Values', *American Sociological Review*, **65**
(2000), 19–51. Daniel Kahneman, Ed Diener and Norbert Schwarz
(eds.), *Well-Being: The Foundations of Hedonic Psychology* (New York:
Russell Sage Foundation, 1999). R. M. Ryan, and E. L. Deci, 'Self-
determination theory and the facilitation of intrinsic motivation, social
development and well-being', *American Psychologist* **55** (2000), 68–78.
V. Chirkov, R. Ryan, Y. Kim and U. Kaplan, 'Differentiating
Autonomy From Individualism and Independence: A Self-
Determination Theory Perspective on Internalization of Cultural

of absolute needs: 'It is necessary, things being what they actually are, that if I avoid being harmed then **I have** x.'[31] For Wiggins, x was a satisfier, a thing that someone needs to *have* or to *use*.

Unfortunately that formulation seems a mis-step in the argument, because it appears to emphasize the possession and use of commodities to the exclusion of other concerns.[32] Commodities themselves can be quite an insensitive metric across persons. As Sen notes in his criticism of Rawls' primary goods, having (eating) equivalent grams of rice would not generate the same nutritional functionings or meet nutritional needs if consumed by a child, a day labourer, a pregnant or lactating woman, or an elderly invalid. Additionally, the possession of a needs satisfier does not convey any information about the surrounding circumstances. In the same way that one might not desire the oyster that consigned one to oblivion, one might not truly need the emergency food delivery that was delivered with such pomposity as to ruin self-esteem (while making available needed nutrition), or the family planning intervention that was violently imposed. One of the concerns regarding the

Orientations and Well-Being', *Journal of Personality and Social Psychology*, **84**, 1 (2003), 97–110.

[31] Op. cit., 10.

[32] I am grateful for David Wiggins' advice on this point in particular. Amartya K. Sen, 'Welfare, Preference and Freedom', *Journal of Econometrics*, **50** (1991), 15–29. Amartya K. Sen, 'Maximization and the Act of Choice', *Econometrica* 65, 4 (1997b), 745–779. Amartya K. Sen, *Rationality and Freedom* (Cambridge MA: Belknap Press, 2002).

MDGs is that they do not safeguard against such distortions in their delivery – but nor, inherently, do Wiggins' needs.

Could x include not only the object of need but also pertinent circumstances such as the *process* by which x was specified – for example, in a way that was gentle and dignifying versus imposed versus empowering? It would seem that, if the process fits the same qualifications for being vital as the object, the process could be part of x. If we changed the description of x away from *have x* and *use x* to *have/ use/ try/ seek/ generate/ act/ etc. x*, the identification of needs could indeed include an account of interpersonal variations or of the process by which the needs were met. Thus we would replace the term *have x* by a number of possible verbal clauses.

Third and finally, if needs are essentially contestable, as Wiggins argues, then how does his account address the ongoing plurality of views once a decision is made as to the set of vital needs and thresholds for a *group* rather than an individual? One might assume that no disagreement persists after a decision is made among the population whose vital needs risk being unmet – that they would graciously welcome all interventions on their behalf. Obviously the much-discussed 'adaptive preferences' raise some barriers here. But setting these aside, even after a group decision is made, the very people whose needs go unmet may continue to hold disparate reasoned views. Indeed this behavior occurs among the absolutely poor as is documented elsewhere.[33] For instance

---

[33] Sabina Alkire, *Valuing Freedoms: Sen's Capability Approach and Poverty Reduction* (Oxford: Oxford University Press, 2002b), Chapters 5 and 7.

disagreement may arise from diversity in respect to plans of life. So persons, whether deprived or flourishing, might choose deliberately to refrain from meeting certain vital needs (although they have the capability to do so) in order to enjoy some other need or functioning, and this deprivation may be occasional or systematic and long-term.[34] As Sen regularly observes, a Brahmin or hunger striker may regularly refrain from eating, because they personally value the religious discipline or the exercise of justice-seeking agency. The side effect of pursuing these other (perhaps non-basic) needs or functionings is that they will not be well-nourished (in the short or long term, depending on the frequency and severity of their fasting).

It is important to know whether people had the real freedom to meet a vital need – as the Brahmin and hunger striker do to meet their nutritional needs – and instead are choosing to exercise a different freedom instead. To gain this information we would need to consider freedom not only as a process, but also in regards to each of the 'vital needs'. This train of thought leads us to consider human functionings and their associated capabilities.

5.   Capabilities

Amartya Sen's capability approach provides an alternative framework in which to frame priorities for public action.[35]

---

[34] Wiggins discusses this briefly (op. cit., 21); see footnote on Paul Streeten's work. C. R. Beitz, 'Amartya Sen's *Resources, Values and Development*', *Economics and Philosophy* **2** (1986).

[35] For the main texts developing the capability approach see Sen 1980, 1980/81, 1985a, 1985b, 1987, 1988a, 1990, 1992, 1993, 1994, 1996a,

In the monograph *Inequality Reexamined* Sen argues that social arrangements should be evaluated according to the extent of freedom people have to promote or achieve valuable functionings. The approach employs three central terms.

Functionings are 'the various things a person may value doing or being'[36] such as being nourished, being confident, or taking part in group decisions. These are the general 'aspects of life' referred to above. The word is of Aristotelian origin and, like Aristotle, Sen claims that 'functionings are *constitutive* of a person's being'.[37]

1996b, 1997a, 1999. Amartya K. Sen, *Resources, Values and Development* (Oxford: Basil Blackwell, 1984).

[36] Sen 1999: 75.

[37] Sen traces the roots of this approach to human flourishing to Aristotle's writings in both *The Nicomachean Ethics* and *Politics* (Sen 1992: 39, Sen 1999: 73). Nussbaum's work investigates this heritage: see especially 1988, 1990, 1992, 1993, 1995. For an inspection of both authors' conceptions of functionings see Crocker 1995. Frances Stewart, *Basic Needs in Developing Countries* (Maryland: Johns Hopkins University Press, 1985). Paul Streeten, Shaid Javed Burki, Mahbub ul Haq, Norman Hicks and Frances Stewart, *First Things First: Meeting Basic Human Needs in Developing Countries* (London: Oxford University Press for the World Bank, 1981). Karin Lederer (ed.), *Human Needs: A Contribution to the Current Debate* (Cambridge, MA: Oelgeschlager, Gunn and Hain, 1980). International Labour Organization, *Employment, Growth, and Basic Needs* (Geneva: International Labour Organization, 1976). Jean Drèze and Amartya Sen, *Hunger and Public Action* (Oxford: Clarendon Press, 1989). Jean Drèze and Amartya Sen, *India: Economic Development and Social Opportunity* (Delhi: Oxford University Press, 1995). Jean Drèze and Amartya Sen (eds.), *Indian Development: Selected Regional Perspectives*

But in assessing social arrangements, Sen argues, a focus on what functionings people have managed to achieve would be incomplete, because it would be blind to people's 'agency'[38] and to their opportunity freedom.[39] In order to attend to the foundational importance of freedom Sen introduces the concept of capability. Capability refers to a person's *freedom to* promote or achieve what they value. 'It represents the various combinations of functionings (beings and doings) that the person can achieve. Capability is, thus, a set of vectors of functionings, reflecting the person's freedom to lead one type of life or another ... to choose from possible livings'.[40] Sen attributes to freedom ('the *real opportunity* that we have to accomplish what we value'[41]) intrinsic value.

To indicate the range of types of valuable freedoms, Sen also has observed that individual advantage can be assessed in at least four different spaces: *well-being achievement, well-being freedom, agency achievement,* or *agency*

(New York: Oxford University Press, 1997). Jean Drèze and Amartya Sen, *India: Development and Participation* (Oxford: Oxford University Press, 2002).

[38] Agency refers to the freedom to bring about achievements one considers to be valuable, whether or not these achievements are connected to one's own well-being or not. See Sen 1992: 56–7, 1999: 191, and Sen's third Dewey lecture 1985: 203–221.

[39] See Sen 1982a, 1982b, 1988b, 1992, 1999, 2002. Sabina Alkire, 'Dimensions of Human Development', *World Development* (February, 2002a).

[40] Sen 1992: 40.

[41] Sen 1992: 31, see 1999: 74 and 2002: 596. Alkire, *Valuing Freedoms*.

freedom. Sen argues that we cannot simply choose to focus on one or another of these four possible spaces; there are good arguments for keeping all in mind. He argues this while accepting that these objectives may conflict. If Rodrigo tried to introduce ethics within his company, his manager might promote him to a 'safe' post with a good package (to keep him quiet) but scant opportunity to affect company policy in an ethical direction. Thus Roger's well-being achievement may increase, but his agency freedom to promote things he values may decrease.

Many immediately object that freedom appears to be given undue prominence in Sen's account. They argue that in fact individual freedom of choice is not necessarily valued equally in different cultures or by different people – and indeed some might value group harmony a great deal, and individual eccentricity slightly less.[42] But this criticism, as common as it is, merely misunderstands Sen's unusually expansive use of the term freedom. For example one commonly discussed manifestation of freedom is freedom of choice. Sen argues that increases in choices per se do not necessarily constitute an increase in freedom, in part because the options added may not be ones we value anyway, and in part because (however valuable or not options may be) we

---

[42] Veenhoven et al. 1994, Smith and Bond 1993, Hofstede 1980, Inglehart 1997, Inglehart and Baker 2000, Kahneman et al. 1999. However see Ryan's empirical studies of autonomy (2000, 2002, 2004), that invoke concepts closely related to Sen. Martha C. Nussbaum, 'Flawed Foundations: The Philosophical Critique of (a Particular Type of) Economics', *University of Chicago Law Review* (1997), 1197–1214.

may lose the option to live 'a peaceful and unbothered life' – perhaps by being a good daughter or a good father and not re-making the social mould.[43] 'Indeed sometimes more freedom of choice can bemuse and befuddle, and make one's life more wretched'.[44] Thus rather than importing in concepts of freedom from other theories, readers might do well to observe how flexible the 'freedom to achieve what one values' and has reason to value actually is – and is intended to be.

As is at once apparent even from this brief summary of Sen's capability approach, a number of kinds of evaluation are inescapable in the specification of capabilities and freedoms that might be entrenched, basic, or vital. At minimum, an evaluation must consider: which achieved functionings people value rather than regard as trivial or evil or undesirable; how valuable alternative people's or future generations' functionings are; how valuable it is to have further (valuable) options as opposed to enjoying the tranquility of not having to choose, or the convenience of having another responsible agent act as one *would choose* without having to consider the matter oneself; and how to guide action according to diverse people's conflicting claims about what functionings are valuable.

Sen has not systematically identified either a set of basic capabilities/freedoms or the relevant facts of human nature. However in the case of human rights (which he, like Wiggins and also following HLA Hart argue, have

---

[43] Sen 1992: 63.

[44] Sen 1992: 59. See Sen 1985b, 1991, 1997d and the references therein.

normative force), Sen does articulate grounds for priority. 'To qualify as the basis of human rights, the freedoms to be defended or advanced must satisfy some 'threshold conditions' of (i) special importance, and (ii) social influence-ability'.[45] Sen acknowledges that the discipline of rights will include ongoing discussions regarding what rights satisfy these threshold conditions. 'Insofar as the idea of human rights demands public discussion and engagement ... the agreement that would be sought is not only whether some specific freedom of a particular person has any ethical importance whatsoever (that condition can be easy to satisfy), but also whether its significance and its influenceability meet the threshold conditions for inclusion among the human rights on which the society should focus'. For example, a person's right not to be telephoned often by persons she detests may be important, but not of sufficient importance to be included as an urgent human right whereas her right to receive urgent medical attention for a serious health condition, is. Similarly a persons' right to live a tranquil life, however important, cannot be guaranteed by external help through social agencies, thus cannot be a human right.

It is precisely at this juncture that the mesh to the previous discussion of MDGs and needs could prove fruitful if, at the international level, needs were framed not with respect to their satisfiers but rather with respect to general functionings.

---

[45] Sen forthcoming 'Elements of a Theory of Human Rights', *Philosophy and Public Affairs* (Expected Fall 2005).

6. General Functionings

I would argue that internationally valid goals, such as the MDGs, can and, for pragmatic reasons mentioned above should, be articulated and advanced. One approach for doing so would be to draw on Sen's defense of the second generation rights and articulate a set of economic and social aims that refer to freedoms considered in a very general way.

What would be lost if needs were framed not with reference to the direct satisfier(s), but rather with reference to that general aspect of human flourishing that is at risk of being blighted? And what is lost if they are framed in a very general way, with the explicit understanding that the relativities and circumstantial conditions are to be 'taken into account' during implementation? Quite a bit would be lost, such as the particular understandings of what, precisely, is required in order to meet a need (understandings of wretchedness, urgency, the feasible alternatives, the concrete satisfiers). Yet a kind of usefulness could be gained – if the process of specification was sufficiently safeguarded.

For example, in 'Capabilities and Well-being'[46] Sen mentions a capability to meet nutritional requirements, to be educated, to be sheltered, to be clothed. These refer transparently to *what is needed at a general level* (nutritional diet, education, shelter, clothes). In this way, we might identify a set of freedoms that pertain to vital needs (as Wiggins' defines it) or are of special importance and social influenceability. If they are conceived of in a sufficiently

[46] Sen 1993a: 36.

general fashion, and if the process of specifying them is likewise sufficiently robust – indeed intrinsic to the account – then this might allay the more considered fears of imposition that Wiggins and many others raise.

7.   Freedom

A standing question is why, in addressing absolute and entrenched deprivation, it might be relevant to talk about capabilities rather than needs. Is our goal to have the capability to . . ., or simply to . . .? Is the capability term merely a way of creating flexibility and accounting for personal differences – or does the freedom itself make an independent contribution? This is the remaining outstanding issue between Sen's capability approach and needs approaches.

It might be mentioned at this point, as an aside, that Sen's capability approach arose out of the 'Basic Needs' approach in international development represented by writers such as Paul Streeten and Frances Stewart. A key reason Sen gave for differentiating the capability approach from the basic needs approach was precisely to introduce a more substantive role for freedom. Wiggins and others have answered, of course, to the familiar criticism that 'needs is a more passive concept than "capability"' – the needs approach asks 'what can be *done for* the person?' whereas the capability approach also adds the question 'what can the person *do*?'[47] In Wiggins' approach, if we changed the

[47] Sen 1984: 514.

description of *x* away from *have x* and *use x* to *have/use/try/ seek/generate/act/etc. x*, the identification of needs could indeed include an account of the process by which the needs were met. Thus we would replace the term *have x* by a number of possible verbal clauses so that they might encompass freedom and other desirable qualities. But that freedom could be introduced does not mean that it would be. Why might freedom be brought centrally into the discussion – especially, for example, in relation to the MDGs and similar practical endeavours to meet acute human needs?

First, Wiggins discusses needs 'within a non-authoritarian, critical society in which discussion was both free and effective'.[48] In such a context one is relieved of the obligation to guard against situations of active political repression. Unfortunately this framing condition does not uniformly pertain in either developed or developing countries at present. Thus presumably Wiggins' account would need modification in these circumstances.

Consider, even superficially, what would happen if governments bent on achieving the MDGs globally *only* evaluated progress in meeting needs relating to health, education, and nutrition (defined either as functionings or as particular satisfiers such as birth assistance[49]). If Country A had higher increases of health, education, and nutrition than Country B, then an international observer would say with utter certainty that the progress in meeting needs (the

[48] Op. cit., 327.

[49] In addition to the eight goals of the MDGs, there are 18 targets and 48 indicators that do track changes in particular 'satisfiers'.

MDGs) in A was better than B. What if A had achieved these indicators by oppressive policies (outlawing fasting, forced displacement of populations, and imposed maternal health regimes)? If food (absence of hunger) and birth assistance (to reduce maternal mortality) were judged to be needs, we would *still* have to say that A was better at meeting needs than B (because A had come closer to our objective than B). This judgement would be accurate, but might not capture the full sense of what we consider important. In order to be able to distinguish country A, which achieved indicators through oppressive policies, from country C, which achieved the same gains without coercion, we would need to change our objective, for example by adding a series of 'process-related' conditions to *every* description of need. That is, rather than having this as a 'framing condition' outside the concept of need, we would need to bring this into the account of need itself. The adjustments to 'have x' could, of course, accomplish this (for example, 'have x in an uncoerced manner').

Now perhaps we could frame our goal as meeting vital needs if we *always* added in the need for decision-making, participation or autonomy among the corealizable set of vital needs.[50] As Wiggins writes, 'freedom, choice and autonomy are themselves vital human needs, and are

[50] Stewart, referring to Streeten et al. 1981, Lederer 1980, ILO 1976 and others notes that BN *always* included 'certain standards of nutrition, and the universal provision of health and education services'. They sometimes included 'shelter and clothing and non-material needs such as employment, participation and political liberty' (1985: 1). See Drèze

candidates for precisely the kind of protection that is accorded qua needs to other real needs'.[51] Then our object- ive might be to increase some set of needs such as vital *health, education, nutrition and freedom.* Indeed this was one option explored by Basic Needs authors.[52] Sen has argued instead, that in addition to considering what he calls 'process' freedoms or agency, one also needs to consider 'opportunity' freedoms with respect to *each* functioning.[53] The reason is that freedom is 'an irreducibly plural'[54] con- cept and different kinds of freedom may increase and decrease at the same time. Increases in democratic partici- pation for a national population (process freedom) may occur during the same time period that indigenous groups are forcibly displaced in order for a dam to be built, and that women gain greater decision-making power within the family, and that maternal health regimes are imposed. If we considered freedom as a separate category (and the MDGs do not even do this) we might only recognize the increase in democratic participation, and not recognize, the other significant losses and gains.

A final and not entirely residual point on the add- itional value of framing needs in terms of human capabilities

and Sen 1989, 1995, 1997, 2002 and Sen 1999, all of which view political participation as a basic capability.

[51] Op. cit., 328.   [52] Particularly Streeten 1984 and Stewart 1985.

[53] This argument is developed in Sen's Arrow lectures, Sen 2002 Chapters 19–21.

[54] Sen 2002: 585.

is that it may help us to explain why it seems at once urgent to meet needs that are defined, strongly, as not intentionally required in order for lives not to be blighted, and yet deliberately to continue to hold out the possibility that people will choose (intentionally) to leave their own needs unmet. But to return to a poor Brahmin, it would seem too strong to suggest that *people's entire lives* will be blighted if they do not meet their vital need for nourishment because, while the Brahmin's 'functioning' of being nourished or healthy would indeed be blighted by intense fasting, it might also hold simultaneously that in other spheres her life might be regal and radiant. By enumerating vital needs with reference to distinct dimensions of flourishing – or 'spheres of concern'[55] – one is able to give a reasoned account for such trade offs.

8. An Iterative Approach

The discussions of this paper might be brought towards a constructive proposal by considering the three ways in which we might frame goals for concerted action to redress absolute human deprivation across the globe.

(1) to provide satisfiers of vital needs (in the absence of which life is blighted)
(2) to expand vital capabilities

---

[55] I have tried to explore some of these ideas elsewhere in *Valuing Freedoms* (2002) and 'Dimensions of Human Development' (2002).

(3) to increase people's capabilities to meet their vital needs, which requires some sequential and iterative set of activities such as the:

    a) articulation of general goals of special importance and social influencability

    b) identification of long term valued capability goals and strategies for the community of interest (i.e. using participation)

    c) establishment of vital needs instrumental to these goals in the short term for the community of interest

    d) implementation of a strategy such that negative freedoms are safeguarded and the goals and strategies can be influenced by public debate in an ongoing iterative manner

    e) mitigation of (especially vital) capability contraction that occurs either among the community of interest or among other groups, while meeting vital needs

The problem with the first alternative (1) – a pure needs approach specified locally only – is that it may overlook coercion, either overtly, as in the case of China's one child policy, or more subtly, in a top-down planning approach that does not allow specification of needs relative to that particular context. It ignores how discussions around 'essentially contestable' needs carry on even after a set of needs has been enumerated and a set of measures implemented. To correct this difficulty it may be necessary for a needs approach to import a rigorous separate discussion as to the processes required to provide for each need, and also for an absence of coercion (although allowing commendation of a set of new practices). The residual problem in the final form is that thus specified, the needs would be so locally particular that they could not guide global initiatives.

The second approach (2) flounders on the absence of procedures by which basic capabilities could be specified. Further it is very hard to put all of the components of the capability approach into practice at the same time. Consider the building of a health clinic in a remote area where traditional medicine is used, and persons visit hospitals infrequently. If a district government wished to be very sensitive to local values, it might quietly arrange the building and staffing of a health clinic 'for those who wished to have access to modern medicine'. But one might doubt that an idle staffed health clinic necessarily constitutes an expansion of capabilities. If Thomás lived in the village, *could* he achieve basic health care, or would his suspicion of, or lack of clarity about the clinic, mean that this was not a real option? The development of functional health clinics, nutritional habits, primary schools, and the like seems more often to *require* field staff to motivate communities, to provide information about the benefits of the initiatives, to demonstrate results and win confidence. This interaction may itself knead and alter the values and of participants and/or decision-makers.[56]

---

[56] With Nussbaum I also think it significant 'that the endogeneity of preferences has been recognized by almost all the major writers on emotion and desire in the history of Western philosophy, including

This paper advances the third (3) option. In this option, the MDGs or similar rights would be framed in a general way, with reference to the freedoms they would protect. This general statement could be of technical and practical value. However, to address the concerns that have rightly arisen, a series of further steps would address the local specification of needs (3b), implementation (3c), the ongoing protection of certain freedoms and possibilities of ongoing adaptation (3d), and concern for wider external impacts (which have not been discussed in this paper). If one accepts this way of constructing a capability framework then articulating and meeting vital needs (3b) does indeed have a central role within a 'capability' approach. This interpretation differs from Wiggins' approach in *formalizing* the need for local specification of needs, participation and negative freedom, and in doing so in a general rather than localized level. But it does not introduce fundamentally new concerns.

Conclusion

Clearly, examination of the needs and capability approaches reveals that they are not at loggerheads. We have to go on using both. As regards the particular problem of framing goals for international action (which may be rights), both

Plato, Aristotle, the Epicureans, the Stoics, Thomás Aquinas, Spinoza, and Adam Smith, not to mention countless contemporary writers in philosophy and in related fields (such as anthropology and cognitive psychology)'. Nussbaum (1997).

face the problem of identifying certain specially important needs or freedoms. Wiggins' account of vital needs introduces some of the considerations that might further delineate how rights of 'special importance' can be met in a particular context at a particular time. At the same time, Sen's approach is useful because it is able to articulate general priorities so that those working at an international level can have some vague common goals, while protecting the ability of those at the local or technical levels to have their say in the 'essentially contestable' specification of needs relative to their particular circumstances.

It may be that needs writers have implicitly assumed that people's participation will be invoked and their freedoms cultivated in the development of vital needs strategies. Yet Wiggins' description of the negative associations with 'need' in Britain suggests that the needs programs may have been executed in such a way that they offered the needy population scant incentive or opportunity to shape, actively, their own response. The danger of not making explicit the value of active engagement by the 'poor' is that it may be overlooked by implementing institutions that understand themselves to be bent on 'urgent' matters.

INDEX